Contemporary Seder Stories

May Day Labor Parade in New York City (1909). Two girls wear banners with the slogan "ABOLISH CHILD SLAVERY!!" in English and Yiddish and one carries an American flag. (George Grantham Bain Collection, Library of Congress)

I. An Introduction: Life as Storytelling

The Mitzvah to Tell Your Children Your Narrative

Rabbi Mishael Zion. Jerusalem, 2012

What matters in life is not what happens to you but what you remember and how you tell it.

— Gabriel Garcia Marquez, *Living to Tell the Tale*

PHARAOH'S FIRST SIN was not remembering. He is the King who "did not know Joseph." *(Ex. 1:8)* The inability of Egyptian culture to hold on to its stories was the beginning of the slippery slope to an oppressive society. For the Torah, not remembering is original sin. As Yosef Hayim Yerushalmi's book *Zachor* (Remember!) put it: "What matters in Judaism is not history — a word that doesn't even exist in Hebrew — but memory, *zikaron*." I would claim, following Gabriel Garcia Marquez, what matters in life is not history, but storytelling — not what happened, but what you remember and how you tell it.

As an antidote to Pharaoh's memory loss, the Exodus is framed first of all as an act of storytelling. The Torah claims that history happens in order that we have a story to tell: "I have hardened his heart . . . ***in order that you may tell your children and grandchildren.***" *(Ex. 10: 1-2)* The stories we tell — to our friends, our children, ourselves — are the determining factor in our worldview, decision-making and happiness. Moral psychologist Jonathan Haidt argues that the basic narratives we tell (the "sacred stories") explain our political and social instincts. Stories determine political choices, but also intensely personal ones: figuring out our own story, and the stories we tell of the world, are a crucial factor in the professional and intimate choices we make in life.

Nowhere is the need for storytelling felt more than in parenting. Storytelling is the central drama of the Exodus story and of the Passover Seder. The Haggadah, like the ac of storytelling — and like parenting — must be dynamic, never frozen. The Rabbinic authors of the Haggadah wanted parents to each write their own "Haggadah." History has proven them right: the Haggadah is the book with the most editions in world history.

Storytelling is not only distinguished from objective history or passive memory, it is also distinguished from one-dimensional ideology. Stories are vessels for questions

---

When I Was A Boy

Garrison Keillor, Lake Wobegon, MN

WHEN I WAS A BOY the storyteller in our family was Uncle Lew who died a couple of years ago at 93. In a family that tended to be withdrawn, Uncle Lew was the friendliest. He had been a salesman and he liked to drive around and drop in on people. He would ask us kids how we were doing in school and then there was a point when he would launch in and start telling stories about the family, generation upon generation. My parents would be in the living room and we would be eating popcorn. As it got later I remember lying on the floor so my mother wouldn't see me and send me to bed. I just wanted him to tell more and more. I wanted to know everything. What it looked like and what it smelled like, what they ate and what they wore. As I got older I looked to those stories about family as giving us some sense of place, that is some way we were meant to be here and had a history. That we had standing.

Our Grandfathers' Shoes

August Wilson, African American playwright, USA

IF WE ARE NOT WALKING in our grandfathers shoes, then whose shoes are we walking in?

Our grandfathers and mothers lived and died to preserve a way of life that was important to them. They taught us everything we know to be true.

Every conceivable act of life was mapped out and handed to us. We got the maps stored in the closet, we got them hidden under the bed. It has been years since we looked at them. Our children know nothing.

---

ot certainty. In the annals of Jerusalem intelligentsia it told that Gershom Scholem would fume about the fact at S.Y. Agnon, the Nobel prize-winning novelist, would ver answer a question head on, especially questions garding his religious belief. "Whenever I would ask him out his faith, or any other pointed question for that atter, he would always evade giving a straight answer d instead smile and say: 'Let me tell you a story!'"

What does it mean when one answers a question only ith a story? Milan Kundera, another great storyteller, ggests that the choice of genre — story/novel, over sertion/manifesto — is an ideology in itself:

"A novel does not assert anything; a novel searches and poses questions. I invent stories, confront one with another, and by this means I ask questions. The stupidity of people comes from having an answer for everything. The wisdom of the novel comes from having a question for everything . . . The novelist teaches the reader to comprehend the world as a question. There is wisdom and tolerance in that attitude. In a world built on

sacrosanct certainties the novel is dead. The totalitarian world is a world of answers rather than questions. There, the novel has no place. In any case, it seems to me that all over the world people nowadays prefer to judge rather than to understand, to answer rather than ask, so that the voice of the novel can hardly be heard over the noisy foolishness of human certainties."*

The memories, the narrative schemes, the twists of plot and the conflicts through which questions are asked in stories, hold the key to redemption. It is through storytelling that the Promised Land is achieved. ◆

Holiday of Free Speech: *Pe-Sach* = A Speaking Mouth

Rabbi Shlomo Zalman Ehrenreich. Hungary, 1943.

ON THE SHABBAT before seder, 1943, Rabbi Shlomo Zalman Ehrenreich spoke to the frightened Jews of Hungary about free speech which was denied them under the fascist regime.

"The great mystic Isaac Luria, HaAri, says that the word Pesach is made up of two words — *peh* and *sach*, mouth and speech, for in Egyptian slavery even speech was in exile. Today it seems obvious that the hatred of Israel has grown and if any Jew says or does even the most minor thing, his punishment is harsh. Immediately false witnesses will testify that they saw and heard him say something against the state. They call him a spy and inform on him

---

* Milan Kundera, from an interview by Philip Roth, NY Times Book Review, Nov. 30, 1980. Reprinted in *The Book of Laughter and Forgetting*, 1981, p. 237

and his punishment is death. Hence we must be careful not to say anything about the war or the state. That was the situation in Egypt as well. But after God redeemed us, we were free of our oppressors and the Egyptians were punished. Then we could open our mouths freely again. Hence the holiday of liberation is called *Pe-sach* for the mouth can say whatever it wishes." ◆

On a farm in Iowa, Bubbie weaves the tale of the Exodus for her grandson. Young Israel, *Cincinnati, Ohio, April 1925. Reproduced from David Geffen's* The American Heritage Haggadah.

II. *Biur Chametz —* Burning the Chametz

The End of Your Hand-me-down Yeast — Leaven and Levain

Rabbi Mishael Zion. Jerusalem, 2012

IT NEVER CEASES TO AMAZE, the all-out war on yeast declared each year by thousands of families. Whether it plays out as a complete eradication of all household dust — spring cleaning under the guise of religious fervor — or simply the purchase of over-priced products marked with KP and inevitably including some amount of coconut — the prohibition on Chametz during Passover remains one of those delicious mysteries of Jewish civilization. As I leave my house with a cardboard box, ready to burn Cheerios in the crisp spring air, here are a few of my favorite interpretations to the idea of destroying unleavened bread.

That Original Levain.

> *For seven days, you shall eat matzot; from the first day you are to get rid of leaven from your homes, for anyone who eats fermented bread — from the first day until the seventh day — that person shall be cut off from Israel.* (Exodus 12:15)

Our good mothers (and an occasional father) — like a good San Francisco baker — would keep a constant batch of sourdough in their kitchen from which they would ferment their bread. These starters (aka *levain*) would often stay for months and years, the best of them improving with time, passed from generation to generation. Each family's lactobaccillus culture symbolizes that source of sizzle and growth, of creativity which quietly sits at the center of every home and serves as the centerpiece of the family's nourishment. Yet once a year — says the Torah — the levain is to be discontinued. As the new wheat grows in the field, it is time to give that old fermented pod a rest. A new starter will be created. In the seven days in between, impoverished of the bread we eat each year, we turn inwards to find a deeper source of nourishment.

Missed Opportunities. The interpretations of Chametz are endless. Search your pockets — not for crumbs but for illegitimate financial gain. Purge your demeanor of all puffiness and swagger in your step. Distill yourself to who you really are, before you were allowed to sit and ferment . . . Modern Hebrew's usage of the word *Chametz* invites a new interpretation: that of missed opportunity — *l'hahmitz* — to miss. Thus burning the Chametz is also about letting go of all the missed opportunities, the could-have-beens and should-have-dones, the blunders and mistakes, the missed targets. In the age of multi-tasking and "being everywhere," burning the *Chametz* is about being OK with being in one place at a time, being one person, flat, unleavened, present. It is the Spring *Kol Nidrei* — an opportunity to cleanse ourselves of what we did not accomplish — in order to enter the new season unburdened by a winter gone stale. As families get together on Passover, the weight of missed opportunities often eats at the edges, turning into a defensiveness which overwhelms the ability to simply be together (or maybe that's just me). Before entering the family seder, before beginning this long-awaited Spring, let's burn those missed opportunities, let go of the times we missed the target, and embrace the joy of simplicity and being. ◆

III. *Karpas:* Washing Hands and Dipping in Saltwater

The seder ritual begins with appetizers that involve water in two ways. First one washes one's hands to purify them before eating finger food, and second one dips greens in salt water. Even those simple ceremonies may arouse powerful memories — moments of acute embarrassment and repressed traumas.

Story-telling
Burning Chametz, Netilat Yadayim

Drinking from the Handwashing Cup?

Daniel Brom, A Memoir of his Grandfather, Chief Rabbi in Luzern, 1930s

SEDERS HAVE STRICT and surprising protocols, and yet participation in a Passover meal is open to all whether or not they have expertise in the special table manners of the seder. Those with less traditional knowledge often make unintentional mistakes and those more knowledgeable must find ways to handle such breaches of halakhic etiquette without shaming the guest who errs.

Daniel Brom, a Jerusalem psychologist who specializes in trauma treatment, told me this tale about his grandfather, a modern Orthodox rabbi in Luzern, Switzerland, in the 1930s. Once the rabbi invited a Christian minister to his home for the seder. Before dipping *karpas* in salt water the

custom is to pass around at the table a large cup of water, used as a pitcher, to wash one's hands ceremonially. The cup was first offered to the guest who took it in his hands and brought it to his mouth to drink the water instead of washing his hands. The rabbi who was his host refrained from correcting this error lest it embarrass the guest. Instead he too took the cup in his turn and drank from it as did all the Jews at the table. As the Rabbis say: "Better to be cast into an oven than to shame one's fellow in public."

(TB Ketubot 67b) ◆

Back to the Salt Mines: Seder Dipping and the Holocaust

Jonathan Lyons. Memoir of his Mother, Germany and Auschwitz, 1943-1945

THE SALT WATER at our seders every year makes tangible the reality of my mother Gloria Hollander Lyon's Holocaust experience. It reminds us of the many tyrants who have attempted to destroy us, as a people, but God has saved us repeatedly. Here is the story of that salt.

During the Holocaust one of the seven camps in which my mother was interned by the Nazis was Beendorf. The camp consisted of a salt mine that was 1200 feet below ground, and inside the Germans built the guidance systems for the V-1 and V-2 rockets shot at Britain. By the time my mother was working in this camp, she was suffering from malnutrition. Old wounds on her leg from years before, suddenly reopened due to vitamin deficiency. Walking through the mine, the salt dust was kicked-up and it would get into the wounds and sting terribly. Yet, the salt also acted as a disinfectant, keeping the wounds from getting infected.

In approximately 1987, before the East Germans flooded that mine with nuclear waste, they invited survivors back for a final visit. My mother went down into the mine and an engineer broke off some of the salt crystals from the wall of the mine for her to take as a memento. My mother brought the salt crystals back to the United States. Every Passover we scrape a little bit of that salt into the bowl for our saltwater — now truly the tears of slavery! "For in every generation they rise up to wipe us out."

Another camp where my mother was engaged in slave labor was Auschwitz. That memory also touched our family life daily. For my whole childhood I knew that my mother had lost her sense of smell, even though as a child she could smell. She traced this sensory loss back to Auschwitz where upon arrival there she puked for three days due to the stench of death. Then she adjusted but she had lost her sense of smell. In Auschwitz she worked in the storage area nicknamed "Canada" where the clothes of the dead were sorted and sent back to Germany for reuse. In 1945 when the camp was to be liquidated by the Nazis, she was loaded on a truck to take all the workers to the gas chambers. But the Polish driver told her that he would leave the backdoor open and so she jumped, hid in a ravine and managed to escape. Eventually she settled in the USA. It was only 40 years later upon her return to Auschwitz with her husband, that she found the ravine that had hidden her during the escape and in it were marigolds. She gathered a bunch and remarked to her husband that there was a strange smell. He remarked, "It is either my aftershave or the flowers. Your sense of smell has returned!" ◆

IV. *Ha Lachma Anya* — Matza's Two Faces

Matza is an edible symbol appearing on the seder plate and used in many rituals. Surprisingly, matza stands both for a slave diet in Egypt (Deut.16:12) and for a hasty flight from Egypt into freedom. (Ex. 12:39)

Chopped Liver: The Bread of Poverty in Argentina

Rebbetzin Gachi Waingortin.
A Memoir of her Grandparents in Argentina, 1910.

TRADITIONAL EASTERN EUROPEAN Jewish delicacies originate in the cuisine of a poverty-stricken people. Gefillte fish, herring, kugel, chopped liver, even schnapps (whiskey) are associated with the most inexpensive foods. Schnapps was a cheap whiskey that had the side benefit of covering the feeling of aching hunger. Gachi Waingortin, now a Rebbetzin and educator in Chile, recalls this childhood memory of her own family's "bread of poverty":

"It was the beginning of the twentieth century when those immigrants who arrived in Buenos Aires intending to make a fortune had to survive as best they could. My great grandfather came from Russia with his family, with no work tools and without knowing the language. The only resource available was the mutual aid and solidarity shown by those Jews, still poor, who had come before him. One Jewish pedlar gave my great grandfather Salomón a pole to sling over his shoulders filled with hats for sale. And he was taught the only word he needed — "Gorras!" (caps). That was a difficult venture as the letter "r" was not in his vocabulary. Thus he set out in the street shouting out "Gorras!" and waiting for somebody to buy one. It was not easy to feed a nine-member family by selling caps.

Living in Argentina, a land known for its cattle herds, he could not afford to buy meat. However he discovered that Argentinians did not eat liver. The butchers gave it away at no charge as pet food for cats. So every day, my great grandmother Sara would tell her son, my Zeide Raúl, to go to the butcher and ask for liver to feed the cat. Thus she managed to feed her seven children. I wonder if anyone knew that there was no cat in their home." ◆

The Bread of Deception

Athens, Greece, 1944

OPPRESSION ALWAYS INVOLVES deception so that those persecuted will not rise in resistance. Thus Pharaoh proposed to "outsmart the children of Israel" (Ex. 1:10) by placing taskmasters over them as if they were being mobilized to work for the state to build store cities. His true goal was to deplete their population by hard labor. Later Pharaoh commanded that the midwives pretend to assist in the delivery of Hebrew babies but instead kill all the Hebrew boys by subterfuge. That way the Hebrews would not know and resist. The midrash explains that Pharaoh oppressed them *be-feh-rakh*, meaning not merely "harshly," but with a "soft mouth" — deceptively.

Similarly the Nazis hid the true destination of the Jews being deported and greeted new arrivals at the extermination camps with a band of Jewish musicians and welcoming signs encouraging people to work: *Arbeit Macht*

Frei / "Work Makes for Freedom." The Nazis combined ruthless violence with big lies to gain Jewish cooperation in their own genocide. The master of this strategy was the German SS commandant Jürgen Stroop, who had systematically deported 450,000 Jews from Warsaw and then burned down the whole ghetto on Passover, 1943. When in 1944 he arrived in Athens, he demanded that the chief rabbi hand over the communal records of all Jews. But a mysterious fire broke out and these coveted records were burned. When asked to assemble a new list, the rabbi cut off his beard, took on a Christian identity and obtained an identity card from the sympathetic Greek police. The Archbishop of Athens himself opposed the Nazi policies toward the Jews.

Now Stroop used an old Greek trick, the Trojan Horse, to lure the Jews into showing up voluntarily at the synagogue, from which he could deport them. First he advertised free Shabbat meals, but only 50 Jews took the bait. Then before Passover he baked matzot and announced they would be distributed at no cost in the synagogue. This time 750 Jews were fooled and they showed up at the synagogue for matza where Stroop arrested them and had them deported. The matza of liberation became once again the bread of affliction and deception. Nevertheless, the majority of Athenian Jewry was not fooled. They hid successfully with their Christian neighbors till October, 1944, the end of the Nazi occupation. ◆

Eating Raw Onions at the Seder

An Israeli Teacher. Israel, 1980

MY GRANDFATHER FROM CZECHOSLOVAKIA used to bring a fresh onion to the seder table just as the family was about to eat maror. All the grandchildren gathered around him and he ceremoniously cut the onion in front of us. Due to the onion's irritating smell, we all began to cry. That, he explained, was to make us feel how bitter life under slavery in Egypt had been. ◆

Seder in Naples with the US Army

Lieutenant General Mark W. Clark. Italy, April 1944

The Commander of the United States Fifth Army addressed Jewish soldiers attending a seder in Naples using the image of unleavened dough:

TONIGHT YOU ARE EATING unleavened bread just as your forebears ate unleavened bread. Because the Exodus came so quickly the dough had no time to rise. There was a time of unleavened bread in this war. The time when it looked as though we might not have time to rise — time to raise an army and equip it, time to stop the onrush of a Germany that has already risen. But the bread has begun to rise. It started at Alamein [the decisive Allied victory battle in 1942 that stopped the Nazi advance from North Africa toward Egypt and thereafter toward Eretz Israel]. It was rising higher when the Fifth Army invaded Italy. It is reaching the top of the pan and soon the time will come when it will spread out . . . and the victory will be ours. ◆

We Are One

Rabbi Dov Greenberg, Chabad House.
Stanford University, CA, 2010

"וַיְהִי שָׁם לְגוֹי" — *"There they became a nation."*
(Pesach Haggadah)

Weeping Man, Ben Shahn
© Ben Shahn Estate/
Licensed by Vaga, NY, NY, 1996

THE JEWS BECAME A PEOPLE only in Egypt. Before the Jews came to Egypt, they were a fragmented group of individuals. However, as the midrash states, in Egypt the Jews were united by their shared suffering and came together to help each other. Our peoplehood was forged by our shared oppression.

The historian Shelby Foote pointed out a fascinating and similar trend in American history. Before the Civil War, the term 'United States' was referred to in the plural. For example, one might have said, "The United States are ready to sign the treaty." Grammatically, it was spoken that way because the nation was still thought of as a collection of independent, fragmented, states. But after the tragic war that claimed over half a million lives, the United States became singular, as we say today, "The United States is ready to raise your taxes."

Our grammatical transformation took place in Egypt. The Jewish people also moved from plural to singular. Our stay in Egypt settled forever this question of Jewish grammar. We are one people.

A few years ago, when the war in Gaza broke out in 2009, Sgt. Dvir Emanueloff became the first Israeli casualty, losing his life to a Hamas rocket as he entered Gaza. Dvir's mother, Dahlia, tells of a moving experience she had a year later. She went to Jerusalem for a concert with her daughter. While waiting for it to begin, someone touched her shoulder. It was a little boy. Dahlia, a kindergarten teacher, was immediately drawn to the boy and started speaking to him. When the boy's father saw what was happening, he called out to his son, "Eshel, why don't you come back and sit next to me and Dvir?" Dahlia was surprised to hear that name and she turned and saw that the father was holding a baby. "What did you say your baby's name is?" she asked the father. The man responded, "Dvir." She said, "I don't mean to be intrusive but why did you name him Dvir?" And the father explained that the first soldier killed in the recent Gaza war was named Dvir, and so they decided to name their new baby son after him. Almost unable to speak, Dahlia said, "I'm that Dvir's mother."

Soon after, Dahlia met with the whole family and the baby's mother. Observing the meeting of these two women, a reporter said to them, "This is an Israeli story par excellence." And both the women responded in unison, "No, it's a Jewish story!" We are one people. We are one family. We are singular, not plural. We were brought together in Egypt, and three thousand years later, in good times and bad, our bonds sustain us and give us strength, hope and joy. ◆

V. *Ma Nishtana:*
The Key to Meaningful Questions

'Warum,' No Place for Why

Primo Levi. Survival at Auschwitz. Auschwitz, 1944.

IN AUSCHWITZ I was driven by thirst. I eyed a fine icicle outside the barracks window, within a hand's reach. I opened the window and broke off the icicle, but at once a large, heavy guard prowling outside brutally snatched it away from me. "Warum [Why]?" I asked him in my poor German. *"Hier ist kein warum!"* (Here is no place to ask "why"), he replied, pushing me inside with a shove. ◆

'I will not question my Rebbe!'

Rabbi Uri Topolsky. USA, 1990's

I LEARNED ABOUT the essential role of asking questions in one's spiritual search from Alex, my college study partner in the University of Maryland. I used to prepare my college assignment with Alex who I initially thought was not a Jew. Once I entered the library and found Alex in a corner reading Hitler's *Mein Kampf.* Shocked, I opened my eyes wide. Alex stammered, "It's not what you think!" and he followed that up by saying, "By the way, I never told you this, but I know where you live!" That of course scared me enough to start running — Alex is taller and broader than I am and built like an ox! (It turns out he grew up just about one mile away from me and knew my family from the neighborhood). Then Alex explained: "It is not what you think. I too am a Jew like you though I never told you. I was just studying about anti-Semitism."

Uri queried, "Why didn't you ever tell me you were Jewish?"

Alex told him the following painful story about the role of asking questions: "I grew up very assimilated without much of a Jewish education, but in seventh grade my playmates in the park were yeshiva students who invited me to study in the yeshiva with them. I felt their warmth and I was curious. For three months I studied in their school, wore *tzitzis* and a black *kippah.* But after a few months I was filled with questions, genuine ones, not provocative *lehakhis* challenges. I kept asking the rebbes questions like none they had ever heard before. Finally one impatient rebbe responded to my question by commanding me: 'Stand up. Go to the board and write 100 times: 'I will not question my Rebbe.' Long before number 100 I left and never came back." ◆

Slavery: No Questions asked.

Maimonides, Laws of Slaves, Chapter 1:6.
Egypt, 12th C.

IT IS FORBIDDEN to work a Hebrew slave harshly *(befarekh).* What is the definition of "harsh labor"?
(1) Work without end [without a pre-assigned time limit].
(2) Work without purpose [useless work] whose only purpose is the master's desire to keep the slave working and prevent idleness. For example, the master should not say: "Rake under these vines until I come back," for that is a task without a set quota [in time or product]. Nor should the master say: "Dig here," when the master has no need of this labor. He may not even order a slave, "Heat up this cup of food or cool it off," when there is no need for it.

Of Questions, Faith and Freedom: A Personal Exodus

Rabbi John Crites-Borak. USA, 2010
Memoir of a Convert to Judaism

LONG BEFORE I BECAME A JEW and a rabbi, when I was still a Roman Catholic, I achieved a bit of infamy in my parish for asking difficult questions. Why does God value what we believe more than what we do? Why would a loving God create a Hell? If God is all-powerful, why doesn't God defeat Satan and do away with evil? My priest's answer to all of them was uniquely frustrating and unsatisfactory: it's a matter of faith, which I clearly didn't have. I asked the priest how to get it. "Pray," he said. I told him I prayed and all I ever got were questions. "Pray harder." I did. I got harder ones. One morning after Mass I asked about a particularly difficult religious issue. He glared at me in a furious silence, then pointed his index finger at my heart. "You," he finally uttered through clenched teeth, "you...are going . . . to burn . . . for this

one." Then he turned and walked away. It was the last time I ever saw him.

As it happened, I was scheduled for a haircut the next day. My barber, a long-time friend, was Jewish. She listened as I told the story. "I don't know why you put up with all that *mishugass*," she exclaimed. "You keep trying to be a Christian, but you're the most Jewish man I know. You think like a Jew. You act like a Jew. You treat others like a Jew. You even think about God like a Jew!"

The only things I really knew about Jews were they wore odd little hats, didn't eat pork and didn't believe in Jesus. Moreover, my family and I viewed all of them with vague suspicion. I didn't believe I'd ever met a Jew before I moved to Los Angeles. Was she sure? "I haven't been inside a synagogue in 20 years," she laughed, "but I know a Jew when I see one."

That afternoon I called five local synagogues at random. "My name is John," I said. "I'm a Catholic, but someone said Judaism might be a better fit for me. What can you tell me about it?" For the record, this is one of the fastest ways to be put through to a rabbi's voice mail. I left five messages.

Only one person, Rabbi Stewart Vogel of Temple Aliyah in Woodland Hills, California, returned my call. He asked me to tell him my story. I did. When I finished he said, "I have bad news for you. We don't have the answer." Then he laughed and added, "Don't get me wrong — we

have answers. More than you can count. But we don't have The Answer. On the other hand," he continued, "if you're looking for a place where you can ask life's most profound, difficult and meaningful questions; and you are willing to accept whatever responses you get to them, then do a bit of studying, thinking and talking about them with others to formulate new questions; and if you're willing to have that be a way of living — maybe you'll find a home with us." Then he recommended the Introduction to Judaism Program at the University of Judaism in Los Angeles. I enrolled out of curiosity.

Studying Judaism began as an adventure in learning. I soon realized it was also a homecoming. My questions were welcomed and encouraged as a road to faith that led both outward and inward. They became my exodus from the narrow straights of dogmatic religious conformity to a rich and fascinating world of unbridled curiosity about God and life. In them I found God, and faith. They led me to Judaism and the rabbinate. They set me free. ◆

(John Crites-Borak, © 2010)

Sandy Koufax's Fateful Question

At the end of a documentary episode on the first African-American major league baseball player Jackie Robinson in Ken Burn's famous research series on American baseball, the camera shows the house of a nine-year old boy in Brooklyn. The television commentator suggests that perhaps when this little boy was asked: "Why is this Night different from all other Nights?" he responded: "Because on this Night a Negro man is playing major league baseball!"

VI. *Avadim Hayeenu* — We were Slaves: Retelling the Exodus in its Contemporary Contexts

'In every generation one is obligated to see oneself as if you went out of Egypt!'

At the seder we have an opportunity to recall the stirring movements of liberation of the last one hundred years, so that the heroes of the modern Exodus can inspire the next generation to follow in their footsteps and in those of contemporary Moshes. For me the most significant "profiles in courage" may be found in the Righteous Gentiles who saved Jews during the Holocaust, the Civil Rights Movement led by Rev. Martin Luther King, Jr., the history-making Soviet Jewry Movement, Nelson Mandela's South African Freedom Movement, the South American struggle against rightwing military dictatorships and the Ethiopian Jewish immigration movement with Operations Moshe and Solomon.

Here are a few tales to trigger your own search for suitable role models to be recounted on seder night. For his seder my colleague Rabbi David White pre-assigns to each guest the task of researching such a hero and dressing the part so as to retell his/her hero's tale. If we do not tell these stories that shaped our Jewish identity, then how will our children and grandchildren ever understand their own origins and their calling to continue the journey from Egyptian persecution to a more Promising Land of Freedom.

A Diary of Operation Moshe: Bringing Jews from Ethiopia through Sudan to Israel

Micha Feldman, On the Wings of Eagles: The Secret Operation of the Ethiopian Exodus

Gefen Publishing House (2012) (www.gefenpublishing.com)

Ethiopia, 1983-1984

Micha Feldman, son of German Jewish Holocaust survivors, organized the absorption of Ethiopian Jewish refugees in Israel after their courageous escape through Sudan and their clandestine aliyah to Israel during Operation Moshe in 1983-1984. Later on in 1990-91 he was sent to Addis Ababa, capital of Ethiopia, to organize and oversee Operation Solomon, the immigration of 20,000 Ethiopian Jews, most of whom arrived in Israel just weeks after Pesach, 1991, in the largest refugee airlift in history.

Agerie's Exodus: When I Was Thirteen

Micha Feldman wrote in his diary:

In a clandestine naval operation from Sudan conducted by the Israeli Mossad, an extended family of seventeen people — the elderly parents, their children and grandchildren — arrived in Israel. For them, it is the end of an exodus that had taken over four years, starting in a small village called Gamo in the north of Ethiopia and ending today in Israel, at last. [In conducting an intake interview for these new immigrants] I paid particular attention to a young woman called Agerie Akale. She gave birth in Sudan only a week ago and looks very sick, but her eyes captivated me: such wisdom with such impishness, as though proclaiming, "Don't worry, I'll live. And how!" [This is the story of her Exodus.]

I WAS THIRTEEN YEARS OLD when my father decided to make aliyah to Eretz Yisrael [from Ethiopia during the general persecution conducted by the communist dictatorship of Daniel Mengistu]. One day, he gathered the whole family together and announced that we were setting out for Jerusalem. We could not all leave together, which might make our neighbors suspicious. There were those who might have reported us to the authorities. So Father moved his children one at a time, walking for three days with each one, always in the direction of a village he knew of on the Sudanese border. It took him a whole year to transfer the whole family [to a crossing point into Sudan].

The Ethiopian 'Matza'

AT LAST we were all together, and the uncles and aunts also joined us. We organized provisions for a journey that would take at least seven days. The women baked **dabo kolo, a sort of dried bread**, while the men prepared furs to rest on at night, as well as several waterskins. Being a poor family, we couldn't buy donkeys or mules. We all had to walk the whole way on foot carrying all our goods. The luckier children were the ones wearing sandals made of old tires. I didn't have any shoes and, believe me, I felt every stone and every thorn all along the way.

Armed guides escorted us. They charged per head. The way went on and on and on. After one week, our food ran out and the waterskins were empty. And of all times, it was just then that we had to pass through a region that was burning hot. My little brothers wanted to go back home, but father encouraged us, saying, "You have to get to Eretz Yisrael. That's where you'll study and make something of yourselves."

The guides left us totally destitute in a small town on the Sudanese border. We were lucky that we ran into kind people who gave us food and drink. The next day father went out to search for Jews who would assist us. This proved difficult and it took half a year before we managed to make contact with Jews employed by the Israeli emissaries to give Jews financial support while awaiting their turn to make aliyah.

The Children of Israel Left Egypt in Great Haste

WE CELEBRATED our last Passover in Sudan with the feeling that our own redemption was close. After all, we had been in the camp over three years and we were next in line to make aliyah. The day after the festival, when they were all busy baking the first bread after having only eaten matza throughout Passover, I gave birth to my son. But on the very next day, they told us we would be departing on the following Monday. My child would then be only five days old and I didn't know how I would carry him. My mother calmed my anxiety, making a special fabric bag — an *enkalwa* — for the baby.

One of the [Ethiopian Jewish] activists arrived disguised as an Arab. He told us to set out immediately for the assembly point, which was an hour's walk away from our house. We packed up our few possessions and my father warned the little ones not to be noisy, reminding them that the Children of Israel had also left Egypt in great haste. It was toward the end of the Hebrew month of Nissan, when moonlight is very faint and the nights are very dark. I could see other families arriving at the meeting point. Altogether, when everyone had gathered,

we were seventy-seven people.

Even before we'd managed to put down the children and our belongings, three vehicles approached with headlights unlit. They were pickup trucks with canvas coverings over the cargo compartments. An Israeli emissary sat behind the wheel of each one. The people were then quickly lifted into the back of the trucks. When the trucks reached the main road, their headlights were switched on. The drivers drove at a crazy speed.

Tsafun: The Hidden Hebrew Baby

UNDERNEATH THE CANVAS the conditions were ghastly. Twenty-five people were jammed into each compartment and the heat mounted. Then the first one threw up and the stench was awful. I felt I was about to lose consciousness. I barely managed to stretch out my hand toward the burning canvas overhead. I wanted to rip it open with my fingernails, but my hand lacked the strength and fell back. The heat was overpowering. I didn't know who should be my first concern. My baby? My parents? Myself? I felt I should be suckling the baby, but it was impossible to unstrap him from my mother's back. Every few minutes, I stretched my hand out to his mouth to check that he was breathing. At midday, my hand suddenly felt wet when I touched him. There was saliva on his face, but he wasn't breathing. I tried to shout, but my voice couldn't be heard. My mouth was open wide, but no sound came out of it. Only my eyes were crying. My mother saw my torment and she felt that the body on her back had ceased to move. She tried to calm me down and, stretching out her hand with difficulty, she stroked my head, saying, "Agerie, my daughter, don't be sad, with God's help we will reach Jerusalem."

All kinds of thoughts were chasing around in my head. Where would we bury the baby? In Sudan? Perhaps it would be better to wait and bury him in Jerusalem? I blamed myself — if I hadn't given birth to him before our departure, I'd have given birth in Jerusalem. What wrong had the child done that God had decided to take him back before he'd been circumcised?

On one of the bends, when all the passengers were thrown to one side, a baby's whimpering was suddenly heard. I heard my mother say, "The child is alive!" Then, when the truck stopped because a flat tire had to be repaired, I put him to my breast and could feel him feeding. A wave of joy swept through my whole body.

At the overnight rest stop, for the very first time in our lives, we ate food from cans — weird things like carrots and peas that were already cooked. But to us they were delicious because they came from Jerusalem. The next day, we left the main highway and traveled for ten battering hours on pitted dirt roads, in order to bypass the Sudanese army's checkpoints. Again we feared that we would not reach Jerusalem. What terrible death was awaiting us in this trap? But after night had fallen, we reached an open area and were told to get down from the truck.

We saw dozens of soldiers and in the darkness they looked to us like Sudanese, but we quickly realized that they were Israelis. They put lifebelts on us and placed us in the boats that were waiting on the beach. We could see lights in the distance. I remembered the stories that the elders used to tell about how Jerusalem is filled with dazzling light and I truly thought that this must be Jerusalem. But when we got close to the lights, we saw it was a ship and realized that Jerusalem was still a long way away. The whole boat, with us in it, was lifted by a crane onto the deck. The children were in a state of shock as we hung between the sea and the sky, but from the deck Zimna [the Ethiopian Israeli] reassured us, saying, "You've reached an Israeli ship. You're safe here."

Refusing to Eat
at the Feast of Liberation

WE'LL NEVER FORGET the reception we had on board. In spite of the fact that we were covered with vomit and smelled foul, the Israelis hugged us. They gave us soap and towels and helped us to shower. Zimna took the baby from me and rushed him off to the clinic so that the doctor could check him right away. After we had showered, they showed us to small cabins that had beds in three tiers. But even before we finished gaping at them, we were invited to go to the dining room. The tables there were covered with white cloths and laden with strange foods. It all looked glorious and so attractive, but when we drew nearer to the tables, many of us felt they had to refuse the meal. I heard my mother say, "Don't touch the food. That's not Jewish food. They want to test us to see if we're Jews who keep kosher." In the end, not one of us touched the food, all just making do with the fresh apples that were on the tables.

When we got back to the cabin, I was attacked by anxiety about my baby — perhaps after all he was no longer among the living — many hours had gone by since he'd been taken from me and I hadn't seen him since. My breasts were sore from retaining so much milk. Again I fell into my mother's arms and sobbed, "My child is dead, he's dead!" Once again she tried to soothe me but in vain. It was only around noon that Zimna came and took me to a room that was completely white. It was the ship's sick bay. My baby was lying motionless in a glass container with a sort of rubber stopper in his mouth. I burst out crying and shouted, "I knew he'd die, I knew he'd die!" The Israeli doctor explained to me that the baby was a little weak and so had been placed in an incubator, but that I could soon nurse him. He also explained that the stopper in his mouth was a pacifier, a temporary substitute for the mother's breast. He understood what was going through my mind and gave orders that I should be brought to the clinic every half hour to see that my son was alive.

Jerusalem, The City of Lights

THROUGHOUT THE TWO DAYS that we sailed, they took us out in couples onto the deck, but all we could see was water. Then, on Saturday night they took us all out onto the deck — lights could be seen from afar, the lights of the city of Eilat. "It's Jerusalem," they said to us, "It's Eretz Yisrael." And we all knelt down on the deck and kissed it. In the plane that flew us from Eilat, my mother rolled up the window blind. The sunlight burst into the plane and my mother said, "You see, it's all just like we told you. Eretz Yisrael is alight with glory. This is our land, the land of Abraham, Isaac, and Jacob." I could swear that I saw my week-old baby smiling. ◆

The Midwives and Pharaoh's Daughter were the First Righteous Gentiles but not the Last

Bosnia, 1940's and 1990's

THE STATE OF ISRAEL honors Righteous Gentiles of the Holocaust who rescued Jews by planting a tree at Yad Vashem. Some righteous gentiles have made aliyah and receive Israeli state pensions. Within this context one story of continued mutual allegiance stands out. The Hardaga family of Bosnian Muslims saved Jewish families from the Serbs and the Nazis in World War Two and were recognized by Yad Vashem. During the bloody conflict in the former Yugoslavia in the 1990's, Serbian nationalists began raping and killing Muslims in Bosnia. Sensing real danger to their own offspring, the Hargadas contacted the Jewish family that they had saved to ask for help. This family had immigrated to Israel. Soon the Mossad, the Israeli secret service, sent a team to extract the extended Hargada family from the war zone and bring them to settle in Israel. Today one of the Hargada daughters works at Yad Vashem and their story is told there. ◆

A Righteous Gentile and a Good Samaritan

IN 1970 Pinchas Nahmani's Israeli jet was shot down over Syria and he was imprisoned under very harsh conditions.

(See his tale of Pesach in a Syrian prison in our Haggadah, A Night to Remember p. 37)

Many years after his release he was on vacation in France when his car broke down. A Good Samaritan stopped to help him change his tire. During their conversation Pinchas realized his helper didn't have a French but a Middle-Eastern accent. After the car was fixed, the Good Samaritan looked Pini in the eye and said: "Don't you remember me? I was the Syrian doctor who treated you in the Syrian prison." ◆

In Prison with a Prohibited Paperback Haggadah.

Rabbi Bill Berk. Phoenix, USA, Pesach 2001

DEAR NOAM,

Yesterday I visited a Jewish prisoner in prison here in Arizona. He is a man who has done much good in the community and he is a devoted observant Jew who made a couple of mistakes to try to save his business and ended up in prison. He is a dynamic guy who was involved in the civil rights movement and who helped convince President Jimmy Carter to pressure the Russians to put up a marker at Babi Yar in Kiev to identify the victims of the Nazi massacre as Jews. But he angered the wrong people and received a sentence far above the norm.

Anyway, I visited him in prison yesterday. I forgot to call ahead and see if they would let me take in a book. When I got there I asked the chaplain if I could bring him a book. The chaplain said, "Only hard bound books are allowed in this prison." I had a Chumash in the car, but he already had a Pentateuch. And I had one copy of your paperback Haggadah, A Different Night. Not just any copy, but the one you gave me with a beautiful inscription. The chaplain wouldn't let me give it to the prisoner. I told him that was a shame.

After my visit the chaplain took me aside and said, "I called the head chaplain and told him about the Haggadah and how it is Passover, and all that. He agreed to let it in, as long as he checked it carefully." So he checked your Haggadah and found it kosher, and of course noticed the inscription. Having an inscription was a problem, but he chose to overlook it, and personally took the Haggadah into my friend in prison. A very good Jew behind bars will have a

My Personal Exodus:

Rabbi Isaac Abrabanel. Zevakh HaPesach. Spain/Italy, 1437-1508

"[EVERY JEW] WILL EXPERIENCE individually in the present time of exile the very same thing that the people of Israel as a nation experienced in Egypt . . . . For it is impossible that a person living in our age of exile will not experience [in his life] some type of suffering — whether it be bodily, or financial, or having to do with his children [by having to watch them undergo forced conversion to Christianity]: or by being forced himself by the Gentiles to violate the sanctity of the Sabbath and the holidays. And since the Lord, blessed be His name, does save us daily in our time of exile and redeems us through miracles and signs and wonders, it is therefore fitting that every person should look upon himself as though he went out of Egypt.

(Abrabanel was a court advisor of King Ferdinand before the expulsion of Spanish Jewry in 1492.)

very powerful Pesach indeed with the help of your Haggadah. I thought you would like to know that somewhere far away from Jerusalem a person who really understands this holiday will be carefully poring over every word. And by the way, I do hope that someday you'll write another inscription for me, so that I can pass it on to my children.

Shalom,
Bill

Otto Geismar, 1927

The Button —
'I Believe in Human Dignity'

Rabbi Moses B. Sachs. Speech delivered in his Minneapolis synagogue after his return from Birmingham, Alabama, USA, 1963

I BELIEVE that the decent American remembers the wrong thing about Birmingham. He remembers the pictures of the dogs and the fire hoses and he continues to respond to the name of that city with a sense of national disgrace. I saw the injustice in Birmingham but I also saw a great populace in the process of moral education and elevation. I saw expressions of the nobility of the human soul that renewed my faith in America.

The exhausted young men and women who met us at the airport wore a button with this message, "I believe in human dignity." I coveted that button. I wanted to buy several for my children. The next day I was chatting with a group of Negro high school seniors in front of the Gaston Motel in which we were quartered, the now bombed out motel. I said, "Where can I get the buttons?" "Mister, do you believe in human dignity?" I teased, "Maybe." He looked into my eye and said, "Then you are not entitled to the button, Mister, not to the button that says 'I believe in human dignity.'"

There are four value words which summarize for me the Negro position. These words are not civil rights and not desegregation. The four value words are freedom, justice, love and human dignity. These words stem from two sources — the Bible and the American Democratic tradition. How are they expressed? From the old spirituals

One Problem Still Unsolved

Theodore Herzl, Altneuland. Austria-Hungary, 1902

THERE IS STILL ONE PROBLEM of racial misfortune unsolved. The depths of that problem, in all their horror, only a Jew can fathom. I mean the Negro problem . . . Think of the hair-raising horrors of the slave trade. Human beings, because their skins are black, are stolen, carried off, and sold. Their descendants grow up in alien surroundings despised and hated because their skin is differently pigmented. I am not ashamed to say, though I would be thought ridiculous, now that I have lived to see the restoration of the Jews, I should like to pave the way for the restoration of the Negroes."

they keep creating new freedom songs. You have got to see the glint in the eye and hear the joy in the voice and the devotion in the song. You have to feel the surging response of the audience as you yourself utter these holy words, "Freedom," "Justice," "Love," and "Human Dignity" and they respond, "Amen, Brother." My button is the most precious material symbol I brought back from Birmingham.

But ideals are not enough. You must have method. Here's how it worked. I entered the 16th Street Baptist Church. The kids have been gathered there since 9:00 A.M. waiting, waiting, waiting for orders to march. All day they sang and cheered and milled around in and out of the Church. Here is the kind of instruction they received, "Today if we go, we are going to have a snake march in line with Dr. Martin Luther King at our head. Now remember, we don't want a riot — we want freedom.

"We believe in non-violence. Those Negroes who throw rocks are our enemies. Non-violence starts with the idea that 'every man — white, black, purple, pink, green or orange — every man is a temple of God and we will not desecrate the temple of God, will we?'"

"If the police stop us and they will block our way, kneel and pray all day, sing hymns, pray that God will change the heart of the policemen. If you don't believe in God and you don't believe in prayer, don't join our demonstration." That is what the youngsters were teaching one another, in Birmingham.

The Reverend Ralph Abernathy retold the story of Moses at the burning bush. He told how Moses avoided looking at the [burning] bush.

"God finally forced Moses to look at the bush. **Moses looked at it until the fire of that bush caught on fire inside Moses.** The bush is burning now in the hearts of the people of Birmingham. Do I know my lesson, man, do I listen?"

For me the high point of my visit was not the interview with Dr. Martin Luther King. It was a moment in a Negro church at the end of a youth meeting. I was giving the priestly benediction in Hebrew and the choir behind me and the whole assembly of about one thousand young people before me were singing *"We shall overcome."* The minister improvised another verse — ***"The rabbis are with us,"*** he sang, *"the rabbis are with us. This, I do believe, we shall overcome some day."* I felt to myself, "We have arrived and what a privilege to be so warmly and generously and completely included in this noble and in this holy assembly of the suffering servants of God." ◆

Esther and the Jewish Beanies: The Voter Registration Marches in Selma, Alabama, 1965

THE AFRICAN-AMERICAN civil rights activist James Bevel reached for his Bible when the persecution by Alabama police reached new depths. In Selma the police used cattle prods on a group of marching students. At a voter registration campaign state troopers shot and killed Jimmy Lee Jackson who was falsely accused of assaulting a police officer. In response Bevel chose for his sermon the verses in the Scroll of Esther where Mordecai warns Esther of the government's decree to exterminate the Jews. He instructs her to go to the king and plead for her people. Esther agrees to accept this life-threatening mission with the words, *"I shall go to the king in spite of the law; and if I perish, I perish."* (Esther 4:17) Bevel identified the king with Governor George Wallace, and kept chanting, "I must go see the king!" until he brought the whole church to its feet vowing to go on foot.

On March 3, 1963, around the time that the Jews celebrate Purim, Bevel led a fifty-mile march from Selma to Montgomery, the homeland of the Confederacy, to petition Governor Wallace to end "police brutality and grant Alabama Negroes the elective franchise." At the press conference, **Bevel wore a yarmulke**, which he had often done since his Freedom Riding days. Whenever asked why he wore a kippah, Bevel might refer to "his affection for the Hebrew prophets" or suggest that it was a protective device to keep himself out of jail. Bevel mused that Mississippi police were "so mystified by the sight of a Negro preacher in a 'Jewish beanie' they preferred to let him alone."* ◆

---

* See Rabbi Marc Schneier, *Shared Dreams: Dr. Martin Luther King Jr. and the Jewish Community*, pp 85-91.

Yearning to be free? Escape from Freedom.

Professor Michael Walzer.
Exodus and Revolution, USA, 1985

THE GREAT PARADOX of the Exodus, and of all subsequent liberation struggles, is the people's simultaneous willingness and unwillingness to put Egypt behind them. They yearn to be free, and they yearn to escape their new freedom. They want laws but not too many; they both accept and resist the discipline of the march. The biblical narrative tells this paradoxical story with a frankness not often repeated in the literature of liberation.

The Socialist Torah of the American Jewish Labor Movement
New York, 1880's-1890's

In his Yiddish newspaper, Der Forverts, Abraham Cahan wrote a weekly column under the title "The Sidra," authored by Der Proletarishker Maggid ("The Proletarian Preacher"). He used the weekly Torah portion to comment on current events. On March 14, 1890 he interpreted a local strike in light of the book of Exodus:

TODAY OUR TORAH PORTION is about strikes: The cloakmakers still have a little strike to finish up, the shirtmakers are on strike, the pantsmakers are striking, even our teacher Moses called a mass meeting to talk about a strike. "Moses assembled the children of Israel and said to them, *Sheyshes yomim t'asu m'lokho*, you shall not work for the bosses more than six days a week, the seventh day you shall rest . . . ." But what is actually the case? The children of Israel work eighteen hours a day . . . and have no Sabbath and no Sunday off. Ay, you may ask, can't they die from exhaustion? Indeed, die they do. But there is one commandment they do fulfill: Moses tells them in today's sedre that on the seventh day they shall not light fire. This they observe an entire week: there is nothing to cook, thank G-d, and no fire to cook with. ◆

VII. Four Children: Communicating with Everyone

The Haggadah showcases four children, each with their own disposition and relationship to Jewish tradition. Parents and educators are challenged to meet each and every one of these children on their own turf, building bridges between the generations.

The Jew is a Dispute Incarnate

Philip Roth, Operation Shylock. USA, 1993

"WHY COULDN'T THE JEWS be one people? Why must Jews be in conflict with one another? Why must they be in conflict with themselves? Because divisiveness is not just between Jew and Jew — it is within the individual Jew. Is there a more manifold personality in all the world? I don't say divided. Divided is nothing . . . But inside every Jew there is a *mob* of Jews. The good Jew, the bad Jew. The new Jew, the old Jew. The lover of Jews, the hater of Jews. The friend of the goy, the enemy of the goy. The arrogant Jew, the wounded Jew. The pious Jew, the rascal Jew. The coarse Jew, the gentle Jew. The defiant Jew, the appeasing Jew. The Jewish Jew, the de-Jewed Jew. Shall I go on? So I have to expound upon the Jew as a three-thousand-year amassment of mirrored fragments . . . Is it any wonder that a Jew is always disputing? He is a dispute, incarnate." ◆

Who is the 'Wicked' Son, Father?

Franz Kafka's Letter to His Father. Prague, Czechoslovakia, 1919.

"I COULD NOT UNDERSTAND how, with the insignificant scrap of Judaism you yourself possessed, you could reproach me for not making an effort . . . to cling to a similar, insignificant scrap. It was . . . a mere nothing, a joke-not even a joke . . . at home it was . . . confined to the first seder, which more and more developed into a farce, with fits of hysterical laughter . . . How one could do anything better with that material than get rid of it as fast as possible . . . Precisely the getting rid of it seemed to me to be the devoutest action." ◆

Leopold Bloom's Silly Seder in Dublin

James Joyce, Ulysses. Ireland, 1922.

"AND IT WAS THE FEAST OF THE PASSOVER . . . Poor papa with his Haggadah book, reading backwards with his finger to me, "Pesach." "Next year in Jerusalem." Dear, O dear! All that long business that brought us out of the land of Egypt and into the house of bondage *Alleluia. Shema Israel Adonai Elohenu* . . . And then the lamb and the cat and the dog and the stick and the water and the butcher . . . Sounds a bit silly till you come to look into it well." ◆

The Rebellious Daughter and Granddaughter

Rabbi Silvina Chemen. Argentina, early 20th C.*

MY GRANDMOTHER TERESA was born in Syria and immigrated to Argentina where she was married and lived in a traditional community where women had no role in the synagogue or in Jewish learning. But after raising her children she became interested in Jewish learning and despite her husband's and the community's objections, she went off to join Bet El, the Conservative synagogue of Rabbi Marshall Meyer, a student of A.J. Heschel and a courageous activist for freedom in rightwing Argentina. She studied there and participated in the services. Though she was neither wealthy nor male, she was honored with an aliyah to the Torah. She was so moved by being included, that she cried when she had her first aliyah.

At her seder she would protest to her loving but traditional husband that she deserved to recite the Kiddush over the wine because she had done all the housework preparing the seder. Eventually my grandparents compromised and each one had their own cup. In later years her granddaughters davened in Bet El. Even her husband would come to enjoy their Jewish involvement. Eventually one granddaughter, Silvina Chemen, became one of the rabbis at Bet El even though her grandmother could not even have dreamed of such an outcome to her "wicked" desire to study Torah. ◆

---

* From *Una Noche de Libertad*, Latin American haggadah by Noam and Mishael Zion, p. 59

Four Daughters

L'Dor va-Dor: From Generation to Generation, A Women's Seder Haggadah, *USA, 2013*[1]

The **Wise daughter** understands that it is up to her to improve the world.

She is the one who steps forward, assuming her opinion counts.

She is the one who can find the root of the problem, and work from within to solve it.

She is the one who can see the greater meaning in the smaller issues.

She is the one who will champion right even if the men try to hush her.

Some call her wise and agreeable. We call her creative and assertive.

We welcome assertiveness to sit with us at our tables and inspire us to act.

The **Wicked daughter** is the one who understands that actions must be taken, voices must be heard.

She is the one who asks too many questions.

She is the one not content to remain in her prescribed place.

She is the one who breaks the mold.

She is the one who frightens the status quo.

Some call her wicked and rebellious. We call her daring and revolutionary.

We welcome rebellion to sit with us at our tables and make us uneasy.

---

1. From *Repairing the World (Tikkun Olam)* — A Temple Emunah Women's Community Seder Haggadah Dedicated to Jewish Women Activists (2013) written by the Temple. Emunah Women's Seder Haggadah Committee, Lexington, Massachusetts.

The **Simple daughter** is the one who accepts the world the way it is without asking for more.

She is the one who trusts easily and believes what she is told.

She is the one who prefers waiting and watching over seeking and acting.

She is the one who believes that the redemption from Egypt was the final act of freedom.

She is the one who follows in the wake of others.

Some call her simple and naive. We call her the one whose eyes wait to be opened.

We welcome the contented one to sit with us at our tables and appreciate what may yet be.

Last is the **daughter who does not know how to ask**.

She is the one who is overwhelmed.

She is the one who is juggling work and family life.

She is the one who is too tired to raise her voice.

She is the one who doesn't know her own strength.

Some call her self-centered or unaware. We call her sister. We welcome the silent one to sit with us at our tables, to be empowered by the community of women. ◆

Loving Our Children and Having Faith In Their Judgment

Hannah Arendt, U.S. political philosopher.
Between Past and Future, *1961*

EDUCATION IS WHERE WE DECIDE whether we love our children enough not to expel them from our world and leave them to their own devices, [enough] not to strike from their hands their chance of undertaking something new, something unforeseen by us. But [education also means] to prepare them in advance for the task of renewing a common world.

Open Doors and the Child Who Does Not Know How to Ask

Rabbi Steve Sager, Director of Sicha: Continuing the Conversation, sichaconversation.org

RABBI ELAZAR HAKAPPAR SAID: "Do not be like a lintel overhead that no one can reach; neither, be like a door beam that injures faces, nor like a raised threshold that bruises feet. Rather, be like a low threshold that everyone crosses easily. In the end, the entire building might disappear, but the threshold will remain in place."

With the soul of a teacher, Rabbi Elazar HaKappar animates the doorway of his academy. The door, like the teacher, has to be generously open, presenting no obstacles. The lintel must be high enough to test but not frustrate the reach; the threshold low enough to assure the step and the stance.

How ironic and fitting that the lintel of Rabbi Elazar's academy survives! In the ancient synagogue of Katzin the black basalt lintel with two eagles stretching a ribbon and wreath between them announces: "This is the academy of Rabbi Elazar HaKappar." This is part of the doorway that Rabbi Elazar has created in his own image, from the lintel-not-beyond-reach to the threshold-humble-and-accessible.

For the Israeli poet, Rivka Miriam, as for Rabbi Elazar, the doorway is both symbol and solid. For Rivka, the doorway offers learning hinged on the language of the Passover Haggadah:

You open for him when he is too small to open you lift him to your shoulders and soothe him with "don't be afraid"

open for him slowly, he is unaccustomed to openings
'til now he imagined that everything was open
the walls, he imagined, were as open
and transparent as the breeze
the walls, he imagined, were as open eyed
as a patient plain, yawning
he recognized neither lintel nor doorposts
neither hinge nor door
you lift him so that he rubs his sides against the doorposts
so that he bows his head beneath the lintel
gently you set him on the threshold
so that he is surefooted,
not like a refugee standing on the threshold.

"You open for him" is the Haggadah's instruction for engaging the last of the four children who together represent the Passover table community. Each of the other three children has a (door) frame of reference: wise, skeptical, or simple. The fourth does not know how to frame a question. For this one with no perspective — nothing to see through — the tradition says, you open the conversation for him. Don't be afraid is the only word spoken. After that, the doorway itself — post, lintel, and threshold — is the learning.

You open for him, lift him up, and he learns the touch of something beyond reach. You open for him the expanse from side to side, and he feels the fact of the doorframe. The world is not, after all, endlessly open and patient. One must respect the solidity of the doorpost and learn to avoid collision with what is overhead. You open for him, so that he might take a knowing stance in the doorway, assured and surefooted on the threshold. ◆

VIII. *Dayeinu*

Cultivating Gratitude

Rabbi Sharon Cohen Anisfeld, Boston, 2000

"JUST LET THIS BABY BE BORN HEALTHY and whole. That's all I ask." I said this over and over when I was pregnant with my first child, as if I didn't know how briefly I would savor the relief when the time came, God willing, as if I didn't know how quickly and greedily I would begin to come up with new anxieties, new requests, new demands.

How easy it is to live in constant anticipation, promising God and ourselves that we will be satisfied and grateful, if only . . . but there is always something else. This is part of what makes us human. When we say *Dayeinu*, on one level we are lying. We say, "It would have been enough." But we know that this is not true. No single step of our journey out of slavery would have been sufficient.

Yet, we tell this lie in order to cultivate our capacity for gratitude. We exercise our thanking muscles, trying at least for a moment to appreciate each and every small gift as if we really believed it was enough. Of course we want more. We have hopes and dreams for ourselves and for our children. But for their sakes, and for our own, we must also be able to stop and say *Dayeinu*: "This is enough for us, thank God." For a moment, to feel that we have everything we need — that is what it means to say *Dayeinu*. ◆

IX. Souvenirs on the Seder Plate

Miriam's African Drum and the Birth of Jazz: Drumming for Freedom

Africa-USA, 18th Century

AT THE SPLITTING of the Red Sea *"Miriam the prophetess . . . took the drum in her hand and all the women went out after her with drums and with dances."* (Ex. 15:20) Moses' sister Miriam was herself a liberated slave from Egypt, a country on the North African coast. Thousands of years later the African drum was still used to symbolize freedom. In his book, *A History of the World in 100 Objects*, Neil MacGregor, curator of the British Museum, describes the Akan drum made in West Africa that reached Virginia (c. 1700-1750):

"The drum was made in Africa, taken to America, and with it we can recover some of the story of one of the biggest forced migrations in history. (Overall, around 12 million Africans were transported to America from Africa). These utterly dispossessed people were allowed to bring nothing with them — but they brought the music in their heads, and one or two instruments were carried on the ships. With them came the very beginnings of African-American music.

"Jazz is a music of freedom and rebellion that can trace its roots back to the terrible days of the slave trade between Africa and America in the eighteenth century, when drums were brought over from Africa to America along with the slaves, and music gave the enslaved and displaced a voice, connected their communities, and provided a language that would ultimately cross continents. Drums like this one stand at the head of that whole African-American musical tradition of blues and jazz — music of poignant regret, or exuberance and rebellion, the music of liberty."

The drums may be romanticized as the key to the transfer of African music to the New World. The historian J. A. Rogers writes:

"The true spirit of jazz is a joyous revolt from convention, custom, authority, boredom, even sorrow — from everything that would confine the soul of man and hinder its riding free on the air."

MacGregor also cites the philosopher Kwame Anthony Appiah of Kenyan origin who explains:

"These drums are important to life, and if you could take one with you to the New World, it would have been a kind of source of memory that you could take with you, and that's one of the things that people taken into slavery tried to hold on to."

But, as MacGregor observes, the masters of these notorious slave ships used the drums in order to serve their own nefarious economic objectives. They would forcibly bring up the chained Africans on deck to "dance the slaves," so that they would be healthier and more likely to overcome depression, survive and fetch a good price on the American market. But drums might also trigger a slave revolt. "In South Carolina in 1739 drums were used as a call to arms at the outbreak of a violent slave rebellion. It prompted the colony to prohibit drums in law and classify them as weapons." The Akan drum in the British Museum may have been "confiscated in one of the drum bans on the plantations." ◆

The Silver Ring and the Magen David: Souvenirs from a Woman's Journey during the Pinochet Years

Deborah Delavegas. Chile, 1970's-1980's

IN 1974 WHEN I WAS LIVING IN EXILE and thirty-three years old, my mother told me we were Jewish. My ancestors had escaped the Spanish inquisition and settled in England. For a time they felt safe, but Jews were also persecuted there. So in the late 1800s, they fled to a new land across the sea. Latin America seemed far from pain, uncertainty and death. But when they settled in Catholic Chile, they had to live as crypto-Jews. They changed their last names and hid their true identities. My mother gave me my great grandparents' haggadot; their old and tattered pages have wine stains of ancient Pesach celebrations. They are a treasure to me, witnesses of a long heritage of struggle, survival and love for life.

Their story explained to me my yearning for identity and for social justice. I too was an exile, a political refugee from Pinochet's fascist military dictatorship. I had been tortured, imprisoned and thrown out of my country. Nevertheless, in 1984, after ten years in exile, I chose to go back to Chile to continue the struggle for freedom. Again I was arrested and tortured. This is the dramatic account of my imprisonment:

"The room was dark, filled with silent cries of other women, prisoners like me. We took care of each other through our agony and pain. Once the woman torturer asked me to make her a silver ring like the one I had worn when they took me in for questioning. Now, it was no longer on my finger. I looked at her through my swollen eyes. They had beaten me brutally. I said I would do what she wanted only if she would let me make something very special for myself. 'You are not going to make some political symbol,' she shouted. 'No,' I said softly, 'I want to make a Star of David; I am Jewish.'

"I worked on the Magen David with enthusiasm; the hours went by in a kind of tranquil dream, my soul felt lighter. The physical pain didn't bother me anymore, even though my fingers were swollen; with their boots the soldiers had stepped on my hands and with her stick, the torturer had beaten them. Now I didn't feel any pain. The Magen David took form in front of my eyes, slowly and beautifully. I worked passionately, and after five days it was finished. It shone like a powerful star. Making the Magen David helped my physical healing and gave me the spiritual strength to carry on and survive. The next day I was released. Though naked and abandoned on a solitary road, I still held the Magen David in my clenched left hand. It felt warm; it gave me a sense of meaning and security."

This persecution happened to me because I thought differently, because I struggled for the oppressed and the poor, because I believed in a world where injustice, discrimination and prejudices should not exist. They tried to make me a slave. But I had learned that:

Freedom is the strength and knowledge that enables us to survive the most difficult trials and be able to love life no matter the sufferings and heartaches.

Freedom is internal peace in the midst of external turmoil.

Freedom is our sense of true identity and belonging.

Freedom is to fight for and demand the inalienable respect for our rights as individuals and as a people.

This is why I tell my story, so that my children and grandchildren do not forget who we are and the high price paid for freedom and redemption by many generations of our people all over the world. ◆

The African-American Seder Plate: Black-eyed Peas and Pork on the Night of Watching

Reverend Terrence Autry. USA, 2014
Celebrating New Year's Eve, January 1, 1863

Story-telling
Souvenirs

WHILE JEWS EAT MAROR to remind them of the bitterness and the humiliation of slavery, African Americans traditionally eat black-eyed peas and pork intestines. Those dishes were reminders of the brutal slave experience. "I grew up being served by my mother, every New Year's Day, 'black eyed peas' and 'chitterlings' (pork intestines) which I DID NOT eat as a kid and will not eat to this day. Now, my kids WILL NOT eat black eyed peas! As an African American (AA) I was taught that 'New Year's Eve' was more than just bringing in a New Year. New Year's is our Passover Day of Exodus and the night of our seder was the Watch Night *(Leil Shimurim)* as it says: *"It will be a night of watching for God; A keeping of the watch of all the children of Israel throughout the generations."* (Ex.12:42)

In 1862 the AA community, free and slave, waited impatiently in anticipation of President Lincoln's signing the Emancipation Proclamation. Some say there was a rumor that President Lincoln was not going to sign it. The AA church responded by initiating Watch Night services imploring God to move the heart of President Lincoln to keep his promise announced 99 days before New Year's, 1863. On "Watch Night" Americans of African descent faithfully "watched" for his proclamation to be issued on the 100th day.

Frederick Douglass called January 1, 1863, the **Day of Jubilee** for in the Bible it was the day when the Children of Israel are commanded to blow the shofar, release the slaves and *"proclaim liberty to all the inhabitants of the land." (Lev. 25:10)* Douglas wrote of the intense anticipation of "a day for poetry and song, a new song. These cloudless skies, this balmy air, this brilliant sunshine, making December as pleasant as May, are in harmony with the glorious morning of liberty about to dawn upon us." Many of the faithful elders believed that God had indeed heard their cries and would deliver them from their taskmasters *(Ex. 2:23-25)* and they congregated in churches in the North and around "praying trees" in secret locations in the South on the evening of December 31, 1862. When the "Trumpet [Shofar] of Jubilee" was heard, "joy and gladness exhausted all forms of expression from shouts of praise to sobs and tears." African Americans were also "watching" for the opportunity to fight for freedom. Later that year, hundreds of AA men joined the Union Army to fight for the Union and their freedom. "January 1, 1863, was an amazing 'God-move' experience. That is the gist of the story that has been handed down to me by my forefathers." ◆

X. Elijah: Opening Doors and Turning Hearts

Franz Rosenzweig, "The Feast of Freedom" in The Star of Redemption. *Germany, 1921*

THE FREEDOM of the Passover meal . . . free is expressed . . . in the fact that the **youngest child is the one to speak, and that what the father says at that table is adapted to this child's personality and his degree of maturity.** In contrast to all instruction, which is necessarily autocratic and never on a basis of equality, the sign of a true and free social intercourse is this, that the one who stands — relatively speaking — nearest the periphery of the circle, gives the cue for the level on which the conversation is to be conducted. For this conversation must include him. No one who is there in the flesh shall be excluded in the spirit. **The freedom of a society is always the freedom of everyone who belongs to it. Thus this meal is a symbol of the people's vocation for freedom.**

The founding of the people affords a glimpse of its **future** destinies, but no more than a glimpse . . . This is the deepest meaning of the farewell which those who participate in the evening meal bid one another: **Next year in Jerusalem!** In every house where the meal is celebrated a cup filled with wine stands ready for the prophet **Elijah**, the precursor of the [messiah], who is forever *"turning the hearts of the parents to their children and the hearts of the children to their parents." (Malachi 3:2-4)* ◆

President Jimmy Carter, the Secret Service and Elijah

USA, late 1970's

Opening the door on seder night is related to the Biblical tradition that seder night is the Night of Watching in which God watched over Israel as the angel of death struck the Egyptian firstborn. Therefore the Rabbis treated seder night as a time when Jews are protected from danger. For that reason they could open their doors even at night, traditionally considered a dangerous time.

IN THE LATE 1970'S Stuart Eizenstadt, the advisor for Middle Eastern Affairs, invited President and Mrs. Carter to his home for seder. At the end of the seder Stuart went to open the *front* door for Elijah, but the secret service agents stopped him because it would be a breach of presidential security. Eventually Stuart convinced the secret service to allow him to open the *back* door for Elijah. ◆

XI. Next Year in Jerusalem

'Next Year a Life of My Own' — Seder in the Battered Women's Shelter

Shelly Horowitz. Lod, Israel, 2012

SEVERAL WEEKS AGO I conducted a Pesach seder in a battered women's shelter in the center of Israel. This shelter is open to anyone, but the majority of women are wives of professional people. I dropped by a week before Pesach with my weekly groceries in the car and casually suggested doing a pre-seder workshop. The response was so enthusiastic that I simply emptied my car and the women began cooking up a storm. Several hours later both these women and their children attended the seder. In the back of my car I had multiple copies of the Zion haggadah in Hebrew. The traditional texts spoke to them very personally.

The women in this shelter, mainly victims of domestic violence, many in the process of obtaining a divorce, hold a very personal view of freedom — freedom from "the tyranny of spousal control" as one woman succinctly stated — the freedom to make difficult choices, the freedom to stand up and advocate for oneself and one's children. Many parts of this haggadah were "adapted" to fit personal experiences. The question of "Why this night is different?" melted into the question of "what is the difference between work and slavery — and what is one's obligation to home and family?" Many women commented on feeling like slaves — every aspect of their lives controlled by their husbands. When we read "everyone must see him or herself as if he or she personally left Egypt," there were cheers all around.

At the end of the seder as we read "Next Year in Jerusalem" and each woman thought of her "next year" hopes for a future. One of the most touching aspects was our reading of Anne Frank's diary about "I Still Believe."

"That's the difficulty in these times: ideals, dreams, and cherished hopes rise within us, only to meet the horrible truth and be shattered. It's really a wonder that I haven't dropped all my ideals, because they seem so absurd and impossible to carry out. Yet I keep them, because in spite of everything I still believe that people are really good at heart. I simply can't build up my hopes on a foundation consisting of confusion, misery, and death. I see the world gradually being turned into a wilderness. I hear the ever-approaching thunder, which will destroy us, too. I can feel the suffering of millions — and yet, if I look up into the heavens, I think it will come out all right, that this cruelty too will end, and that peace and tranquility will return again. In the meantime, I must uphold my ideals, for perhaps the time will come when I shall be able to carry them out." *(Diary of Anne Frank, Amsterdam, 1944)*

These battered women reflected together on their effort to maintain hope (and faith) in light of personal adversity.

◆

Next Year in Jerusalem – A Vision of Israel from the Perspective of Washington

President Barack Obama, Passover, Jerusalem, March 21, 2013 — addressed to the Israeli people

SHALOM. It is an honor to be here with you in Jerusalem. Over the last two days, I have reaffirmed the bonds between our countries . . . Those ties began only eleven minutes after Israeli independence, when the United States was the first nation to recognize the State of Israel. As President Truman said in explaining his decision to recognize Israel, **"I believe it has a glorious future before it not just as another sovereign nation, but as an embodiment of the great ideals of our civilization."**

I have borne witness to the ancient history of the Jewish people at the Shrine of the Book, and I have seen Israel's shining future in your scientists and entrepreneurs. This is **a nation of museums and patents, timeless holy sites and ground-breaking innovation**. Only in Israel could you see the Dead Sea Scrolls and the place where the technology on board the Mars Rover originated. But what I've looked forward to the most is the ability to speak directly to you, the Israeli people — especially so many young people — about **the history that brought us here today, and the future that you will make in the years to come.**

I know that I come to Israel on the eve of a sacred holiday — the celebration of **Passover** . . . Just a few days from now, Jews here in Israel and around the world will sit with family and friends at the seder table, and celebrate with songs, wine and symbolic foods. After enjoying seders with family and friends in Chicago and on the campaign trail, **I'm proud to have brought this tradition into the White House. I did so because I wanted my daughters to experience the Haggadah, and the story at the center of Passover that makes this time of year so powerful.**

It is a story of centuries of slavery, and years of wandering in the desert; a story of perseverance amidst persecution, and faith in God and the Torah. It is a story about finding freedom in your own land. For the Jewish people, this story is central to who you have become. But it is also a story that holds within it the universal human experience, with all of its suffering and salvation. It is a part of the three great religions — Judaism, Christianity, and Islam — that trace their origins to Abraham, and see Jerusalem as sacred. And it is **a story that has inspired communities around the globe, including me and my fellow Americans**.

Of course, even as we draw strength from the story of God's will and His gift of freedom expressed on Passover, we know that here on Earth we must bear our responsibilities in an imperfect world. That means accepting our measure of sacrifice and struggle, and working — through generation after generation — on behalf of that ideal of freedom. As Dr. Martin Luther King said [echoing Moses' speech before dying at edge of the Promised Land] on the day before he was killed — **"I may not get there with you. But I want you to know that . . . we, as a people, will get to the promised land."** So just as Joshua carried on after Moses, the work goes on — for justice and dignity; for opportunity and freedom.

For the Jewish people, the journey to the promise of the State of Israel wound through countless generations. It involved centuries of suffering and exile, prejudice, pogroms and even genocide. Through it all, the Jewish people sustained their unique identity and traditions, as well as a longing to return home. And while Jews achieved extraordinary success in many parts of the world, the dream of true freedom finally found its full expression in the Zionist idea — **"to be a free people in your homeland"** [as it says in the Jewish national anthem, *HaTikvah*]. That is why I believe that Israel is rooted not just in history and tradition, but also in a simple and profound idea: the idea that people deserve to be free in a land of their own. And over the last 65 years, when Israel has been at its best, **Israelis have demonstrated that responsibility does not end when you reach the promised land, it only begins.** ◆

Hope: The Trials of Patience

*Vaclav Havel, The Art of the Impossible.
Prague, Czechoslovakia, 1997*

ALTHOUGH I AM TRAINED in the dissident type of patience based on the awareness that waiting has a meaning, nevertheless . . . I have been seized again and again by a desperate impatience. I have agonized over how slowly things are changing . . . .

I longed desperately for at least some of these problems to be resolved so that I could cross them off the list and put them out of the way. I longed for some visible, tangible, indisputable evidence that something was finished, over and done with. I found it difficult to accept that politics, like history itself, is a never-ending process, in which nothing is ever definitely over. It was as though I had forgotten how to wait, to wait in the way that has meaning.

"Next Year in Lod"

Shelly Horowitz. Lod, Israel, 2012

"The author must be Ethiopian — He understands!
Maybe God is also Ethiopian."

SEVERAL WEEKS AGO I led an unforgettable mock Seder and a real meal for kids and their immigrant parents from Ethiopia and Russia who now reside in a poor neighborhood in Lod. The idea started when Noam Zion gave me 40 copies of his haggadah. I started thinking. Why not do a pre-seder in Lod where I teach? So I made three turkeys, a "traditional seder plate" and loaded up the haggadot. We started with 15 who listened politely. Those who could read (mostly the children, not the adults), read. Two adults left the room and returned with 25 more. My first impression was that people came for the meal — and even that was worth the effort! *("Let all who are hungry come and eat!")* But the comments showed that what they took home from the evening was much more.

When we read, *"Let My People Go,"* and *"Everyone must see themselves as if they went out of Egypt,"* there was incredible interest — and identification. We looked at the photograph of Ethiopians walking to Addis Abba on their way to leave Ethiopia for Israel and then at the Israeli stamp commemorating — in Russian — the Exodus of Soviet Jewry. The eyes of the Ethiopian adults lit up and there were murmurs and nodding. The Russian Jews also spoke up. One father told his story as a refusenik (a Soviet Jew who asked for permission to make aliyah, was refused, lost his job and suffered for many years until permission was granted). So I told him the story of my father Herb Kohn and of Noam's father, Rabbi Moshe Sachs, whose Soviet Jewry Action Committee (1970) spoke by telephone weekly with Russian Jewish refuseniks. With explanations in Russian and Amharic everyone understood. It was most amazing to see the Russian and Ethiopian Jews bonding as they realized that in many ways (language NOT being one of them) a common experience united them.

After the stories and the food, I took out my guitar and taught them "Who Knows One" *(Ehad Mi Yodeia)*. Everyone seemed happy, but after three hours, it was time to leave. I told everyone they could take their haggadah home as a gift and they were literally speechless, until one Ethiopian, hugging the haggadah, said, "Now I own my own book!" This was a HUGE occasion. They were stunned that they would OWN a book. Books were not in the average Ethiopian's budget or culture. It was a mark of having arrived.

People commented: "This is my story — I too went out!" / "I do not know if this is true but they tell it so beautifully." / "The illustrations are so very nice and comics too!" / "This is really NOT boring!" / "The author must be Ethiopian — He understands! / Maybe God is also Ethiopian."

I think a tradition has just been created . . . "Next Year in Lod, again!"

'If you will it, it is no dream.'

Herzl the Dreamer

Selections from the 1895 diaries of the Founder of the Zionist Movement.

• Hebrew School Memories

"I recall that I received a thrashing because I did not remember the details of the Exodus of the Jews from Egypt. Nowadays many schoolmasters would like to thrash me because I remembered that Exodus only too well."

• A Madman's Letter

Herzl wrote:

"I have the solution to the Jewish question. I know it sounds mad . . . This simple old idea is the Exodus from Egypt . . . I can see your troubled face, as you stroke your beard and murmur, 'completely out of his head . . . the poor family.'"

The Rabbi of Vienna replied:

"I could think you were Moses."

• A Novel or a Reality?

"I have been pounding away for some time at a work of tremendous magnitude. It bears the aspects of a mighty dream. For days and weeks it has saturated me to the limits of my consciousness. What will come of it is still too early to say. However, even as a dream, it is remarkable and should be written down — if not as a memorial for mankind, then for my own pleasure and meditation in years to come. Or perhaps as something for literature. If no action emerges from this romancing, a novel, at least, will emerge entitled: *The Promised Land*."

Within Ourselves

"NO ONE HAS EVER THOUGHT of looking for the Promised Land in the place where it really is — and yet it lies so near. It is here: within ourselves! For everyone will carry over there, in himself, a piece of the Promised Land. This one, in his head, that one, in his hands, the third in his savings. The Promised Land is where we carry it!"

(Theodore Herzl, 1895)

The Return

Behold the days come, says the Lord,
when I will return the captivity of my people Israel;
They will build the destroyed cities and inhabit them.
They will plant vineyards and drink their wine.
They will make gardens and eat their fruit.
I will plant them upon their land,
And they will never again be uprooted from the land which I have given them,
Says the Lord, your God.

(Amos 8:13-15)

Story-telling

Jerusalem, Herzl

Acknowledgments

"Either companionship and collaboration or death"   *(B.T. Taanit 23a)*

A special thanks to the Zion, Dishon and Gelles family members who celebrated Pesach with us creatively, and especially to Tanya Zion, the in-house artist, Mishael Zion, our personal computer expert, Heftziba and Eden Zion, who folded hundreds of brochures, and Yedidya Zion for his patience. Above all, thanks to those "righteous women" Marcelle Zion, Gila Dishon, and Mia Buchwald Gelles, who sustained us in our *Mitzrayeem* and who saw us through the wilderness.

"Be warned! The making of many books is without limit . . . and very wearying . . . ."

(Ecclesiastes 12:12)

Foreword: A Haggadah to Grow With

Dear Reader,

We at the Shalom Hartman Institute in Jerusalem have been researching the Haggadah and its educational principles for a decade. At last we venture beyond scholarly essays to an experimental Haggadah which is designed to enable the contemporary Jew to lead an interactive and intellectually stimulating seder. While holding to the traditional text of the seder, we have discovered that much can be done to make the seder **more responsive to contemporary needs and simultaneously truer to the spirit of the Rabbis as educators**. Rabbinic tradition mandates the kind of innovations that appear throughout this Haggadah.

Our Haggadah facilitates a seder that is as an educational dialogue between parent and child, leader and participant. *A Different Night* offers stories and readings as well as commentaries and activities that can fuel a dynamic evening of storytelling and discussion, dramatics and singing. The illustrations drawn from medieval and modern artists serve as visual commentaries that evoke discussion. We have assembled many artistic portrayals of the Four Children to encourage comparison and debate.

True to the spirit of the Haggadah we have sought to be eclectic, building on the creative artistry and intellectual insight of others: Maimonides, Ben Gurion and I.B. Singer, Ben Shahn and Marc Chagall, gifted children's writers, cartoonists and philosophers.

Everyone — whether adult or child — can feel at home in this **inclusive, pluralistic Haggadah**. Transliterations and contemporary translations make the traditional Hebrew accessible to all.

With this Haggadah the seder may be customized to match each family's needs and religious commitments. One can choose a short seder (an hour) or a long seder following various trails through the wealth of options provided. Every year you can focus on different aspects of the seder — preserving what you love and experimenting with new ideas. (*The Leader's Guide*, a separate companion volume, provides practical advice as well as background essays for preparing the Passover evening most appropriate for you.)

This is **a Haggadah to grow with from Pesach to Pesach**; a resource to enable each seder to be different than its predecessor. With *A Different Night* your seder will maximize the active participation of everyone.

On this night all of us must feel that we experienced the Exodus and that **the holiday of freedom belongs to us personally**.

Noam Sachs Zion and David Dishon

P.S. Please share with us your responses to this Haggadah.

The Shalom Hartman Institute, founded by the Jewish philosopher Rabbi David Hartman and headed by Rabbi Donniel Hartman, is an educational, learning and research center serving all sectors of the Jewish world that wish to enrich their dialogue with Jewish texts and to have it impact on their lives. The Hartman Institute is devoted to pluralist, non-denominational study of Judaism and it includes men and women from all varieties of Jewish faith and practice.

Library of Congress 96-7 1600
© Noam Zion and David Dishon
Published in the U.S.A., 1997
Pesach, 14th Nisan, 5757.
Revised 2015

Haggadahs-R-Us
1888 So. Compton Rd.
Cleveland Heights, OH 44118
Toll-free: 877-308-4175
Email: jbgelles@gmail.com

Shalom Hartman Institute
http://hartman.org.il/
Email: noam.zion@gmail.com

Table of Contents

A Friendly Warning

Do not try to do it all in one night. This Haggadah offers resources for many years of Pesach seders. Pick and choose the readings and activities that are most appropriate for the seder at hand. *(See the user's guide on the following pages.)*

Dedications and Sponsors

We wish to thank our many sponsors whose faith in the educational power of this Haggadah expressed itself in generous grants for its development.

Eunice & Ernest Benchell

Dr. Emile & Gail Bendit

Marilyn, Ellen & David Bierman

Brenda Brown-Lipitz

Deborah & Gerald Charnoff

Gary & Margey Cheses

Ann & Ari Deshe

Leonard Fein

Rina & Samuel Frankel

Jean & Jerry Friedman

Mia & Joe Buchwald Gelles

Susie & Michael Gelman

Herb & Dee Dee Glimcher

Gary & Cari Gross

Dr. Merle & Anna Hillman

LeRoy E. & Rebecca Hoffberger

Holly & Bradley Kastan

Elie Katz

The Kayne and Kane Families

Philip & Phyllis Margolius

The children of Harvey & Lyn Meyerhoff

Bonnie & David Milenthal

The Moskowitz Family

Karen & Neil Moss

Henry & Bella Muller

Charles & Ilana Horowitz Ratner

Bernice Rosenthal

Leonard & Lainy LeBow Sachs

Marc Saltzberg

Jeffrey & Jodie Schein

Robert & Janice Schottenstein

Steven & Jill Schottenstein

Alvin Cramer Segal

Kathy Levin Shapiro & Sandy Shapiro

Children & grandchildren of Dr. Hyman Shapiro

Chuck & Joyce Shenk

Charna Sherman

Mark Silverstein

Carol & Norman Traeger

The Wexner Heritage Fellows of Phoenix

Gordon & Carol Zacks

The User's Guide to 'A Different Night'

'Only the lesson which is enjoyed can be learned well'

A Rich Menu: Don't Overeat!

*How can you enjoy the resources of **A Different Night** without being overwhelmed?*

This special Haggadah contains a rich **menu** of stories, songs, activities, explanations and topics for discussion which supplement the traditional seder. These add spice and variety. As in any menu we are not expected to order everything but to select what we feel is appropriate for this particular evening. While following the basic traditional order, there is room for a few additions and a few substitutions chosen to fit the tastes and talents of the participants.

Please don't "overeat" or over-plan for the seder. You can always return to the menu and order something else the next night or the next year. Regard **A Different Night** as a collection of options, not as a required course adding more obstacles on the path through the Haggadah before reaching the food. Pick a few things and see how they develop!

Don't Starve!

How can we add more activities to the seder when people already complain that it is too long?

A major obstacle to making the seder more creative and more educational is the **rumbling stomachs** that murmur: "When do we eat already?" Sitting at a beautifully set table naturally evokes a Pavlovian response as our mouths start to water.

Extensive **dipping** is our solution. To prevent hunger from undermining your best efforts to create "a different night," you may offer extensive hors d'oeuvres. Along with the **karpas** — the traditional dipping of parsley, celery or potato in salt water — serve more substantive appetizers. This was the original Rabbinic custom. The stomach which gets its due early in the seder liberates the mind to engage in the main course of the seder: telling the story and discussing freedom and slavery. (A light meal — with no matza! — in the late afternoon before seder night is also helpful.)

Short Cuts through the Haggadah

How can we plan a reasonably short but lively seder?

Many of us have **only one hour** or so to devote to the Haggadah before the meal begins. Yet the traditional text is so long and the supplementary materials, though fascinating, make it longer. Speed-reading through the Haggadah misses the whole point of the seder as a family learning experience with dialogue, dramatics and discussion.

Our proposed solution is designed for families who generally skip sections of the traditional text anyway. It will help them to balance **skipping** and **supplementing** within a very limited time frame. We call it the **"Bare Bones Basic Seder."** It identifies the basic essentials of the Haggadah (minimal readings, songs and rituals) that can be completed in approximately half an hour. This leaves plenty of time to add a few enriching activities and readings that make this seder special, before beginning the main meal.

It is easy to locate the B.B.B. sections by following the ❖ in the body of the Haggadah. You will find an item-by-item summary of the B.B.B. Seder on page 8.

Note: The Bare Bones Basics do not correspond precisely to formal halachic requirements (traditional Jewish law). They are aids to locate the most popular and the most meaningful elements of the traditional seder. (For those concerned with the minimal halachic standards, consult your rabbi).

On the RIGHT HAND PAGE you find the main line of the traditional seder (directions, Hebrew, English and transliterations for pieces which are often sung or recited together). Please treat the "Directions" as helpful guidelines, not as obligations that must be done at all costs.

A Navigation Bar is located on the side with some of the previous activities in pale color and the present activity named in dark color.

For example,

| Kadesh |
| Urchatz |
| Karpas |
| Yachatz |

On the LEFT HAND PAGE you will find explanations, stories, readings and personal meditations. **Activities** to be performed (not merely **read**) by the participants are specially marked in shaded colored areas. In addition, **The Leader's Guide** (which is a separate companion volume) provides many more activities and stories for future years including special suggestions for younger children.

ILLUSTRATIONS provide not only artistic variety for child and adult, but a form of running commentary to be "read" and discussed like the written texts. In particular, see the ten-page art section (pages 62-71) with twenty artistic renditions of the Four Children that invite comparison and debate. The editors of this Haggadah do not endorse any one of these artistic interpretations, but we do encourage a lively discussion about them. A commentary on each picture of the Four Children is provided in the original edition of this haggadah, and can be found online at haggadahsrus.com.

Starting from the end of this revised edition of the haggadah you will find a supplement of 33 pages of CONTEMPORARY SEDER STORIES. It is organized according to the themes in the haggadah. Choose from its amazing anecdotes to enrich your seder.

At first glance the traditional Haggadah may seem like a hodgepodge of texts and activities. That first impression is not surprising for the Haggadah is an eclectic anthology constructed by many hands over two thousand years.

Therefore, we have highlighted the underlying structure of the Haggadah built around the four cups. Each of the four major sections is keyed in the corner of the page by a graphic representation of a cup.

First Cup: 'Kadesh'

The evening opens with the sanctification of the holiday by an initial invocation and with appetizers (dips).

Second Cup: 'Maggid'

Questions and storytelling in multiple versions fill this longest part of the seder. After telling the story of Exodus and explaining the symbolic foods that trigger memories of Egypt, we sing a song of praise to God our liberator.

Third Cup: 'Shulchan Orech'

The meal begins with matza and maror and concludes with the blessing after eating called "Birkat HaMazon."

Elijah's Cup:

After dinner an extra cup is poured in honor of Elijah and the door is opened to welcome the messianic age.

Fourth Cup: 'Hallel'

The Psalms and their blessings are sung responsively.

Concluding Songs

The famous folksongs like "Chad Gadya" constitute a medieval appendix to the Rabbinic four cup structure.

On Maximizing Participation

A seder run completely by the leader — even though informative and entertaining — is less desirable than a seder which encourages many people to participate. Participation should not be limited to letting everyone read a different paragraph in turn. We suggest that the leader **delegate responsibilities** in advance. Ask several guests to take charge of different sections of the seder for 3-5 minutes each. Send each a copy of the appropriate section of *A Different Night*, which includes explanations, stories and activities, to help them prepare.

From our experience, those most resistant to a lengthy seder can be turned into allies, if they have a creative part to play that taps their special interests and talents. Time goes by very quickly and painlessly when there is lots of participation.

The Bare Bones Basic Seder

To identify the recommended B.B.B. sections, follow the colored ❖ that appears throughout *A Different Night* and skip the rest. Then select a few enrichment activities and readings appropriate for this year's guests. In subsequent years you will probably want to vary and expand on the B.B.B., but this is a good way to get started.

Remember: sections 1-17 (before the meal) should take about an hour. Add in a few activities, readings, and discussions according to your choosing. It is wise for the leader to select some sections in advance. Don't be surprised if people begin to improvise and extend the seder voluntarily.

Guide for the Perplexed Seder Leader

Homemade Judaism: Infusing Your Passover Seder with Meaning. The seder is the setting for annually renewing our membership in the extended family, the historic Jewish people and the universal prophetic vision of social justice and liberation. It is the site for initiating young Jews into a tradition that in the coming generation they will be asked to lead. Therefore it is best to involve them in shaping and steering that experience as soon and as much as possible. It is an opportunity for many Jews, who have not always found their Judaism welcoming, exciting and inspiring, to come as guests and to leave as co-partners in the Jewish project begun by Abraham and Sarah. Often it is the place to showcase the best Jewish tradition has to offer both to nonJews who have joined our family and to those who are friends.

Home is where Jews are made, for such family events leave indelible (positive as well as negative) memories. It is at home around the seder table that we must prepare and season-to-taste our own brand of Homemade Judaism. The traditional ritual order, which is the original meaning of the word "seder," is only the external scaffold which we must fill in with our own thoughts of freedom and identity and our own agenda of stories and ethical dilemmas. When asked the eternal question 'what is being served at the seder?' the answer must include aromatic food for thought as well as for the palate. No Jewish event is without extensive nourishment, but the seder is for thought-provoking table talk as much as for timeless recipes. When asked what kind of seder are you giving, one must answer back: **And what will you, as our guest and co-participant, bring to the mix at our table** — stories, questions, experiences, musical and dramatic talents and a sense of humor. When people help "make" the seder, they also "make it meaningful."

'Was it a good seder this year?' Don't ask 'how much was read aloud' (and certainly not 'how quickly did we get to the meal and how early did we get home'). The seder ritual went astray from the rabbinic ideal centuries ago when it became a public reading of a sacred text. The seder is supposed to be a series of oral activities: tasting and telling, asking and answering, discussing and singing. Traditional ritual activities punctuate and integrate more flexible and open-ended activities. The Rabbis measured the successful seder by how many children and adults asked serious questions (not just those memorized by rote), how dramatically and extemporaneously the Exodus was retold (even if it took all night long). At the emotional level, it matters most how deeply did each and every one personally relive the liberation

from their Egypt and the beginning of their journey to a promised land. If that was accomplished, then they were confident that the participants would feel gratitude for their freedom and sing a 'new song to God' (while imbibing at least four cups of wine). To help achieve that experiential high, Jewish tradition mandated the use of many props (seder plate, kiddush cups, sometimes afikoman bags and a priestly gown called a kittel) and edible symbols (maror, matza, and haroset). But neither the text to be read nor the food to be broken, hidden, sandwiched, swilled and blessed, was enough. A seder aims at personal identification with slavery and freedom, with the poor and the persecuted, and a profound hope for Next Year in Jerusalem and for world peace.

But who can lead such a seder? What talents are needed to orchestrate and maximize participation of such a varied and often motley crew of guests at the table? The rabbinic seder is so challenging, for it is four kinds of activity rolled into one: (1) an **intellectual symposium** modeled on the Greek symposium; (2) a reenactment of the **priestly service of the Passover sacrifice in the Temple** with ceremonial foods eaten in the proper order at the right time; (3) **retelling, re-experiencing the original Exodus** as a moving drama; and (4) an **intergenerational family meal** in which grandparents, parents and children of all ages engage in dialogue designed to "turn the hearts of the children to their parents and the hearts of the parents to their children." *(Malachi 3:24)*

Presiding over the building of bridges across the generation gap is Elijah. You have to do that with people of different ages, backgrounds, attitudes to Judaism, and often religions. It's almost a 'mission impossible' to balance all those elements. Who can do all that, in one night (or even two nights) and with such limited talents and knowledge (while so many complaining relatives are so worried about the food)?

Building a Coalition and Delegating Responsibility. My practical advice is to do what you do best and to find — in advance — those with talents that complement yours. Find someone to share cooking, shopping, salad cutting, dips. Equally important, assign four people to do what they are best at: one **storyteller** with a dramatic flair to re-enact the exodus; one **traditionalist** (preferably with a good voice) to do the Hebrew songs and kiddush; one **educator** or **psychologist** to provoke questions and to analyze the best approach to the so-called rebellious, "wicked child;" one **political activist** to raise contemporary issues of freedom and slavery, poverty and social justice (but without preaching divisive political views that alienate and polarize). Don't do it all yourself even if you can. Don't spare your guests the work of preparation, because when they help, they also have buy-in; they also can make meaning. You should be an orchestrator, not a one-man/woman band. So pick the people to contribute not necessarily based on their prior Jewish knowledge, but on their positive energy and openness to experiment. Since all changes generate discomfort (do you need a family

therapist?), you do not want to go it alone.

Planning What To Do, What to Read, and, equally important, What to Skip. Generally, less is better, as long as what you do is good. This is not your last seder, so you can do more and differently the next night or the next year. You must definitely innovate some things in keeping with the wisdom of Saul Bellow, **"Ah, we Jews are very impatient with doing the same thing over and over again. It's gotta to be different!"** That is Maimonides' instruction as well: make it different so people will ask, "Why is this seder different than all other seders?" Manage family conflicts and anxiety levels which, while unavoidable, may be controlled. Push for change, however never change more than 10% of your seder in any one year. In some families even that is too much, but you owe it to yourself and your children to make this memorable. Do not let seder become merely a Jewish Thanksgiving where football and turkey are its only content. There are plenty of chances for family gatherings in a more flexible setting, but the seder is more than that. Let people know in advance what you expect: this year will be a little different and a little more serious but probably a lot more fun and engaging.

Surprise Guests: What to do with Bob Dylan and Marlon Brando at Your Seder

The Reform rabbi, Haskell Bernat, recalls his first Passover at the prominent Temple Israel of Hollywood. He was expected to conduct a public seder at the synagogue, just as had his predecessor who put on a show and invited eminent Los Angeles personalities. Bernat, however, believed in intimate family seders at home. He agreed reluctantly to lead the public seder but declined to prepare a dramatic program.

Bernat was about to start with an expected 300 attendees, when in walked unexpected guests — Bob Dylan along with two well-known non Jews — an Indian chief and Marlon Brando. In panic mode the rabbi asked the president of the congregation, "Are we built on an Amerind burial plot?" Thinking on his feet, Bernat thought of creative ways to involve his surprise guests at the seder. He asked Marlon Brando to do a dramatic reading in English of the Kiddush, while the rabbi explained that Passover is about the liberation of all nations (to make it relevant to the chief). Later he asked his cantor to bring her guitar and then invited Bob Dylan to sing *Blowing in the Wind* with its appropriate Passover lyrics, "Yes, 'n' how many years can some people exist, before they're allowed to be free?" Next year 500 people showed up for the public seder.

Beware of Complaining About Boring Seders

[In medieval Catholic Europe] religion was not a laughing matter, at least for the officials assigned to enforce orthodoxy. They did not treat even trivial jokes lightly. In France, a villager was arrested for having exclaimed, when a friar announced after mass that he would say a few words about God, "The fewer the better."

In Spain, a tailor named Garcia Lopez, coming out of church just after the priest had announced the long schedule of services for the coming week, quipped that: "When we were Jews, we were bored stiff by one Passover each year, and now each day seems to be a Passover and feast-day." Garcia Lopez was denounced to the Inquisition.

(Steven Greenblatt, The Swerve, 236)

The Night Before the Seder
The Search for Chametz

1. **The Search for Chametz** (products containing leavened grain) is the ceremonial culmination of several weeks of transforming the house into a sanctified setting for Pesach. The physical efforts help create a psychological readiness for the seder.

2. **Prior to** this evening's ceremony, we **clean** all the rooms where food might have been eaten or stored, so that no chametz is left. We **collect** all the chametz products (like spaghetti or whiskey) and put them in a cabinet. We **seal** it, mark it as chametz, and **sell** its contents to a non-Jew for the duration of the holiday. Generally a local rabbi will serve as your agent for the ritual "sale."

3. **After dark**, on the night before the seder (or two nights before the seder when it falls on Saturday night), conduct a candlelight search for chametz into all the corners of the house. (In Eastern Europe Jews used a candle, a feather to sweep the crumbs and a wooden spoon to collect them. For greater safety you may prefer a flashlight to a candle.) We recommend that ten pieces of chametz be hidden before the search begins, to enhance the fun of the search for the children.

4. **Before the search** recite the blessing. After the search recite the Aramaic formula for disowning any chametz still undiscovered in the home.

B'deekat Chametz

The Search

The Blessing before the Search in the Evening:

BLESSED ARE YOU, Adonai our God, Ruler of the Universe, who sanctified us by commanding us to remove all chametz.

Ba-ruch ata Adonai
Elo-hei-nu me-lech ha-olam,
asher kee-d'sha-nu b'meetz-vo-tav
v'tzee-va-nu al bee-ur cha-metz.

בָּרוּךְ אַתָּה יי
אֱלֹהֵינוּ מֶלֶךְ הָעוֹלָם,
אֲשֶׁר קִדְּשָׁנוּ בְּמִצְוֹתָיו,
וְצִוָּנוּ עַל בְּעוּר חָמֵץ.

The Formula for Disowning Unseen Chametz After the Search:

ALL CHAMETZ in my possession, whether I have seen it or not and whether I have removed it or not, shall be nullified and ownerless as the dust of the earth.

Sefer HaMinhagim, Amsterdam

כָּל חֲמִירָא וַחֲמִיעָא דְּאִכָּא
בִּרְשׁוּתִי דְּלָא חֲמִתֵּה וּדְלָא
בְעַרְתֵּהּ וּדְלָא יְדַעְנָא בֵּיה
לִבָּטֵל וְלֶהֱוֵי הֶפְקֵר כְּעַפְרָא
דְאַרְעָא.

Sherlock Holmes and the Haggadah

In the picture on this page, we have dispersed ten small pictures of a challah. Later on in the Haggadah we have hidden ten small matzot (afikoman). Good luck ferreting them out!

Searching for Chametz

Complications

WHEN SEDER NIGHT FALLS ON Saturday evening, the search is conducted on Thursday night and the bonfire on Friday morning. Challah is put aside in a special "chametz zone" in the house to be eaten by approximately 10 a.m. on Shabbat morning. The leftovers may be removed by means of a flush of the toilet.

Keeping Your Pockets Clean

RABBI MOSHE ISSERLES (16th C. Poland) required that the search for chametz include checking one's pockets. The Kabbalist Isaiah Horowitz added an ethical dimension to this internal audit: check carefully that your pockets contain no funds deriving from theft, robbery or fraud.

Hide and Go Seek

A medieval custom perfectly suited to a children's game involves hiding ten pieces of bread throughout the house before the candlelight search for chametz begins. Originally this was done to guarantee that even after the scrupulous cleaning, the ritual search on the last night before seder would still uncover some chametz. Today it provides an occasion for a game in which ten pieces of bread secured in closed plastic bags are carefully concealed.

On each bag a word or a clue or a question may be attached (the words add up to a secret message or a Pesach song; the clues hint at the next hiding place; the ten questions constitute a quiz about basic Pesach facts).

Remember that besides finding the pre-hidden bags of chametz, one must genuinely check the typical "hang-outs" of forgotten chametz (like the car's glove compartment).

The Morning Before the Seder
The Burning of the Chametz

בְּעוּר חָמֵץ

1. **The Burning** of the Chametz marks the symbolic division between chametz and matza, winter and spring, the evil inclination and the desire for purity.

2. **Before** approximately 10 a.m. on the day of the seder, we stop eating chametz and gather the leftovers for a ritual bonfire outside.

3. **After** the chametz has been burned (or rendered inedible in some other way), the owners of the house repeat the formula disowning any undiscovered chametz on their premises. From now on, no chametz may be eaten.

4. **Aramaic**, the language of the Talmud, is used for this legal formula.

B'deekat Chametz
Bee-ur Chametz

Burning Leaven

The Formula for Disowning the Leftover Chametz:

ALL CHAMETZ in my possession,
whether I have seen it or not
and whether I have removed it or not,
shall be nullified and be ownerless
as the dust of the earth.

כָּל חֲמִירָא וַחֲמִיעָא דְּאִכָּא בִּרְשׁוּתִי,
דַּחֲזִיתֵּהּ וּדְלָא חֲזִיתֵהּ, דַּחֲמִתֵּהּ
וּדְלָא חֲמִתֵּהּ, דְּבִעַרְתֵּהּ וּדְלָא
בִעַרְתֵּהּ, לִבְטִיל וְלֶהֱוֵי הֶפְקֵר כְּעַפְרָא
דְאַרְעָא.

Prague, 1526

Meditation on the Spiritual Yeast:
Removing the Evil Inclination from Our Hearts

GOD, MAY IT BE Your will, that just as we remove all the chametz from our house and from all that we control, so may You help us to remove all the impure forces from the earth and our evil inclinations from within us and renew our heart of flesh. May all negative forces disappear like smoke. Remove tyrannical governments from the world and all who cause anguish to the Divine Presence. Blow them away with a spirit of justice, just as you did to Egypt and their idols in those days long ago.

יְהִי רָצוֹן מִלְּפָנֶיךָ יי אֱלֹהֵינוּ וֵאלֹהֵי אֲבוֹתֵינוּ, כְּשֵׁם
שֶׁאֲנִי מְבַעֵר חָמֵץ מִבֵּיתִי וּמֵרְשׁוּתִי כָּךְ תְּבַעֵר אֶת
הַחִיצוֹנִים וְאֶת רוּחַ הַטֻּמְאָה תְּבַעֵר מִן הָאָרֶץ וְאֶת
יִצְרֵנוּ הָרָע תְּבַעֵר מֵאִתָּנוּ וְתִתֶּן לָנוּ לֵב בָּשָׂר, וְכָל
הַסִּטְרָא אָחֳרָא וְכָל הָרִשְׁעָה כְּעָשָׁן תִּכְלֶה וְתַעֲבִיר
מֶמְשֶׁלֶת זָדוֹן מִן הָאָרֶץ, וְכָל הַמְּעִיקִים לַשְּׁכִינָה
תְּבַעֲרֵם בְּרוּחַ בָּעֵר וּבְרוּחַ מִשְׁפָּט כְּשֵׁם שֶׁבִּעַרְתָּ אֶת
מִצְרַיִם וְאֶת אֱלֹהֵיהֶם בַּיָּמִים הָהֵם בַּזְּמַן הַזֶּה.

14

Procrastination and Chametz

SIMILARITIES between matza and chametz are many, while the difference is ever so slight. On Pesach that distinction takes on great significance. Both matza and bread are made of flour and water, and both may contain egg, onion, fruit juice, sugar, salt and other ingredients. However matza may contain no yeast nor may it be left to rise by itself after water has been added. The Rabbis fixed 18 minutes as the maximum time for making matza from the moment water and flour are mixed. They taught Jews to be very precise about time — not to procrastinate when making matza or doing any other mitzvah. (A word play conveys the idea that a procrastinator can easily "miss the boat" turning matza into chametz. They coined the motto: "When an opportunity to perform a *mitzvah* comes to you, don't miss it — tach*meetz*." *Mitzvah* is a word play on *matza, tachmeetz* on *chametz*).

Perhaps the Exodus from Egypt should be seen as a **window of opportunity** that the Jews had to be careful not to miss. Pharaoh kept changing his mind about liberating the Jews, and the children of Israel continued to hesitate about leaving their homes in Egypt. When the tenth plague struck, the Egyptians relented for a moment and released the Jews who had not even finished preparing bread for the journey. Nevertheless, they took the dough which had not yet risen and took advantage of their opportunity. When three days later Pharaoh sent his chariots to retrieve his slaves, God split the Red Sea to open an unexpected escape route. Again the Jews had to leap into the unknown and rush forward before the walls of water came crashing down again.

Search and Destroy: Forbidden Chametz

THE TORAH REQUIRES that chametz neither be eaten, nor seen, nor even located in one's house during Pesach *(Exodus 13:3, 7, 15)*. All yeast-based baked goods must be removed from our premises *(Exodus 12:15)*. The Rabbis detailed the process of removing chametz:

1. Bdeekat Chametz. The Search involves a careful cleaning of every place in the house where foods are eaten or stored, and a ceremonial investigation of "nooks and crannies" by candlelight on the night before the seder. *(Mishna Pesachim 1:1)*

2. Bee-ur Chametz. The **Removal of Chametz** is accomplished both physically and mentally. Physically the remains of the chametz are burned on the morning before the seder approximately two hours before noon. In the days of sacrifices, the Pesach lamb was sacrificed during the daylight from noon until sundown at which time the seder began. Since the sacrifice could not be accomplished in the presence of chametz *(Exodus 34:25)*, the *bee-ur chametz* had to precede the sacrifice, which began at noon. Since preparations before the seder often ran late, the Rabbis moved up the burning of the chametz two hours before noon "just to be on the safe side."

Mentally, the chametz is removed by pronouncing a formula written in Aramaic. The owners of the house (in which chametz may have gone undetected) disown what is left and declare it to be like the ownerless dust of the earth.

The Spiritual Significance of Yeast

THE OBSESSIVE SEARCH and destruction of chametz from our homes has spiritual as well as ritual overtones. Yeast came to symbolize **arrogance** because the bread raised itself above the level of matza though it was only filled with pockets of hot air. Yeast is also a catalyst that symbolizes the restless force of the evil inclination *(yetzer ha-ra)*. Just as yeast causes fermentation in bread and wine, it also turns them sour when not controlled. Similarly, the instinctual forces, desire and ambition, can contribute to progress but also to discontent and corruption. On Pesach, which celebrates the rejection of Egyptian civilization and a new pristine beginning of Jewish freedom, the matza is more appropriate fare than bread. Don Isaac Abarbanel *(15th C Spain and Italy)* explains that matza represents simplicity which is a desirable spiritual quality. Freedom involves the rejection of the *"fleshpots of Egypt" (Ex.16:13)* and the removal of the restless yeast of the evil inclination.

Candle Lighting

1. **Lighting the candles** marks the beginning of Pesach as well as the end of the frantic work of preparation. It contributes to the transition to sanctity.

2. **Before sunset,** it is traditional to light at least two candles placed on or near the table. Some families light one candle for each family member. Others prepare two candles for each woman over the age of bat mitzvah. Ideally, the candles should be longer lasting than usual, so they will provide light for the length of the seder.

3. **Usually on Pesach** one first recites the blessing and then lights the candles without covering one's eyes. However, when seder night occurs on Friday night, then one lights the candles first, covers one's eyes and then recites the blessing (as in Chagall's picture opposite).

Candle Lighting

BLESSED ARE YOU, Adonai our God, Ruler of the Universe, who sanctified us by commanding us to light the [Shabbat and] holiday candles.

Many say the following when lighting the candles, while others recite it together with Kiddush. (There is no need to recite this blessing twice).

BLESSED ARE YOU, Adonai our God, Ruler of the Universe, who has kept us alive and brought us to this happy moment in our lives.

Ba-ruch ata Adonai, Elo-hei-nu me-lech ha-olam, asher kee-d'sha-nu b'meetz-vo-tav v'tzee-va-nu l'had-leek ner shel [Shabbat v'shel] Yom Tov.

בָּרוּךְ אַתָּה יי
אֱלֹהֵינוּ מֶלֶךְ הָעוֹלָם,
אֲשֶׁר קִדְּשָׁנוּ בְּמִצְוֹתָיו,
וְצִוָּנוּ לְהַדְלִיק נֵר
שֶׁל (שַׁבָּת וְשֶׁל) יוֹם טוֹב.

Ba-ruch ata Adonai, Elo-hei-nu me-lech ha-olam she-he-chee-ya-nu v'kee-ma-nu v'hee-gee-anu laz-man ha-zeh.

בָּרוּךְ אַתָּה יי
אֱלֹהֵינוּ מֶלֶךְ הָעוֹלָם,
שֶׁהֶחֱיָנוּ וְקִיְּמָנוּ
וְהִגִּיעָנוּ לַזְּמַן הַזֶּה.

A Traditional Woman's Prayer at Candle Lighting

May it be Your will, God of our ancestors, that You grant my family and all Israel a good and long life. Remember us with blessings and kindness, fill our home with your Divine Presence. Give me the opportunity to raise my children and grandchildren to be truly wise, lovers of God, people of truth, who illuminate the world with Torah, good deeds and the work of the Creator. Please hear my prayer at this time. Regard me as a worthy descendant of Sarah, Rebecca, Rachel and Leah, our mothers, and let my candles burn and never be extinguished. Let the light of your face shine upon us. Amen.

Romance and Candlelighting

THE SADDUCEES *(1st C.)* and Karaites *(9th C.)* regarded the Biblical prohibition against *making* a fire on Shabbat *(Ex: 35:3)* as a prohibition against the use of its light as well as its creation. They sanctified Shabbat in darkness. Shabbat was a day of holy abstinence. It involved no warm food, no lamps and no sexual activity.

The point of view of the Rabbis, however, stands out in bold contrast. The Rabbis **prescribed** the lighting of candles and made the Shabbat lights and holiday candles in the home one of the most significant features of the day. They were seen as essential to *Shalom Bayit* — peace and intimacy between husband and wife in the home, and to *Oneg Shabbat* — physical and emotional enjoyment. Lovemaking by spouses on Shabbat was commended, as was the enjoyment of hot food.

A Woman's Mitzvah?

THE RABBINICAL commandment that the house be lit up on Shabbat requires that whoever takes care of holiday preparations should light the candles. Maimonides noted that in his era women are generally responsible for the household, so the mitzvah is incumbent primarily on them *(Shabbat 5:2)*. But in families where men share household tasks equally, the mitzvah may be equally incumbent on them. (In your home, who should be lighting candles?)

Shabbat Candles

Marc Chagall, 1946 © ADAGP, Paris 1996

Blessing the Children

בִּרְכַּת יְלָדִים

The custom of blessing one's children originates in the Bible. On the eve of Yom Kippur, on Shabbat and holidays many parents lay their hands on the head of each child, blessing them with the priests' benediction.

For male children:

MAY GOD make you like Ephraim and Menashe.

(Genesis 48:20 from Jacob's blessing for his grandchildren)

(לַבֵּן)

יְשִׂמְךָ אֱלֹהִים כְּאֶפְרַיִם וְכִמְנַשֶּׁה.

For female children:

MAY GOD make you like Sarah and Rebecca, Rachel and Leah.

(See Ruth 4:11, the women's blessing for Ruth, a Jew by choice)

(לַבַּת)

יְשִׂמֵךְ אֱלֹהִים כְּשָׂרָה רִבְקָה רָחֵל וְלֵאָה.

For all:

MAY GOD bless you and keep you.
May God's face shine upon you and favor you.
May God's face turn to you and grant you Shalom.

(Numbers 6:24-26, the priestly benediction)

יְבָרֶכְךָ יי וְיִשְׁמְרֶךָ.
יָאֵר יי פָּנָיו אֵלֶיךָ וִיחֻנֶּךָּ.
יִשָּׂא יי פָּנָיו אֵלֶיךָ
וְיָשֵׂם לְךָ שָׁלוֹם.

WHO IS GOD? WELL IT IS AN INVISIBLE
PERSON AND HE LIVES UP IN HEAVEN
I GUESS UP IN OUTER SPACE HE
MADE THE EARTH AND THE HEAVEN &
THE STARS AND THE SUN AND THE
PEOPLE HE MADE LIGHT HE MADE DAY
HE MADE NIGHT HE HAS SUCH POWER-
FUL EYES HE DOESN'T HAVE MILLIONS
AND THOUSANDS AND BILLIONS AND HE
CAN STILL SEE US WHEN WE'RE BAD
HE STARTED ALL THE PLANTS GROWING TO
ME I THINK OF HIM WHO MAKES FLOWERS
& GREEN GRASS & THE BLUE SKY &
THE YELLOW SUN GOD IS EVERYWHERE
& I DON'T KNOW HOW HE COULD DO IT

Who Knows God?

Ben Shahn © 1996
Ben Shahn Estate
Licensed by VAGA, NY, NY

*Jacob kissed and hugged his grandchildren. "I never expected to see your face again, Joseph, and now God has shown me your offspring." (Gen 48:11).
Rembrandt van Rijn, Jacob blessing his grandchildren, Ephraim and Menashe, the sons of Joseph (Holland, 1656).*

Signposts for the Seder

סִימָנֵי הַסֵּדֶר

1. *The official opening* of the seder should begin by welcoming all the guests. Make sure to introduce all the participants, so that everyone will be made to feel part of the Jewish family — especially on a night when we recall what it felt like to be strangers in the land of Egypt. You may ask all the participants to say their Hebrew names as well.

2. *We review* briefly the order of the seder by singing the medieval poem by Rabbenu Shmuel of Falaise (France) that summarizes the Signposts of the Seder ("Kadesh Urchatz").

3. *You may wish* to give credit to all who have helped prepare this seder — its foods, its readings and its activities.

Candle
Lighting

Blessing
the
Children

Sign
Posts

The Agenda
of the Seder

❖ THE 15 STEPS OF THE SEDER

All sing:		
Kadesh	First cup and Kiddush	קַדֵּשׁ וּרְחַץ
UrChatz	First handwashing (without a blessing)	
Karpas	First dipping: vegetable and salt water	כַּרְפַּס יַחַץ
Yachatz	Breaking the middle matza	
Maggid	Storytelling	מַגִּיד רַחְצָה
Rachtza	Second handwashing (with a blessing)	
Motzi	First blessing over the matza	מוֹצִיא מַצָּה
Matza	Second blessing over the matza	
Maror	Second dipping: maror in charoset	מָרוֹר כּוֹרֵךְ
Korech	Hillel sandwich	
Shulchan Orech	Festive meal	שֻׁלְחָן עוֹרֵךְ
Tzafun	Afikoman (dessert)	צָפוּן בָּרֵךְ
Barech	Birkat hamazon (the blessing after eating)	
Hallel	Psalms of praise	הַלֵּל נִרְצָה
Nirtza	Concluding prayer and folk songs	

SEDER MEANS ritual order, just as "siddur" means the order of prayers (the prayerbook). There may be surprises along the way, but the seder offers a basic road map for running the course(s) of the Pesach evening. Let us survey the signposts along the way, so that no one gets too lost and everyone gets their cue for inserting questions, dramatics, jokes, songs and games.

Welcome to the Seder

We welcome you to be full and equal participants in this communal event combining both ritual sanctity and a familiar home atmosphere. While the religious requirements governing eating and reading at the Pesach meal emphasize the sanctity of this meal, you will also discover the playful and intellectually stimulating aspects of the seder. The Rabbis added to this sacred banquet a lively symposium for the adults as well as many educational games to draw in the children. **Please feel free**, or better, obligated to ask questions, to insert personal reflections, to challenge assertions and to tell good stories.

We are all invited to take **a leap of solidarity** back into the founding event of Jewish nationhood — the Exodus. First we relive slavery and indignity and then we re-experience the exhilarating gift of Divine liberation. Our goal is to return to the experiential sources of the Jewish values of freedom and justice. We make this journey as individuals, as families and as a worldwide community. In reliving our national autobiography we renew our covenant with one another and with God, who took us out of the house of bondage.

We commit ourselves to God's words: "Love the stranger as yourself for you were once strangers in Egypt." *(Leviticus 19:34)*

The 15 Step Method

IN THE TEMPLE DAYS the spiritual pilgrimage reached its climax at the 15 stairs leading up to the Holy of Holies. On these steps the musicians of the tribe of Levi played and sang Shir HaMa'alot, the "Song of the Steps." Reaching a spiritually worthwhile destination requires a process, an effort to achieve new heights. One cannot expect to sense the power of the seder without strenuous preparations beforehand. May our intensive cleaning purify us and prepare us for a personal journey down into Egypt and back up to freedom.

Kadesh: Sanctifying Time
Kiddush

קַדֵּשׁ

1. *The Kiddush* sanctifies not the wine, but the holiday. Pesach is dedicated "to remember the Day of your Exodus from Egypt." *(Ex.13:3)* (On Shabbat add the texts in shaded boxes and in parentheses in the body of the Kiddush).

2. *Offer to pour* the wine or grape juice into someone else's cup. In turn each one is served by another as befits royalty. Having attained the high status of freedom we celebrate it in style, preferably with red wine, because the rabbis considered it more elegant.

3. *Mitzvah Readiness:* Before each special Pesach act — drinking the wine, eating the matza and maror, and telling the story — we have inserted an abbreviated meditation. Based on the Jewish mystical tradition, these preludes to ritual action direct our full attention to the spiritual task before us. They help raise mundane behaviors like eating and storytelling, to the level of a sacred moment.

4. *Stand* to recite the Kiddush, then *recline* to the left to drink the wine as befits nobles who once reclined at symposia (intellectual drinking banquets). If there are no pillows on the chairs, ask the children to bring as many as possible.

Kadesh

First Cup

HERE I AM, ready to perform the mitzvah of the first cup of wine and to dedicate this whole evening "to telling the story of miracles and wonders that were performed for our ancestors in Egypt on the night of the 15th of the month of Nisan" more than 3,300 years ago. This is what the Torah commands us: "Remember the day of your Exodus from Egypt"
(Ex. 13:3; Maimonides, Chametz 7:1).

הִנְנִי מוּכָן וּמְזוּמָּן
לְקַיֵּם מִצְוַת כּוֹס
רִאשׁוֹן שֶׁל אַרְבַּע כּוֹסוֹת.

On Shabbat rise and recite from Genesis 2:1-3:

[There was evening and there was morning, and the sixth day was over. The sky and the earth and all their contents were completed. On the seventh day God completed all the work. God ceased on Shabbat from all activity. God blessed the seventh day and declared it holy because on that day God ceased from all the work of creation.]

(וַיְהִי עֶרֶב וַיְהִי בֹקֶר)
יוֹם הַשִּׁשִּׁי, וַיְכֻלּוּ הַשָּׁמַיִם וְהָאָרֶץ וְכָל צְבָאָם. וַיְכַל אֱלֹהִים בַּיּוֹם
הַשְּׁבִיעִי, מְלַאכְתּוֹ אֲשֶׁר עָשָׂה, וַיִּשְׁבֹּת בַּיּוֹם הַשְּׁבִיעִי, מִכָּל
מְלַאכְתּוֹ אֲשֶׁר עָשָׂה. וַיְבָרֶךְ אֱלֹהִים אֶת יוֹם הַשְּׁבִיעִי, וַיְקַדֵּשׁ אֹתוֹ,
כִּי בוֹ שָׁבַת מִכָּל מְלַאכְתּוֹ, אֲשֶׁר בָּרָא אֱלֹהִים לַעֲשׂוֹת.

The Anniversary of the Birth of Freedom

זְמַן חֵרוּתֵינוּ

IT SEEMS SOMEWHAT paradoxical that Rosh Hashana, the Jewish New Year, occurs in the fall, while the first month of the Hebrew year is counted from Pesach, the spring holiday. The Jewish calendar reflects a double commitment — a celebration of the Creation of the world (traditionally associated with the fall, the beginning of the rainy season in the Middle East) and a commemoration of national liberation (associated with the springtime Exodus from Egypt). The origins of life and freedom, the universal and the national, orient our values and our measurement of time. Freedom is a second birth, a watershed from which life begins again.

Who Pours the Wine?

Roman and Rabbinic Table Manners and the Role of Women

On Pesach the Rabbis asked us to play a double role — remembering our slave status by eating the bread of poverty and bitter herbs, yet reiterating the freed status that we achieved on this very night in Egypt. How does one behave in a style befitting a free being?

The Rabbis took their cues from Greco-Roman citizens, a privileged minority whose freedom and dignity were displayed in their participation in elegant symposia. **Aristocratic dining** meant reclining on cushioned couches, sipping excellent wines with hors d'oeuvres dipped in appetizing sauces, eaten from one's finest silver and ceramic dishes, while conducting a leisurely intellectual exchange of views according to a well-known format set by the host. (The term "school" derives from the Greek word for leisure — "schole").

On seder night the Rabbis require this format from even the poorest Jews. Practically speaking, this means that the community tzedakah fund must provide at least four cups of wine for needy men and women. All must be able to celebrate their freedom with the same basic material comforts, because **"all Israel are regarded as children of royalty."** For that reason it is customary that someone else pour your wine for you, just as aristocrats are served while reclining.

However, we must note the vigorous dissent from this custom, by Rabbi Y. M. Epstein *(Poland, 19th C)*. He feared it would lead to what a contemporary might call blatant sexism or the exploitation of women to pour wine for the men:

"It is haughty and arrogant to order one's wife to serve him wine. After all he is no more obligated to drink wine than she. Therefore we ask that everyone pour for him or herself."

There is a simple solution to this problem. Participants may form pairs and each person pours for the other.

Reclining to the Left: An Outmoded Custom?

ONE OF THE FOUR questions is: "Why on seder night must we eat reclining, while on all other nights we may eat either reclining or sitting up?" Clearly the question presupposes a social world in which as in the Greco-Roman nobility, meals were often taken while the guests reclined on their left arms on couches, leaving their right hand free to dip and taste. At each couch was a small table with individual portions, like today's seder plate.

However, since the European Middle Ages, it is no longer the **way of nobility** to recline. In fact, eating while reclining on pillows is the **way of the sick**. Avi HaEzri led the Ashkenazi tradition in declaring the commandment to recline, obsolete and no longer binding. *(Rabbi Eliezer Ben Joel, 12th C. Germany)*

All things considered, we commend the view of Rabbi Y. M. Epstein that everyone should be provided with a pillow precisely because it is an outmoded and outlandish custom. For the point of the seder is to introduce changes into the meal, so the children will be aroused to ask: "Why is this night different from all other nights?" By the same token it would be ideal for everyone to have their own seder plate.

BLESSED ARE YOU, Adonai our God, Ruler of the Universe, who creates the fruit of the vine.

Ba-rukh ata Adonai
Elo-hei-nu me-lech ha-olam
bo-rei pree ha-gafen.

בָּרוּךְ אַתָּה יי,
אֱלֹהֵינוּ מֶלֶךְ הָעוֹלָם,
בּוֹרֵא פְּרִי הַגָּפֶן.

BLESSED ARE YOU, Adonai our God, Ruler of the Universe, who has chosen us from among the nations and the languages, sanctifying us by your mitzvot. Lovingly, You have given us [Shabbat for rest and] **festivals for happiness**, including today — [the Shabbat and] the **Holiday of the Matzot**, the **season of our liberation**, a sacred day to gather together and to commemorate the Exodus from Egypt. For You have chosen us and sanctified us among the nations. You have granted us [lovingly the Shabbat and] joyfully the holidays. Blessed are You, Adonai, who sanctifies [the Shabbat and] the people of Israel and the festivals.

בָּרוּךְ אַתָּה יי, אֱלֹהֵינוּ מֶלֶךְ הָעוֹלָם, אֲשֶׁר בָּחַר בָּנוּ
מִכָּל עָם, וְרוֹמְמָנוּ מִכָּל לָשׁוֹן, וְקִדְּשָׁנוּ בְּמִצְוֹתָיו.
וַתִּתֶּן לָנוּ יי אֱלֹהֵינוּ בְּאַהֲבָה (שַׁבָּתוֹת לִמְנוּחָה וּ)מוֹעֲדִים
לְשִׂמְחָה, חַגִּים וּזְמַנִּים לְשָׂשׂוֹן, אֶת יוֹם (הַשַּׁבָּת הַזֶּה
וְאֶת יוֹם) חַג הַמַּצּוֹת הַזֶּה, זְמַן חֵרוּתֵנוּ (בְּאַהֲבָה),
מִקְרָא קֹדֶשׁ, זֵכֶר לִיצִיאַת מִצְרָיִם. כִּי בָנוּ
בָחַרְתָּ וְאוֹתָנוּ קִדַּשְׁתָּ מִכָּל הָעַמִּים,
(וְשַׁבָּת) וּמוֹעֲדֵי קָדְשֶׁךָ (בְּאַהֲבָה וּבְרָצוֹן,)
בְּשִׂמְחָה וּבְשָׂשׂוֹן הִנְחַלְתָּנוּ.
בָּרוּךְ אַתָּה יי, מְקַדֵּשׁ
(הַשַּׁבָּת וְ)יִשְׂרָאֵל
וְהַזְּמַנִּים.

Kadesh

First Cup

Tully Filmus

24

The Centrality of Women on Pesach

RASHBAM *(11th C., France)* says women must be involved in the celebration of Pesach for they were the catalysts of the redemption by continuing to procreate and to hide their children in order to thwart Pharaoh's genocidal plan. Therefore women are obligated to drink four cups of wine at the seder.

In contrast to the traditional exemption of women from time-specific mitzvot, all the commandments of the seder night are their privilege and duty. The redemptive role of Moses' mother Yocheved and sister Miriam, like that of Queen Esther in the Megillah, won women exceptional recognition on both Pesach and Purim.

Do Kids Need Wine?

THE RABBIS were of two minds over the appropriateness of wine for children. The Talmud reports their dispute:

"Everyone is obligated to drink four cups of wine: men, women and children . . . But Rabbi Yehuda said: 'What good is wine for children? Give them popcorn* and peanuts on Pesach night in order to prevent them from falling asleep and in order to arouse them to ask questions." (T.B. Pesachim 108b)

Now is an appropriate time to distribute to the children candies and nuts along with wine or grape juice. Some families fill the children's cups with candies.

*(Popcorn refers to toasted grains, permissible on Pesach according to the Talmud and eaten on Pesach by Sefaradim.)

Today Everyone is a Priest

THE SEDER is no ordinary meal. It is a highly orchestrated rite of eating, questioning, telling, and singing. As Philo put it:

"At this time the whole household takes on the sanctity of a temple. The sacrifice becomes a seder meal. The invited guests cleanse themselves in water. They come not to fill their gullets with wine and their stomachs with food as at other symposia, but to celebrate with song, prayer (and story)."

"The whole people, old and young, ascend to the status of priests to conduct the holy service (the seder). For they all celebrate the great migration, when over 600,000 men and women happily exited from a land of cruelty and animosity towards strangers . . . ."

(Philo of Alexandria, Special Laws, the first Jewish philosopher)

'Don't Cry Over Spilt Wine'

A PUBLIC MESSAGE from the Hosts to All Their Guests:"Don't Cry over Spilt Wine."

Rabbi Akiba Eiger *(Germany 18th C.)* used to be very strict about the mitzvah of hospitality especially on Pesach. Once when he was leading a large seder, one of the guests happened to spill a cup of wine. The clean white tablecloth was stained. Seeing the guest's enormous embarrassment, Rabbi Eiger himself bumped the table spilling his own glass of wine. He exclaimed: **"Oh, this table must be off-balance."**

Havdalah: The Gift of Fire

IF PESACH FALLS on Saturday eve, havdalah is recited over the Pesach candles (not over a special havdalah candle). This blessing over the light celebrates the technological revolution by which human beings learned to make fire and to illuminate the darkness. The Rabbis trace this advance to a gift of knowledge from God to Adam and Eve who were frightened by the dark that set in after the first Shabbat of creation.

Since fire is a divine gift for human benefit, the blessing is recited over the use of the light. Often people examine their fingernails in the light of the candles when reciting *Me-orei Ha-eish*, the blessing over the "fire."

Creating Wine-Stained Heirlooms

IT WAS AN OLD heirloom, with ancient wine stains. It had come down from the days of her grandfather. The book contained many boldly and brightly colored pictures. As a little girl, she had often looked at it so eagerly on Passover evenings.

(Heinrich Heine, German Romantic poet, 19th C., "The Rabbi of Bachrach")

Havdalah הַבְדָּלָה

On Saturday night:

Havdalah is the blessing over the distinction between Shabbat and the weekdays. The light of the fire is blessed using the festival candles already lit. (No special havdalah candle or spice box are necessary):

Blessed are You, Adonai our God, Ruler of the Universe, who creates the lights of fire.

Blessed are You, Adonai our God, Ruler of the Universe, who **differentiates** between the holy and the secular, between light and darkness, between Israel and the other nations, between the seventh day and the six days of creation, between the sanctity of Shabbat and the sanctity of Yom Tov (the festivals). You sanctified the people of Israel with your holiness.

Blessed are You, Adonai, who **differentiates** between the holiness of Shabbat and the holiness of Yom Tov.

בָּרוּךְ אַתָּה יי, אֱלֹהֵינוּ מֶלֶךְ הָעוֹלָם, בּוֹרֵא מְאוֹרֵי הָאֵשׁ.

בָּרוּךְ אַתָּה יי, אֱלֹהֵינוּ מֶלֶךְ הָעוֹלָם הַמַּבְדִּיל בֵּין קֹדֶשׁ לְחֹל, בֵּין אוֹר לְחֹשֶׁךְ, בֵּין יִשְׂרָאֵל לָעַמִּים, בֵּין יוֹם הַשְּׁבִיעִי לְשֵׁשֶׁת יְמֵי הַמַּעֲשֶׂה. בֵּין קְדֻשַּׁת שַׁבָּת לִקְדֻשַּׁת יוֹם טוֹב הִבְדַּלְתָּ, וְאֶת יוֹם הַשְּׁבִיעִי מִשֵּׁשֶׁת יְמֵי הַמַּעֲשֶׂה קִדַּשְׁתָּ. הִבְדַּלְתָּ וְקִדַּשְׁתָּ אֶת עַמְּךָ יִשְׂרָאֵל בִּקְדֻשָּׁתֶךָ,

בָּרוּךְ אַתָּה יי, הַמַּבְדִּיל בֵּין קֹדֶשׁ לְקֹדֶשׁ.

 BLESSED ARE YOU, Adonai our God, Ruler of the Universe, who has kept us alive and brought us to this happy moment in our lives.

Now be seated, recline comfortably leaning to the left on a pillow, and drink most of the cup.

Ba-ruch ata Adonai,
Elo-hei-nu me-lech ha-olam
she-he-chee-ya-nu v'kee-ma-nu
v'hee-gee-anu laz-man ha-zeh.

בָּרוּךְ אַתָּה יי,
אֱלֹהֵינוּ מֶלֶךְ הָעוֹלָם,
שֶׁהֶחֱיָנוּ וְקִיְּמָנוּ
וְהִגִּיעָנוּ לַזְּמַן הַזֶּה.

The First Thing God Wants Us to Know

THE VERY FIRST THING God tells us about Himself at Sinai is this: "I am Adonai your God who brought you out of Egypt." God tells us that, before telling us not to steal and not to kill, before telling us to observe the Sabbath day and not to worship other gods. It is as if God thinks we need to be reminded of the great favor done for us in order to be sure that we will reciprocate by observing God's commandments.

"I brought you out of the house of bondage" is the first of the Ten Commandments. It commands us to know for all time that our God is a **God of freedom**, that the commandments God offers us are gifts, not burdens, that the acceptance of those commandments is not a form of self-denial but a form of liberation. God does not want our gratitude; God wants us to understand that nothing matters to God more than our freedom, and then to teach us that freedom depends upon law.

Tonight, at the great festival of our freedom, we are, all of us, from the youngest to the oldest, colleagues in the celebration of freedom.

At the same time, we are partners in a seder — which means order. We might have chosen to celebrate and remember our liberation with noisy carnivals; others have. But we have been taught something different.

(Leonard Fein, author, social activist, U.S.A.)

Remembering Our Slavery

זֵכֶר לִיצִיאַת מִצְרַיִם

IN THE KIDDUSH, Pesach is called the **"time of our liberation."** Reading aloud one of the following stories may help us focus on the meaning behind the Kiddush on Passover.

'Happy Birthday Dear Israel'

ON JANUARY 27, 1990, the rabbi came to shul as usual to greet the older men who were his morning minyan regulars. One challenged the rabbi playfully: "Aren't you going to wish me Happy Birthday?"

"Sure, how old are you?" replied the rabbi.

"Oh, I'm 45 today."

"Who are you kidding, you must be at least 75?"

"No, today is the day I celebrate as my birthday. Forty-five years ago I was **reborn** when the Allies liberated me from Auschwitz. The **gift of life** and the **gift of freedom** are for me inseparable."

In the same spirit as the story told above, the Torah calls on Israel to regard the spring month (Nisan), the month of its liberation, as its first month, its birthday — starting over its life as a nation: *"Adonai said to Moses and Aaron in the land of Egypt: This month shall mark for you the beginning of the months. It shall be the first of the months of the year for you."*
(Ex. 12:1-2)

Tanya Zion

From Rags to Riches: A Folktale

IRAQI JEWS tell the tale that in one country the king was always chosen in a special way. When the old king died, a bird called the "bird of good fortune" would be released. On whomsoever's head it landed, the people would place the crown making him their next ruler.

Once the bird of good fortune landed on the head of a slave. That slave had been a simple musician who entertained at the master's parties. His costume consisted of a feathered cap and a belt made of the hooves of sheep.

When the slave became king, he moved into the palace and wore royal robes. However, he ordered that a shack (a kind of sukkah) be constructed next to the palace and that his old hat, belt and drum be stored there along with a giant mirror.

The new king was known for his kindness and love for all his people — rich and poor, free and slave. Often he would disappear into his little shack. Once he left its door open and the cabinet ministers saw him don his feathered hat, put on his old belt and dance and drum before the mirror. They found this very strange and asked the king:

"After all, you are a king! You must maintain your dignity!"

The king replied:

"Once I was a slave and now I've become a king. From time to time I want to remind myself that I was once a slave lest I grow arrogant and treat with disdain my people and you, my ministers."

(The English term, "auspicious day" or "inauguration day" preserves an echo of the Roman custom of consulting the flight of birds as an "augur" for the future.)

Urchatz
The First Handwashing

1. **The ritual handwashing** prepares us for eating finger foods, Karpas, the hors d'oeuvres of the Pesach banquet. It sanctifies the act of eating.

2. **Ask for two volunteers:** one to carry a pitcher of water and to pour water over each guest's hands, and one to carry a basin and a towel. No blessing is said for this handwashing.

Kadesh
Urchatz

First
Washing

Pesach: The Spring Holiday

Shraga Weil, Song of Songs, © 1968

28

Why Wash Hands Before Karpas

Why Not Say a Bracha?

JEWISH LAW REQUIRES the ritual washing of the hands before eating bread. This washing is accompanied by a blessing. But why do we wash before eating the green vegetable and why in this case is no blessing recited?

Fruits or vegetables dipped in water can acquire ritual impurity *(Lev. 11:34)*. Washing before eating vegetables which have come into contact with water is a hold-over from Talmudic times. In that period many Rabbis attempted to eat all their foods in a state of ritual purity — trying to experience in their daily eating the sense of sacredness associated with the Temple. To emphasize that this is only a pious custom, and not even a rabbinic requirement, no blessing is recited.

Except for the seder night the custom has fallen into general disuse, even among the strictly observant. But on seder night we wash at the beginning of the evening to create the spirit of a sacred gathering conducted in purity and devotion.

Not a Pagan Resurrection of the Spring Deities

MOST PAGAN PEOPLES celebrate Spring as a festival of liberty. But it is remarkable that, with these peoples, it is not human beings nor the nation, but a deity who is liberated at the festival of Spring; the resurrection of the deity symbolizes the Spring revival of life.

Only the Jews, in their national consciousness, have dared to connect the liberation of nature with the liberation of the nation, with the Exodus from Egypt. Only the Jews have known how to transform the festival of Spring into the "Festival of our freedom."

(Ber Borochov, Marxist Zionist, 1913)

A Meditation on Renaissance

Spring is the renaissance, the rebirth of life, after a winter of discontent:

> For now the winter is past,
> The rains are over and gone.
> The blossoms have appeared in the land.
> . . . Arise, my darling,
> My fair one, come away!
>
> *(Song of Songs 2:11-13)*

On the national level the Jewish people lay dormant in Egyptian slavery until God awakened their desire for freedom and led them out in the springtime. On the individual level liberation is often experienced as a gift of new options, a sudden expansion of possibilities. However, the **fresh taste of new-found freedom** symbolized by Karpas is still mingled with memories of bitterness, the salt water of tears.

The Return to Nature

THE EMPHASIS on spring and the rebirth of nature in this Haggadah is typical of Zionist Haggadot. Zionism sought to return the urbanized Diaspora Jews to their roots in the land and in its seasonal cycles. Israeli schoolchildren and their parents often go on field trips to discover the flora and fauna as well as the history and archeology of Eretz Yisrael.

Karpas
The First Dipping
Hors d'oeuvres of Spring Greens

כַּרְפַּס

1. **Distribute Karpas** (a vegetable) and dip it in salt water, while reciting the appropriate blessing. Some Jews dip in charoset.

2. **While some** medieval rabbis strictly forbid eating more than an olive's size of parsley for Karpas, you may wish to revive the ancient custom of eating extensive appetizers — each with its own dip. You may continue dipping and tasting various fresh vegetables and other appetizers during the seder until sufficiently full to persevere during the extensive storytelling (Maggid), but not so full as to ruin one's appetite for the matza eaten later.

For vegetables (like celery, parsley, or potatoes):

 BLESSED ARE YOU, Adonai our
God, Ruler of the Universe,
who creates the fruit of the earth.

Ba-rukh ata Adonai
Elo-hei-nu me-lech ha-olam,
bo-rei pree ha-ada-ma.

בָּרוּךְ אַתָּה יי,
אֱלֹהֵינוּ מֶלֶךְ הָעוֹלָם,
בּוֹרֵא פְּרִי הָאֲדָמָה.

Optional:
For appetizers (like gefilte fish in horseradish or boiled eggs in salt water):

 BLESSED ARE YOU, Adonai our
God, Ruler of the Universe,
who creates everything by the
power of the Divine word.

Ba-rukh ata Adonai
Elo-hei-nu me-lech ha-olam,
she-ha-kol nee-hee-ye bee-d'va-ro.

בָּרוּךְ אַתָּה יי,
אֱלֹהֵינוּ מֶלֶךְ הָעוֹלָם,
שֶׁהַכֹּל נִהְיֶה בִּדְבָרוֹ.

30

A Menu of Meanings: Why Karpas?

The word "Karpas" derives from the Greek "Karpos" meaning fruit of the soil. Though the historical origins of dipping Karpas at the seder simply reflect the accepted cuisine of the Greco-Roman symposium, the rabbis added their own symbolic interpretations in order to connect the dipping to the Pesach story.

1. Spring Greens: April/Nisan

Metaphorically, Karpas, the spring vegetable, represents both the historic birth of Israel born out of the womb of Egypt in the Exodus and the rebirth of nature renewed each spring. According to Philo and to Rabbi Joshua the original birthday of nature — the Creation — occurred at Pesach-time, not Rosh Hashana. Similarly, the Italian name for spring **primavera** and the French **printemps** preserve the sense of the return to the original "first time" of the world.

Spring (old English) is originally applied to the place of origin from which a stream arises. Later it was applied to the season, the "spring of the year."

2. A Time to March

The Latin term for March preserves the memory of spring as a time for war under the auspices of the god of war, Mars. Spring also has military associations in the Torah. God's spring victory over Egypt is portrayed in martial terms. For example, Israel's armies left Egypt "armed" *(Ex. 13:18)* in the month when kings go out to war.

"God took Israel out of Egypt precisely in the best month for an exodus. Not in Tamuz (June-July) when there is the chamsin (hot summer winds), not in Tevet (December-January) when it is cold (and rainy), but in Nisan (March-April) when it is neither too hot nor too cold to be on the march." *(BaMidbar Rabbah 3)*

3. A Guilty Memory: Dipping in Blood

The dipping of greens is reminiscent of the historic dipping that led Israel into exile in Egypt and the dipping that facilitated their redemption. The descent to Egyptian slavery began when Joseph's brothers sold him into slavery and dipped his **coat of many colors** into a slaughtered goat's blood in order to mislead their father Israel about his beloved son's true fate. The ascent from exile — moral and physical — began when every family gathered together with their neighbors to share a lamb on seder night and to dip in its blood a hyssop plant and to dab it on the **doorposts and the lintel** as a protection against the tenth plague.

Shraga Weil, Song of Songs, © 1968

Yachatz
Breaking the Matza

1. **Breaking the Matza** *is one of many ritual acts that turn the food of the seder into a symbol of meaning.*

2. **Count off** *the matzot from top to bottom: 1, 2, 3, naming them, if you wish, "Cohen," "Levi" and "Yisrael" (the three ritual classes of the Jewish people). The top matza is for the usual blessing over bread (motzi). Tonight that blessing is recited over matza. The bottom matza is for the Hillel sandwich (korech) made with matza, maror, and charoset.*

❖ **3.** **Break the middle matza** *in two and explain that this is for a dual purpose: the bigger portion is to be hidden for the "afikoman" and eaten when retrieved from the children for dessert. It will be the last taste of food at the seder. The smaller portion will be eaten with the top matza when we say the special blessing over matza at the beginning of the meal.*

4. **You may wish** *to add a Tunisian custom: While breaking the matza recite*

כָּךְ קָרַע ה' אֶת הַיָּם לִשְׁנֵים עָשָׂר קְרָעִים, וְיָצְאוּ מִמֶּנּוּ בְּנֵי יִשְׂרָאֵל בַּיַּבָּשָׁה.

"This is how God split the Red Sea."

5. **Warn the children** *that they must keep their eye on the disappearing afikoman.*

Kadesh

Urchatz

Karpas

Yachatz

Breaking
the Matza

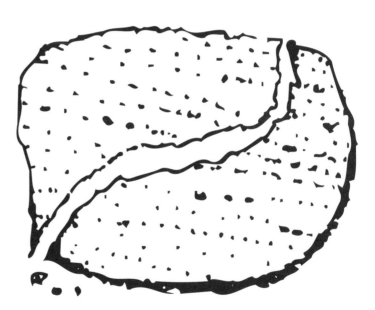

'A Half a Loaf Is Bettrer Than One'

ON SHABBAT and holidays, we celebrate the double gift of abundance with two whole loaves just as in the desert the Jews received a double portion of manna *(Ex. 16:22)* every Friday for the weekend. ("**Manna from heaven**" was suspended on Shabbat).

However, the seder night is unique in that the Rabbis mandated that half a loaf is better than one, for matza is called the "**bread of poverty**." *(Deut. 16:3)*

Therefore, the seder begins by breaking the matza in two and explaining that "this is the bread of poverty and persecution."

Of the **three** matzot, two remain whole, in order to symbolize the abundance of freedom, but one must be broken to recall the deprivation of slavery. The Rabbis noted that the poor in their era were "**savers**," experts at delayed gratification, who would never consume a complete loaf at one sitting, but would always put something aside against the uncertainty of the following week. In the midst of the seder banquet, the broken matza — the symbol of poverty — is meant to jar us out of our sense of complacency. Maimonides explains that the Torah repeats so often: "Remember that you were a slave in the land of Egypt," because it fears that growing up in wealth tends to breed arrogance and insensitivity.

The Story of the Compulsive Saver

IN THE JERUSALEM neighborhood of Talpiot lived an eccentric old man in a large villa. He visited the synagogue religiously whenever a kiddush was served with cakes and kugel. At shul everyone filled themselves with sweets but this elderly man took twice as much, filling his pockets and his mouth. His fellow Jews smiled at his anxious hoarding and wondered how a man living in a large house could be so desperate for a little cake. Once a curious Jew asked him to explain. The old man replied heavily: "In the concentration camps in Poland there was never enough bread. I have never liberated myself from my fear that tomorrow there may not be any more food."

A Principled Debate: Two Matzot or Three?

THOUGH ALMOST ALL contemporary rabbis sanction the use of three matzot at the seder, the Gaon of Vilna *(18th C.)* insisted that only two matzot be used.

For the two matza tradition, matza is primarily **a recollection of poverty**. While on all other holidays we eat from two whole loaves, here we eat from one broken matza and one whole one. The seder re-enacts our common suffering out of which we generate our solidarity and our moral commitment to the stranger and the deprived. The concern for the outsider breaks into our family banquet symbolically in the form of a broken matza marring our sense of wholeness.

While even the three-matza tradition includes one broken matza, it chiefly emphasizes the seder as a Thanksgiving Dinner. The three matzot recall the minimal thanksgiving offering described in the Torah. *(Lev. 7:12)* That offering was shared within a community of friends and relatives; the hosts praised God who had redeemed them from illness, imprisonment, or danger. *(Ps. 107:22)* On Pesach, families retell how their children were threatened by Pharaoh and how they suffered degradation and injustice in Egypt. While sharing the thanksgiving offering of matza, they sing Hallel to thank God.

The two-matza tradition makes this evening resemble a communal "Solidarity-with-the-Poor Box Lunch," while the three-matza tradition is reminiscent of a family "**Thanksgiving Night Banquet**."

A Personal Thanksgiving

The Pesach family gathering is in fact a thanksgiving banquet during which we retell our national salvation. It is also appropriate to weave into the seder memories of personal deliverance from danger.

Invite the family and guests to recall their own family stories of redemption from illness, from danger, or from persecution. Perhaps they can discuss the personal lessons they drew from these crucial events in their lives.

Maggid
Telling the Story

1. **The heart** of the seder is the "maggid" from the term "Haggadah," meaning "storytelling." The storyteller must be flexible and inventive, for this, the longest part of the seder, is also the most creative.

2. **According** to many oriental Jewish traditions, it opens with a traditional Pesach skit. It is also time to **hide** the afikoman (the larger portion of the middle matza).

בְּבְהִילוּ יָצָאנוּ מִמִּצְרַיִם

Recalling the First Seder Night

We begin by recalling the first seder night in history when we **"hurriedly left Egypt:"**

"Adonai said to Moses and Aaron in Egypt . . .
This is how you shall eat it (the Pesach meal):
your loins girded, your sandals on your feet, and your staff in your hand; and you shall eat it **hurriedly:** it is a Passover offering to Adonai . . .

In the middle of the night Adonai struck down all the first-born in the land of Egypt . . .

The Egyptians urged the people on, impatient to have them leave the country, for they said,
"We shall all be dead!"

So the people took their dough before it was leavened, their kneading bowls wrapped in their cloaks upon their shoulders . . . ."

(Exodus 12:11-29, 33-34)

הִנְנִי מוּכָן וּמְזוּמָן לְקַיֵּם אֶת הַמִּצְוַה לְסַפֵּר בִּיצִיאַת מִצְרַיִם.

HERE I AM, ready to perform the mitzvah of retelling the story of the Exodus from Egypt.

"FORGETFULNESS leads to exile, while memory is the secret of redemption," says the Baal Shem Tov. *(18th C. founder of Hassidism)*

Therefore, we celebrate Passover by teaching ourselves to become inventive storytellers and empathetic listeners.

Prague, 1526

The Game Begins: Rules for Hiding the Afikoman

While the broken matza is designed to remind the adults of the culture of poverty, the afikoman is the key to gifts of plenty for the children, as well as the lever for parents to arouse tired children and maintain their alertness through the lengthy stories, rituals, and explanations of the seder. The rabbis mandated playing games with the matza precisely for this educational purpose and felt little compunction about disturbing the sanctity of the evening or the dignity of the matza as a symbol. Each Jewish community made their own rules — sometimes the child stole the afikoman and sometimes the parent hid it. Here is one contemporary version of the game with practical instructions:

1. After breaking the matza, either the seder leader or head of each nuclear family hides the afikoman(s) in a napkin. Some parents sew cloth envelopes embroidered with the word "afikoman."

2. The children are told that a portion of the afikoman will be hidden in more or less plain sight. Children should be encouraged to work together so that the negative aspects of competition will not ruin their evening when they are rewarded for finding the afikoman.

A Passover Skit

In Egypt the Jews ate quickly and anxiously because they were nervous about the plague of the first born and they were expecting their imminent departure into freedom. Today Jews of Africa and Asia customarily act out the Exodus itself dressing their children (or a dramatically inclined adult) in baggy clothes, a scarf or hat, hiking boots, a walking stick, a belt with a canteen and, most important, the afikoman wrapped in one's clothes on the shoulder (or perhaps in a backpack).

Try sending the youngest children out of the room (or the house) with a bag of props and the help of an adult to prepare this dialogue. Here is a semi-traditional script that may be used by the "actors" at the seder.

Knock on the door

Adults: Who's there?

Children: Moshe, Aaron, and Miriam.

Adults: Come in. Tell us about your journey!

Children: We have just arrived from Egypt where we were slaves to Pharaoh. He made us do such hard work. *[Improvise about how bad it was.]*

Adults: How did you escape?

Children: God sent Moshe and Aaron to tell Pharaoh: "Let my people go." When he refused, God sent 10 plagues. *[Improvise describing some of the plagues.]* Finally God brought the most awful plague on the first born of Egypt. Then Pharaoh was really scared so he kicked us out.

Adults: Why are you dressed like that? What is on your shoulder?

Children: We escaped in the middle of the night and had no time to let the dough for our bread rise. The dough that we wrapped in our cloaks and slung over our shoulders turned to matza in the heat of the sun.

Adults: Tell us about your adventures.

Children: Pharaoh changed his mind after releasing us and chased us to the edge of the Red Sea. We would have been caught for sure, but then God split the sea. *[Describe how it felt.]*

Adults: Where are you going now?

Children: To Jerusalem.

ALL: L'Shana Ha-ba-ah Bee'Yerushalayeem!

Ha Lachma Anya:
The story of the matza
'This is the Bread of Poverty and Persecution'

הָא לַחְמָא עַנְיָא

1. **The storytelling** continues with a look at the matza and its multiple meanings as explained in Aramaic, once the everyday language for Jews in Israel and Mesopotamia.

2. **Remove** the cloth covering the matzot so that they are in plain view during the telling of the story, the Maggid. **Raise** the three matzot and point out the broken middle matza (left after the afikoman has been hidden).

3. **Some Rabbis** require the seder plate as well as the matzot to be lifted up as if they were about to be removed from the table even before the meal has begun. This was originally designed to arouse the children to ask questions.

4. **Morrocan Jews** pass the matzot over everyone's head while reading together "ha lachma anya." Some families open the door as a sign of welcoming guests to the seder.

Kadesh
Urchatz
Karpas
Yachatz
Maggid

Ha
Lachma
Anya

❖ Ha Lachma Anya

THIS IS THE BREAD of poverty and persecution that our ancestors ate in the land of Egypt. As it says in the Torah *"seven days shall you eat . . . matzot — the bread of poverty and persecution"* (Deut. 16:3) so that you may "remember that you were a slave in Egypt . . . ." (Deut. 16:12)

LET ALL who are hungry, come and eat
LET ALL who are in need, come and share the Pesach meal.

THIS YEAR we are still here —
Next year, in the land of Israel.

THIS YEAR we are still slaves —
Next year, free people.

Ha lach-ma an-ya
Dee-acha-lu av-ha-ta-na
B'ar-ah d'meetz-ra-yeem.

Kol deech-feen, yei-tei v'yei-chool,
Kol dee-tzreech, yei-tei v'yeef-sach.

Ha-sha-ta ha-cha,
L'sha-na ha-ba-ah
be-ar-ah d'yis-rael

Ha-sha-ta av-dei,
L'sha-na ha-ba-ah
B'nei cho-reen.

הָא לַחְמָא עַנְיָא
דִּי אֲכָלוּ אֲבָהָתַנָא
בְּאַרְעָא דְמִצְרָיִם.

כָּל דִּכְפִין יֵיתֵי וְיֵכָל,
כָּל דְּצָרִיךְ יֵיתֵי וְיִפְסַח.

הָשַׁתָּא הָכָא,
לְשָׁנָה הַבָּאָה
בְּאַרְעָא דְיִשְׂרָאֵל.

הָשַׁתָּא עַבְדֵי,
לְשָׁנָה הַבָּאָה
בְּנֵי חוֹרִין.

36

Uplifting Bread

THE GESTURE of raising the matza of poverty and persecution is an allusion to God's lifting up the poor from the garbage heaps. *(Psalms 113:7)*

The Moroccan custom of passing the matza over the heads of the participants may allude to the Angel of Death who "passed over" the Jewish houses on the night of the tenth plague.

The Bread of Answers

THE RABBIS punned that *anya* means not only poverty but giving answers. This is the bread over which many "answers" will be said. The parent answers the child while pointing at the matza and says: *"For the sake of this, God did so much for me when I left Egypt."* *(Ex. 13:8)*

Fast Food, Oppression and 'Schindler's List"

SEFORNO, a rabbi of the Italian Renaissance, noted that matza is the original **"fast food."** Made of flour and salt it bakes quickly, as it must, for slaves have no time to themselves to let their dough rise at its leisure. Quick to prepare and easy to eat, matza is the **bread of a tight schedule** due to the oppressor's unrelenting demands for meeting the production quota. *(Ex. 5)* Perhaps for that reason the Rabbis insisted that today's matza be prepared from start to finish in no more than **18 minutes**.

Matza's Double Identity

As everyone knows, the Jews eat unleavened bread because the dough they brought out from Egypt in their rush to leave, never had a chance to rise. Matza is then the **bread of liberation**. It is a mark of an exodus whose rapid pace overtook them unprepared. The Egyptians who enslaved them, suddenly expelled them after God brought the plague on the first born. The Passover skit *(p. 35)* reenacts the matza of expulsion and exodus.

Yet *"ha lachma,"* the first official explanation for matza in the Haggadah, calls it the **"bread of poverty and persecution"** based on Deuteronomy 16:3, *"You shall eat unleavened bread, bread of 'oni' (distress) — for you departed from the land of Egypt hurriedly."* Here matza is a memorial not of liberation, but of slavery. The life of oppression is marked by a pressured, "hurried" pace, for the slaves do not control the rhythm of their existence.

When the Israeli actor, Ezra Dagan, was chosen by Steven Spielberg to play the rabbi in the Holocaust movie *Schindler's List*, he went to visit a friend whose father was a survivor. Ezra wanted to get the personal feel of the Jews who had lived through Auschwitz. Arriving just as his friend's father sat down to eat, Ezra marvelled at the rapid pace at which he consumed everything on his plate. **"Does your father always eat at so frenzied a rate?"** he inquired. "I never noticed it but you are right. It must be a life saving lesson he never unlearned from his years in Nazi forced labor camps."

Seforno explained that God rewarded the Jews who were forced to bake and to eat so quickly *(be-cheepazon)* in Egypt by granting them a quick exodus *(be-cheepazon)* after the original seder. *(Deut. 16:3)* The leisurely pace of the seder today as well as the abundance of food and the comfort of the pillows expresses our liberation from an **(op)pressing schedule.**

An Open Door Policy

BEFORE COMMENCING any meal, Rav Huna of Babylonia used to open the door and announce: "Let all who are in need come and eat." *(B.T. Taanit 20b)*

Concern for the needy is characteristic of every Jewish celebration. The Torah emphasizes: *"You shall rejoice in your festival — with your son and daughter, your male and female servant, the Levi, the stranger, the orphan and the widow in your communities." (Deut 16:14)* Maimonides expands and explains this principle:

"When a person eats and drinks at the festive meal he is obligated to provide food for the stranger, the orphan, and the widow, along with the rest of the poor and despondent. But whoever locks the doors of the courtyard, and eats and drinks with his wife and children, and does not provide food and drink for poor or suffering people, this is not a "mitzvah celebration" ("sim-chat mitzvah") but a **"celebration of the belly"** *("simchat kray-so") . . . and this kind of celebration is a disgrace." (Maimonides, Festivals 6:18)*

We continue this Biblical tradition of hospitality today by collecting money to fund preparations for the holiday by the indigent *("Maot-cheeteem")*, and by inviting guests to the seder table. Communities should provide networks of hospitality so that no Jew, whether a newcomer or an elderly person, need spend the holiday alone and forsaken.

Ben Shahn's poster, "Hunger," was used to appeal for help for refugees after World War II. It is modelled on a photograph taken in the Warsaw Ghetto.

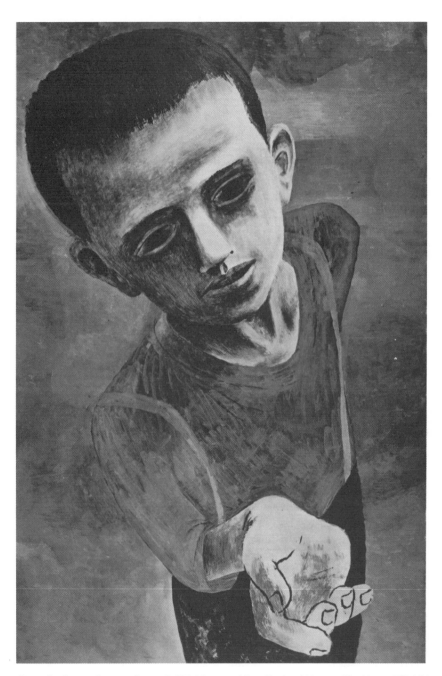

"Let all who are hungry"   © 1996 Estate of Ben Shahn / Licensed by Vaga, NY, NY

Kadesh
Urchatz
Karpas
Yachatz
Maggid
Ha
Lachma
Anya

'All of Us Are Equal'

AT A SEDER the poor are often invited to eat at the home of the rich. This may reinforce their sense of shame and dependence on others. Therefore we begin by the eating of dry, broken matza which is supposed to be an **equalizer**. Don Isaac Abrabanel explains that the hosts must make clear to the guests: "All of us are equal. Though you are poor, you will not feel estranged at my table for all of us were impoverished in Egyptian bondage."

(Don Isaac Abrabanel, Zevach Pesach Haggadah. In 1492 Abrabanel was a cabinet minister to King Ferdinand and Queen Isabella. When the decree expelling the Jews from Spain was issued, he was offered an exemption. Nevertheless he chose to be expelled in solidarity with all the Jews).

'Needy but Not Necessarily Poor'

SOMETIMES the rich are needy. Though they have lots of food they may not know how to make a seder. Therefore the text says *"all those in need"* and not only *"all who are hungry."*

"One should also invite travellers in a strange town far from home for they are certainly sad so far from their families . . . you are obliged to bring them to your home and make them happy on this holiday."

(anonymous medieval Talmudist)

The Jewish Mayflower

DAVID BEN GURION, first prime minister of the State of Israel, described the importance of the memories preserved on Pesach as he argued for the right to a Jewish State in 1947:

"Three hundred years ago a ship called the Mayflower set sail to the New World. This was a great event in the history of England. Yet I wonder if there is one Englishman who knows at what time the ship set sail? Do the English know how many people embarked on this voyage? What quality of bread did they eat? Yet more than three thousand three hundred years ago, before the Mayflower set sail, the Jews left Egypt. Every Jew in the world, even in America or Soviet Russia knows on exactly what date they left — the fifteenth of the month of Nisan; everyone knows what kind of bread the Jews ate. Even today the Jews worldwide eat matza on the 15th of Nisan. They retell the story of the Exodus and all the troubles Jews have endured since being exiled. They conclude this evening with two statements: *This year, slaves. Next year, free men. This year here. Next year in Jerusalem, in Zion, in Eretz Yisrael.* That is the nature of the Jews."

(Testimony to the British Peel Commission, 1936)

"This year we are slaves"

WHAT CAN these words mean?

We are slaves because yesterday our people were in slavery, and memory makes yesterday real for us.

We are slaves because today there are still people in chains around the world and no one can be truly free while others are in chains.

We are slaves because freedom means more than broken chains. Where there is poverty and hunger and homelessness, there is no freedom; where there is prejudice and bigotry and discrimination, there is no freedom; where there is violence and torture and war, there is no freedom.

And where each of us is less than he or she might be, we are not free, not yet.

And who, this year, can be deaf to the continuing oppression of the downtrodden, who can be blind to the burdens and the rigors that are now to be added to the most vulnerable in our midst?

If these things be so, who among us can say that he or she is free?

(Leonard Fein, founder of MAZON: A Jewish Response to Hunger, 1985)

Four Questions

מַה נִּשְׁתַּנָּה

1. **Pour** the second cup for everyone.

2. **Let** the younger children sing "Ma Nishtana."

❖ MA NISHTANA

מַה נִּשְׁתַּנָּה

HOW IS THIS NIGHT different
from all other nights?

Ma nish-ta-na ha-lai-la ha-zeh,
mee-kol ha-lei-lot?

הַלַּיְלָה הַזֶּה
מִכָּל הַלֵּילוֹת?

ON ALL other nights,
we eat
either leavened bread or matza,
but on this night we eat only **matza**.

She-b'chol ha-lei-lot,
anu och-leen,
cha-metz u-matza,
Ha-lai-la ha-zeh, ku-lo matza.

שֶׁבְּכָל הַלֵּילוֹת
אָנוּ אוֹכְלִין
חָמֵץ וּמַצָּה,
הַלַּיְלָה הַזֶּה כֻּלּוֹ מַצָּה.

ON ALL other nights,
we eat
other kinds of vegetables,
but on this night we eat **maror** (bitter herbs).

She-b'chol ha-lei-lot
anu och-leen
sh'ar y'ra-kot,
Ha-lai-la ha-zeh maror.

שֶׁבְּכָל הַלֵּילוֹת
אָנוּ אוֹכְלִין
שְׁאָר יְרָקוֹת,
הַלַּיְלָה הַזֶּה מָרוֹר.

ON ALL other nights,
we need not dip
our vegetables even once,
but on this night we **dip** twice.

She-b'chol ha-lei-lot
ein anu mat-bee-leen
afee-lu pa-am echat,
Ha-lai-la ha-zeh, shtei-p'ameem.

שֶׁבְּכָל הַלֵּילוֹת
אֵין אָנוּ מַטְבִּילִין
אֲפִילוּ פַּעַם אֶחָת,
הַלַּיְלָה הַזֶּה שְׁתֵּי פְעָמִים.

ON ALL other nights,
we eat
either sitting upright or reclining,
but on this night we all **recline**.

She-b'chol ha-lei-lot
anu och-leen,
bein yo-shveen u-vein m'su-been,
Ha-lai-la ha-zeh, ku-la-nu m'su-been.

שֶׁבְּכָל הַלֵּילוֹת
אָנוּ אוֹכְלִין
בֵּין יוֹשְׁבִין וּבֵין מְסֻבִּין,
הַלַּיְלָה הַזֶּה כֻּלָּנוּ מְסֻבִּין.

Kadesh
Urchatz
Karpas
Yachatz
Maggid

Four
Questions

The Four Questions — An Occasion for Reciting or for Inquiring?

The custom of having the youngest child recite the "four questions" has its origin in Rabbinic sources from Second Temple times. However the Mishna in describing the ancient seder service shakes up our usual assumptions:

They fill a second cup of wine for him (the leader of the seder) — and here the child (the inquisitive child) asks his father. If the child lacks intelligence ("daat"), his father teaches him: "How different this night is from all other nights! For on all other nights we eat leavened bread and matza, etc. . . ." (Pesachim 10:4)

The surprising point here is that the four questions are not formulated as questions but as statements of wonder. They are stated by the parent, not by the child — and only if the child lacks the intelligence to ask spontaneously!

The intelligent child is expected to notice the changes in the routine and inquire about them. According to the Mishna, then, if all children were intelligent and curious, there would be no recital of a ritual text of four questions!

Nevertheless, *Ma Nishtana* has earned an honored place at the seder. But one who is satisfied with **only** a formal recitation of questions is far from realizing the educational potential the Rabbis sought to develop.

Prague, 1526

Eliciting Questions

1. Go around the table asking everyone to share one personal question about Pesach or the Exodus.
2. Afterwards, spend some time replying to a few questions by pooling everyone's collective knowledge.

'Izzy, Did You Ask a Good Question Today?'

To the Editor:
Isidor I. Rabi, the Nobel laureate in physics was once asked, "Why did you become a scientist, rather than a doctor or lawyer or businessman, like the other immigrant kids in your neighborhood?"

"My mother made me a scientist without ever intending it. Every other Jewish mother in Brooklyn would ask her child after school: **'Nu? Did you learn anything today?'** But not my mother. She always asked me a different question. **'Izzy,'** she would say, **'Did you ask a good question today?'** That difference — asking good questions — made me become a scientist."
(Donald Sheff, New York Times, Jan. 19, 1988)

מַה נִּשְׁתַּנָּה ??

Kadesh
Urchatz
Karpas
Yachatz
Maggid

Four
Questions

Otto Geismar, 1927

In Search of the Four Answers

As often happens after the youngest child recites the four questions, the family and guests applaud but do not bother to answer the questions. Since a young child's questions should not go unanswered, we shall present one answer to each of the four questions.

ON ONE HAND, the matza and the maror belong to the menu of the slaves and the oppressed:

1. Why eat plain matza which is hard to digest?

Poor laborers and slaves are fed matza not only because it is cheap but because it is filling and requires a long digestion period. The diet was designed by the oppressor to exploit the people efficiently.

2. Why eat raw, bitter vegetables?

Maror is eaten plain only by the most oppressed workers who are given little time to prepare their meals. With more time they would have made these herbs into a tasty salad.

ON THE OTHER HAND, dipping and reclining typify the manners of the leisure class in Roman times:

3. Why dip twice before eating?

On seder night we are obligated to dip twice — karpas in salt water and maror in charoset — before the meal begins. Even today, finger foods dipped in tangy sauces are typical hors d'oeuvres with cocktails (the first cup of wine) at banquets.

4. Why recline on pillows while drinking wine?

The body language of the free reflects their ease and comfort. Reclining on sofas or pillows, everyone — big and small alike — experiences the freedom of the upper classes. On seder night these foods and these table manners are props and stage directions in the script acted out by all.

(based on Don Isaac Abrabanel, Zevach Pesach)

42

The Questioning Personality

A Key to Freedom

Why were the Rabbis so insistent that the Exodus story open with a spontaneous question?

First of all, one can view this as an educational device. Teachers know that if they can just get their students to pay attention, get their minds working on something they find interesting, then the teachers have gone a long way towards creating an openness to learning new things. The Rabbis wanted to remind the leaders of the seder not just to focus on the story — but first to make sure to have an active, **attentive audience**.

On a deeper level, the Rabbis may have reflected that questioning is an essential part of the freedom celebrated on the seder night. The whole Talmudic literature is in the form of **questioning and dialogue** — not the meek questioning of inferior to superior but the give-and-take interaction of adamant rivals pitted against one another, and sometimes even against God! *(B.T. Bava Metzia 59 b)*

An essential characteristic of free people is that they notice the world around them, make distinctions and search for meaningful patterns. They want understanding, not inscrutability. **For a slave mentality, nothing is "different"** — all tasks are part of the same meaningless arbitrariness. There is no point in asking if no one answers, no place for questions in a world where the master's arbitrary orders are the ultimate justification for the way things are.

In beginning the seder with genuine (not rote) questions, the Rabbis show that we not only **tell** the story of freedom, but we **act** like free people.

Questions in Many Tongues

Traditionally the questions and answers of the seder must be in the vernacular, a language understood by all whatever their age or literacy. Try asking the questions in as many foreign languages as possible (see *The Leader's Guide* for many translations).

Four Questions: Kibbutz Style

IN EVERY GENERATION one is obligated to ask **new questions**. Though the Haggadah never explicitly makes such a demand, the Mishna does require intelligent children to ask their own questions. Naturally these will reflect their own era. Even the recommended four questions of the youngest child have changed over the generations.

In the early days the Kibbutz Haggadah retooled the four questions to transcend ritual issues and to focus on contemporary historical concerns, such as the battle with the Arabs (1930's), the Holocaust (1940's) and the ingathering of 1,000,000 Jewish refugees (1950's).

Below are four questions asked by children in Kibbutz Ein Harod. It is a shame that we don't have a copy of the answers the parents gave to these contemporary questions.

Kibbutz Ein Harod 1930's - 1940's:
- *Why do people all over the world hate Jews?*
- *When will the Jews return to their land?*
- *When will our land become a fertile garden?*
- *When will there be peace and brotherhood the world over?*

Who needs 'Ma Nishtana'?

ONCE THE YOUNG pupil, Abaye, was invited to the seder of his teacher Rabbah. While still at the beginning of the seder Rabbah ordered the servants to clear the dishes from the table. Amazed, Abaye asked, "Why are you removing the seder plate before we have even eaten?" Rabbah exclaimed, "Your question has served the same function as the usual four questions of… 'Ma nishtana.' Let's dispense with those set questions and proceed directly to the telling of the story." *(Babylonian Talmud Pesachim 115b)*

Find the Differences

Before singing the "Ma Nishtana," prompt the youngest children to see how different this table is from other family meals (length of table, foods, dishes, guests, books, pillows, etc).

The Rabbis As Storytellers
Shmuel's Story: "We were slaves"

עֲבָדִים הָיִינוּ

❖ When, in time to come, your children ask you: "What is the meaning of the decrees, laws, and rules that Adonai our God has enjoined upon you?" You shall say to your children: **"We were slaves to Pharaoh in Egypt and Adonai freed us from Egypt with a mighty hand and an outstretched arm.** Adonai produced before our eyes great and awful signs and wonders in Egypt, against Pharaoh and all his household; and God freed us from there, so that God could take us and give us the land that had been promised on oath to our ancestors."

(Deut. 6:20-23)

עֲבָדִים הָיִינוּ לְפַרְעֹה בְּמִצְרָיִם.
וַיּוֹצִיאֵנוּ יי אֱלֹהֵינוּ מִשָּׁם,
בְּיָד חֲזָקָה וּבִזְרוֹעַ נְטוּיָה.

Optional Song:

עֲבָדִים הָיִינוּ, הָיִינוּ
עַתָּה בְּנֵי חוֹרִין, בְּנֵי חוֹרִין.

Avadeem hayeenu, hayeenu,
Ata bnei choreen, bnei choreen.

Kadesh
Urchatz
Karpas
Yachatz
Maggid

We Were
Slaves

What if

❖ **IF GOD** had not taken our ancestors out of Egypt, then we would still be enslaved to Pharaoh in Egypt, along with our children, and our children's children.

EVEN IF all of us were wise, all of us discerning, all of us veteran scholars, and all of us knowledgeable in Torah, it would still be a mitzvah for us to retell the story of the Exodus from Egypt.

So, **THE MORE** and the longer one expands and embellishes the story, the more commendable it is.

וְאִלּוּ לֹא הוֹצִיא הַקָּדוֹשׁ בָּרוּךְ הוּא אֶת אֲבוֹתֵינוּ
מִמִּצְרַיִם, הֲרֵי אָנוּ וּבָנֵינוּ וּבְנֵי בָנֵינוּ,
מְשֻׁעְבָּדִים הָיִינוּ לְפַרְעֹה בְּמִצְרָיִם.

וַאֲפִלּוּ כֻּלָּנוּ חֲכָמִים,
כֻּלָּנוּ נְבוֹנִים, כֻּלָּנוּ זְקֵנִים,
כֻּלָּנוּ יוֹדְעִים אֶת הַתּוֹרָה,
מִצְוָה עָלֵינוּ לְסַפֵּר בִּיצִיאַת מִצְרָיִם.

וְכָל הַמַּרְבֶּה לְסַפֵּר בִּיצִיאַת מִצְרַיִם,
הֲרֵי זֶה מְשֻׁבָּח.

Children ask the Best Questions

A kindergarden child once asked the teacher: "What does it mean to be a slave? Is it like being the cleaning lady who doesn't speak English?" Try to answer the child's question.

"By Tomorrow Today Will Be a Story"

Isaac Bashevis Singer:

"When a day passes, it is no longer there. What remains of it? Nothing more than a story. If stories weren't told or books weren't written, humans would live like the beasts, only for the day."

Reb Zebulun said, "Today we live, but by tomorrow today will be a story. **The whole world, all human life, is one long story.**"

Children are as puzzled by passing time as grownups. What happens to a day once it is gone? Where are all our yesterdays with their joys and sorrows? Literature helps us remember the past with its many moods. **To the storyteller yesterday is still here** as are the years and the decades gone by.

In stories time does not vanish. Neither do people and animals. For the writer and his readers, all creatures go on living forever. What happened long ago is still present.

(I.B. Singer, Nobel prize laureate, Yiddish literature, from Zlateh the Goat)

Shmuel vs. Rav: Competing Stories

After the youngest child has asked the four questions and everyone else has added their own questions, then it's time to tell the story that will explain why for us this night is different from all other nights. The Rabbis recommended:

"The parent should teach according to the intelligence and personality of each child. Begin with describing the **degradation** and culminate with the **liberation.**" *(Mishna Pesachim 10:2)*

However, Rav and Shmuel, the Babylonian rabbis, disagreed about the central story to be told at this point in the seder:

Shmuel said: Start with "We were slaves in the land of Egypt" *(Deut. 6.20)* and move from physical enslavement to political liberation. *(see page 44)*

Rav said: Start with Terach, Abraham's father and the state of idolatry to which we had descended. "**Once upon a time our ancestors were slaves of idolatry who worshipped pagan gods.** Now — since Mount Sinai — God has brought us close to the Divine service." *(see page 72)*

The editors of the Haggadah bring both stories: first Shmuel's "We were slaves" and later, after the Four Children, Rav's story.

Trieste Haggadah, 1864

The Longest Seder: The Five Rabbis of Bnai B'rak

בְּנֵי בְּרַק

A TALE IS TOLD of Rabbi Eliezer, Rabbi Yehoshua, Rabbi Elazar son of Azarya, Rabbi Akiva and Rabbi Tarfon who dined (reclined) at the seder in Bnai B'rak. The whole night long **they spent retelling** the story of the Exodus from Egypt, until their students arrived and announced to them: "Our masters, it is already time to recite the morning Sh'ma!"

מַעֲשֶׂה בְּרַבִּי אֱלִיעֶזֶר וְרַבִּי יְהוֹשֻׁעַ, וְרַבִּי אֶלְעָזָר בֶּן עֲזַרְיָה, וְרַבִּי עֲקִיבָא, וְרַבִּי טַרְפוֹן, שֶׁהָיוּ מְסֻבִּין בִּבְנֵי בְרַק, וְהָיוּ מְסַפְּרִים בִּיצִיאַת מִצְרַיִם, כָּל אוֹתוֹ הַלַּיְלָה, עַד שֶׁבָּאוּ תַלְמִידֵיהֶם וְאָמְרוּ לָהֶם: "רַבּוֹתֵינוּ, הִגִּיעַ זְמַן קְרִיאַת שְׁמַע, שֶׁל שַׁחֲרִית."

Kadesh
Urchatz
Karpas
Yachatz
Maggid

The Five
Rabbis

Recalling the Exodus Every Night

RABBI ELAZAR son of Azarya said: "Even though I am like a man of seventy, I had never understood why the going out from Egypt should be mentioned at night-time [in the Sh'ma], until **Ben Zoma** explained it to me from the verse, *'That you may remember the day when you came out of Egypt all the days of your life.'* (Deuteronomy 16:3) *'The days of your life'* means just the days! BUT *'All the days of your life'* means the nights as well!"

However the **Rabbis** explain: *"'The days of your life'* means this life! BUT *'All the days of your life'* means the days of the Messiah as well!"

(Mishna Brachot 1:5)

אָמַר רַבִּי אֶלְעָזָר בֶּן עֲזַרְיָה: הֲרֵי אֲנִי כְּבֶן שִׁבְעִים שָׁנָה, וְלֹא זָכִיתִי, שֶׁתֵּאָמֵר יְצִיאַת מִצְרַיִם בַּלֵּילוֹת עַד שֶׁדְּרָשָׁהּ בֶּן זוֹמָא, שֶׁנֶּאֱמַר: "לְמַעַן תִּזְכֹּר, אֶת יוֹם צֵאתְךָ מֵאֶרֶץ מִצְרַיִם, כָּל יְמֵי חַיֶּיךָ."
"יְמֵי חַיֶּיךָ" – הַיָּמִים, "כָּל יְמֵי חַיֶּיךָ" – הַלֵּילוֹת.
וַחֲכָמִים אוֹמְרִים: "יְמֵי חַיֶּיךָ" – הָעוֹלָם הַזֶּה,
"כָּל יְמֵי חַיֶּיךָ" – לְהָבִיא לִימוֹת הַמָּשִׁיחַ.

Otto Geismar, 1927

Ben-Zoma vs. the Rabbis: Will the Seder Be Superseded?

THE TALMUD RELATES that Ben-Zoma felt that the Messianic redemption would wipe out the memories of all previous troubles and rescues. The Rabbis insisted that while the Messianic redemption would be the greater one, we must still recall the earlier ones, including the Exodus.

This argument has to do with the importance of memory. For Ben-Zoma, contemporary events have the decisive weight. Some modern Zionist thinkers like Ben-Gurion seem to prefer this position, arguing that the founding of Israel has made 2000 years of exilic experience irrelevant. In their view, the Bible, reflecting the experience of a sovereign people in its land, must be the pivotal educating force for Jewish culture, not the Talmud which grew in the shadow of destruction and conquest by the Romans. Similarly, some might argue that the enormity of the Holocaust makes the recalling of all previous sufferings of the Jews seem trivial and irrelevant.

The Rabbis maintained that history should add, but not erase memories. Recent dramatic historical events may indeed be accorded prominence, but we should never forget our earlier experiences. In their view, even in the Messianic Era when war, poverty, and human suffering have been eradicated, it will still be incumbent to remember daily the saga of bondage and liberation.

"Moses kills the Egyptian taskmaster" (Ex. 2:11)   *Julius Schnorr*

Personal Recollections: "My Most Unusual Seder"

The seder is as much a family renewal ceremony as a remembrance of ancient Egypt. Sharing family memories with the younger members as well as involving the guests, who may feel homesick, will contribute to the bonding of all participants.

1. Ask the participants, especially the guests, to share a special seder memory. (See Contemporary Seder Stories in supplement, pages S-5,13,17,29,32 for great seders in Jewish history.)

2. Ask the participants, especially the oldest ones, to recall their best or their worst moment at the old family seder. (For example, the seder when I had stage fright in the middle of the four questions).

Storytelling: Multiple Options

'The more one expounds and embellishes the story, the more commendable it is'

The Haggadah recommends that parents now go beyond the text of the Haggadah and improvise dramatically in retelling the story of the Exodus. The **traditional Haggadah does not include a script for the storyteller** nor even bring the appropriate Biblical chapters.

Some parents like to tell the story in their own words. Others ask the children to retell what they have learned in school under three major headings:

1. What was it like to be a slave?
2. What do you know about Moshe as a baby and as a young man?
3. How did the Jews finally become free?

(Before the seder, ask the children to prepare drawings to illustrate these themes and then to show and tell what they drew.)

Many parents prefer to use a script. Try reading aloud one of the following selections (pages 48-55).

Kadesh
Urchatz
Karpas
Yachatz
Maggid

Storytelling

A Philosopher at Home: David Hartman

OUR FAMILY labors a long time at our seder trying to grasp the first part of the Haggadah: *"We were slaves in the land of Egypt."* I ask my children: **What do you think it feels like to be a slave?**

ONCE I TOLD my four-year-old a story about a boy who did not see his Daddy for a year: "The boy had a birthday and Daddy couldn't come. Then Daddy called and said, 'I'm going to come home.' The boy invited all his friends to come and see his Daddy, because he loved him. He said, **'Abba is coming home.'** He watched his Mommy cook kugel, his Daddy's favorite. Just after his friends had come, Abba called to say, 'The boss won't let me come.' The little boy said, 'What do you mean, the boss won't let you come? Tell him your son wants you home. Everybody wants you. We miss you!'"

SUDDENLY I could not help it, I started crying and my son started crying about the kid in the story. I created this dialogue of the Abba trying to explain to his little son: "I can't make my own decisions. The boss decides my movements for me." We felt the loneliness of the little boy who wanted so much to see his father but who knew that his love is not enough to bring him home. **That is what it means to be a slave. You can't control your life.**

(That is the story I tell when my child is four. At twelve, I tell another story. At sixteen, still another. On Pesach night I am a multi-faceted storyteller because my autobiography encompasses so many dimensions).

Otto Geismar 1927

48

The Duty to Give Memories

The haggadah transforms parents into storytellers. It is a very serious task to tell stories. My parents bring me into contact with my historical roots, with my grandparents and a world other than me. **Whether it is relevant, the child will decide; but the parent must witness to a history and a memory that is needed in order to realize that there is a dimension to existence beyond the self.** People who learn to honor their parents escape narcissism and acquire a memory. The parents are the feeders of history.

Parents should not determine their children's future, but they must open for them their past.

In many ways we are today human beings in search of a narrative who may find our personal story by reconnecting to our people's great story of wandering and homecoming, of oppression and liberation, and of near annihilation and rescue. By returning to our origins and following the journey of our people we offer deeper resonance to our personal lives and develop a common language to share our fears and our dreams. In retelling the Exodus we learn to commemorate the moments of family and national crisis and to celebrate with profound gratitude our emergence into a better life.

(David Hartman, Jewish Philosopher, Jerusalem)

Ben Shahn, "Weeping Man"

*© 1996 Estate of Ben Shahn /
Licensed by Vaga, NY, NY*

Not By Bread Alone

IN THE SPRING OF 1945 a father and his teenage son shared the harsh labor in the Nazi camp. The father suggested a pact between them to save part of what little bread they received. After several days of saving the father reported to his son sheepishly: "I am sorry but I have given away our whole store of bread to a new arrival." "Why?" asked the son in desperation. The father explained, "There are two reasons: First, he needed food even more than we and second, I exchanged the bread for a miniature haggadah." Several days later using this haggadah, the father was able to raise people's spirits by conducting a seder for many inmates. Even though matza was unavailable, the seder gave everyone a special kind of nourishment — hope.

Heroic Women and Baby Moses

retold by Diana Craig (The Young Moses)

In one small corner of Egypt, just where the great river Nile runs into the sea, there lived some people called Israelites. They had come from Israel to Egypt many years before to look for food.

God had promised to look after the Israelites in their new home, and at first everyone was very happy. There was plenty to eat, and they grew strong and had lots of children. Soon their families filled the land.

But then everything changed. The king of Egypt, who was called the Pharaoh, died, and a new Pharaoh became king. He hated the Jews.

"There are so many of them," he grumbled. "Just think what would happen if they turned against us.

"They might even take sides with our enemies. We must stop them!"

So he thought of a plan. **"We'll make them our slaves,"** he announced with an evil grin. "We'll work them so hard they won't even have time to think of fighting us . . . with a bit of luck they may even die of exhaustion!"

So the Jews slaved from sunrise to sunset, making bricks and moving huge stones to build Egyptian cities. When they were not building cities, they had to dig the fields and plant all the wheat and barley.

The Jews were exhausted, just as the Pharaoh had hoped. But they didn't die. In fact, they didn't even get ill. They stayed just as strong and healthy as ever. The Pharaoh's wicked plan wasn't working.

So he had another idea. He told the nurses that they must kill all Israelite baby boys as soon as they were born. But the nurses knew that God would not approve if they did such a terrible thing, so they made up an excuse.

"We're so sorry, Your Majesty," they lied, not daring to look the Pharaoh in the eye. "But the babies are born so quickly that we never get there in time."

"All right then," replied the Pharaoh angrily.

"They'll just have to be thrown in the river instead!"

All the Jewish mothers were terrified and tried to hide their babies. One mother hid her newborn boy in a corner of her house. If anyone heard him crying and wondered about the noise, she knew what to say.

"It's a sick sheep I'm looking after," she would tell them. "Funny, isn't it, how they sound just like babies when they're ill?" No one suspected anything.

But soon the baby grew too big to hide. "I know what I'll do," thought his mother. "I'll make a little ark of reeds and float the baby on the river, near where the Pharaoh's daughter comes to wash every morning, and she's sure to find him. She has no children of her own, and she's not nearly as cruel as that wicked king. Perhaps she'll feel sorry for my baby and save him."

So the mother took a big basket and painted the outside with black, sticky stuff called pitch, to stop the

(Continued on page 52)

Kadesh
Urchatz
Karpas
Yachatz
Maggid

Storytelling

50

Leon Baxter

The Batya Parent Association

THE NAME of the Biblical heroine, the daughter of Pharaoh who adopts Moses, is not mentioned in the Bible.

One rabbinic midrash calls her "Batya" which means "the daughter of God" and regards her as a convert to Judaism. Her adoption of Moses was motivated, they suggest, by her infertility. Appropriately the American association of adoptive Jewish parents with infertility problems is called "Batya."

Who will be Today's Midwives?

ONE SUNDAY morning in 1941 in Nazi-occupied Netherlands, a mysterious character rode up on his bicycle and entered the Calvinist Church. He ascended the podium and read aloud the story of the midwives who saved the Hebrew babies and defied Pharaoh's policy of genocide. "Who is today's Pharaoh?" he asked. "Hitler," the congregation replied. "Who are today's Hebrew babies?" "The Jews." "Who will be today's midwives?" He left the church, leaving his question hanging in the air.

During the war (1941-1945) numerous families from this little church hid Jews and other resisters from the Nazis.

(See the full story In the Leader's Guide)

The Shifra and Puah Award

AL AXELROD, the Hillel rabbi at Brandeis University in the 1960's, established this annual award for non-violent resistance to tyranny. He named it after the midwives who resisted and outsmarted Pharaoh and saved the Hebrew infants from drowning. (In Tel Aviv the maternity hospital is located at the intersection of Shifra and Puah Street).

To whom would you give this award this year? *(In 1849 Harriet Tubman deserved such an award. See page 99).*

Churchill's Favorite Story

ABOUT THE EXODUS Churchill wrote: "the most decisive leap-forward ever discernable in the human story."

(Winston Churchill, Prime Minister of Great Britain, who led the Allies in World War II, the greatest war of liberation ever fought, sent this quote from his essay on Moses in a personal letter to Prime Minister David Ben Gurion).

Leon Baxter

water from getting in. Then she laid the baby inside and put the basket among the reeds near the river bank. She told her daughter, Miriam, to stay and see what happened.

Sure enough, the princess came down to the water's edge and stopped the basket. She sent one of her servants to fetch it, and she was amazed to see a little baby tucked up snugly inside.

"Whatever are you doing here?" she exclaimed, picking him up and giving him a cuddle. And then she guessed the truth. "You must be one of the Jewish babies, and your mother has hidden you here for safety. Well, I don't care what my father says, I won't throw you in the river."

Kadesh
Urchatz
Karpas
Yachatz
Maggid
Storytelling

Moses Comes of Age

When the little boy was old enough, his mother took him back to the princess. "From now on, I shall be his mother," the princess said, "and I'll call him Moses, because I took him from the water." So Moses was brought up like an Egyptian prince, and had everything he could wish for.

But as the years went by, one thing began to bother Moses more and more. **Although he lived with the Egyptians, he knew he wasn't one of them.** He knew he was really a Jew. He saw how cruel the Egyptians were to his people and it made him very angry. How could the Egyptians treat them so badly? They hadn't done anything wrong. **It just wasn't fair.**

One day, when Moses had grown up, he decided to visit one of the building sites and see for himself what was going on. He caught sight of one of the Egyptian slave drivers beating a Hebrew slave. Moses completely lost his temper. He picked up a stone and smashed it on the slave driver's head. The man fell to the ground, dead. Moses was horrified at what he had done.

Quickly, he buried the body in the sand.

"Don't breathe a word of what's happened, or the Pharaoh will have me killed!" he warned the slave. But the man just couldn't help telling his brother, and his brother told his aunt, and his aunt told her friend . . . and soon everyone knew.

The next day, Moses visited another building site, and saw a big, strong slave bullying a small, weak slave.

"Stop that, you great bully!" shouted Moses.

"Just you try and make me!" the slave answered back cheekily. "You can't boss me about, or I'll tell the Pharaoh how you killed one of his men!"

Moses was terrified. His secret was out, and he knew that when the Pharaoh heard, that would be the end of him.

So, that night, he packed a few clothes and some food and, with a last, longing look at his home, he crept away.

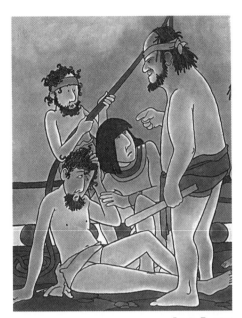

Leon Baxter

Returning Moses to the Haggadah

SOME HAVE ARGUED that Moses was deliberately excluded from the Haggadah to avoid deifying a human leader. Certainly the hero of the traditional Haggadah is and should be God. But it is likely that Moses was often mentioned in the rabbinic seder when parents told their children the story of the Exodus. We have introduced Moses explicitly into our Haggadah as recommended by Moses Maimonides: *"It is a mitzvah to tell the children about the Exodus even if they did not ask . . . If the children are mature and wise, tell them all that happened to us in Egypt and all the miracles God did for us by means of Moses . . . ." (Laws of Chametz and Matza 7:2)*

Moses' Identity Crisis

What kind of spiritual transformation can come from an act of murder? What has ensued in the years between Moses' being taken to live in Pharaoh's palace and this act?

Being free, Moses was not prey to the slave psychology. However, growing up as Pharaoh's grandson thrust him into an equal danger — the ambivalence of **dual identity**. He was Hebrew and Egyptian. By birth he belongs to the oppressed, but he is nurtured as a member of the oppressing group. It is wishful thinking to assume that Moses was immune to the comforts and privileges of his station in life.

There must have been times when Moses felt like a **traitor** to his people, especially as he relaxed on a hot day, a fine robe draping his body, servants offering him pomegranates, figs, and dates, while his people worked in the hot sun building pyramids. I wouldn't doubt that sometimes Moses wept in silent helplessness as he tried to unravel the dilemma of appearing to be an Egyptian while knowing himself a Jew. He is a **stranger** in Egypt and a stranger to himself because he cannot live his true identity.

Nothing is so vital to psychological well-being as identity. Through **identity** we know our place in the world. If that identity is seriously divided or defined by a society as negative, we are insecure in the world and insecure in ourselves. Moses was possibly the first person in history to have to ask, Who am I? Everyone else in the ancient world knew.

They knew because society conferred identity on them. Moses had no alternative but to confer identity on himself.

His first attempt to do so comes when he goes to face the suffering part of himself in the persons of his enslaved people. He looks on their burdens and weeps, saying *"Woe is me for you! Would that I could die for you." (Midrash Rabbah)* He feels their suffering as his own. It is a moment of intense compassion, charged with the emotion of a life-and-death conflict. Because true compassion compels one to act, he does. He kills an Egyptian.

Psychologically he "kills" a hated part of himself. Moses projects his self-hatred outward onto one who most closely resembles that hated Egyptian part of himself. He wants to be a part of his people, and murdering an Egyptian was the way to come home. But this solution does not work adequately.

I imagine him looking at what he has done. He feels no exultation, no sense of freedom or wholeness. Instead, he is engulfed by remorse, shame, and guilt. He is more of a **stranger** now than he could have ever imagined possible.

(Julius Lester, Civil Rights Activist, U.S.A.)

Chronicles

News of the Past

15 Aviv 2524 © The Reubeni Foundation　　　　Dr. Israel Eldad and Moshe Aumann, Editors

"Chronicles"

WE QUIT EGYPT TODAY

Pharaoh gives in to Moses as 10th plague wipes out Kingdom's First-born.

Rameses, 15 Aviv — Moses' oft-repeated plea to Pharaoh Merneptah, to "let my people go," was finally heard today, just after midnight, when the king of Egypt, badly shaken by the death of his eldest son, not only agreed to Moses' request, but actually insisted that the Israelites leave the country immediately. Pharaoh had sent for the Israelite leaders as soon as word had reached him that all of Egypt's first-born — including Pharaoh's — had been "mysteriously" struck down at midnight.

Moses and Aaron had expected the call. They had left for Rameses several hours earlier, after Moses had told reporters: "The period of hag-gling is over. This time we are going to tell Pharaoh briefly and precisely: Tonight we leave. And I think that this time Pharaoh will relent."

Pharaoh Capitualtes

Merneptah, surrounded by his Council of Magicians, addressed Moses and Aaron in these words:

"Rise up and get you forth from among my people — you and the Children of Israel — and go serve Adonai as you have said. Take your flocks and your herds and be gone!"

But then Merneptah began to mention terms and limitations.

To the consternation of those present, Moses dared to interrupt Pharaoh, as he curtly rejected all conditions. This was unprecedented in the palace, and contrary to the sacred protocol, in which Moses is well-versed.

Moses declared emphatically that he had been willing to discuss terms before God smote the land of Egypt - but not any more. A smitten people, he added, does not dictate terms; it has to accept them.

Sudden Death Strikes Men and Cattle

Last night, at the exact hour of midnight, God stretched out his hand against Egypt for the tenth time and struck down every first-born Egyptian son, from the first-born of Pharaoh to the first-born of the lowliest prisoner in the land. Even the first born among the cattle died.

It is difficult to describe the woe and wailing of the bereaved mothers and the terrible fear and sense of catastrophe that have descended upon Egypt. This night will be marked forever in the annals of Egypt as a night of indescribable horror and suffering.

Hebrews Spared

A summary check of Israelite homes in the Goshen province reveals that the Angel of Death, on his way to smite the sons of Egypt, passed over the families of the Hebrews and left them intact.

It seems the Children of Israel were under God's special protection tonight, for not only are all the firstborn sons still alive — but no Israelite died in the course of the night, even of so-called natural causes.

Exodus Instructions

1. All Israelites of military age are to report immediately to their respective tribes.
2. Each tribe will camp separately under its own standard.
3. Everyone is to follow the instructions of our police, so as to avoid crowding, and to arrange themselves speedily in the order prescribed.

600,000 Gathering at Succoth

The Children of Israel — 600,000 strong — are on the move. Under the leadership of Moses, the man of God, they are preparing to leave Egypt after a stay there of over 200 years, the last 86 years of which were spent in bitter slavery.

Palace is Stormed by Egyptian Mobs

Rameses, 13 Aviv — A huge crowd yesterday staged a mass demonstration before the Palace of Merneptah. The demonstrators threw stones at the police and troops in an attempt to break through to the Palace.

Order of the Day
Sons of Jacob: Tribes of Israel!

This month shall be unto you the beginning of months. This day shall be unto you the first day of all days till the end of time. For today you have been delivered from slavery unto freedom. Today you have become a nation.

Egypt, with its taskmasters and its heathen beliefs, is behind you. In front of you is the desert, vast and terrible. But this terrifying wilderness leads to a land flowing with milk and honey, to the land of your fathers. Be not dismayed. For if you will remain faithful to the covenant and willingly undertake all the sacrifices Adonai may exact from you — then He will allow no harm to come to you, and your enemy shall not overpower you.

As you have emerged today from bondage unto freedom, so shall you be free tomorrow in the land of your fathers.

Hear, O Israel: Adonai our God, Adonai is one!

MOSES, The Son of Amram

Hard to Believe!

How strange it all is, how difficult to believe! Only yesterday we were toiling for a cruel master; today we are free men, leaving the House of Bondage behind us forever, on our way to a new life — a life we have never before known.

Through the centuries we have not forgotten the land of Canaan and God's promise to our forefathers. The long years of servitude only strengthened our longing for liberty. These many months we have witnessed with our own eyes the signs and portents, as we have watched the powerful kingdom of Egypt, with its host of servants, its mighty army, and its cunning magicians, reel under the impact of the ten plagues.

Nonetheless it all seems like a dream. It seems as if our people, in their thousands and tens of thousands, were moving eastward, not of their own volition, but irresistibly, as though bewitched by the inspired man who waved his magic wand and commanded us to go forth.

How shall we overcome the dangers threatening us on our path — the merciless desert, the turbulent sea, the powerful nations barring our way? How shall we traverse the desert, cross the sea, and conquer the promised land, when we are only a handful of tribes, unlearned in the arts of war and government?

We are an erring people, a nation of slaves without law or government; we are but wandering tribes, clans and families.

Moses, man of God, make us into a nation, give us the Law, guide our steps so that we shall not come to the Promised Land like a flock of sheep. We are ready — each tribe under its own standard, yet one people, descended from one ancestor, and believing in one God.

THE EDITORS

The Four Children

Kadesh
Urchatz
Karpas
Yachatz
Maggid

Four
Children

כְּנֶגֶד אַרְבָּעָה בָנִים

1. *The Haggadah offers us educational advice about intergenerational storytelling. The midrash of the Four Children invites us to distinguish different character types and to suggest different approaches to our offspring.* *Consider the artistic interpretations of the Four Children, comparing and contrasting them.*

2. *The Rabbis turn the commandment of "ve-heegadta" (you shall tell) into a mitzvah of dialogue — with give and take on both sides. Successful dialogue means that each side, and especially the side anxious to "pass on the message," be keenly attentive to what the other is saying and feeling — to the particular personality and his or her needs.*

❖ BLESSED be God,
Blessed be that One.
Blessed be the Giver of the Torah to the people Israel,
Blessed be that One.

THE TORAH alludes to **Four** Children:
One Wise or Thoughtful,
   One Wicked or Rebellious,
      One Simple or Innocent,
         One Who Does Not Know How to Ask.

בָּרוּךְ הַמָּקוֹם,
בָּרוּךְ הוּא.
בָּרוּךְ שֶׁנָּתַן תּוֹרָה לְעַמּוֹ יִשְׂרָאֵל.
בָּרוּךְ הוּא.

כְּנֶגֶד **אַרְבָּעָה** בָנִים דִּבְּרָה תוֹרָה:
אֶחָד חָכָם
וְאֶחָד רָשָׁע
וְאֶחָד תָּם
וְאֶחָד שֶׁאֵינוֹ יוֹדֵעַ לִשְׁאָל.

Istavan Zador, Four Children (Budapest, 1924)

Education Through Dialogue

A Reminder for Parents!

Thus far the Haggadah has given guidelines to the parent who is full of earnest enthusiasm to pass on an historical and cultural "message" to the younger generation. If ever there was an event which appeals to the parent's desire to bring their youth-culture-centered children to appreciate the old values of cultural and ethnic pride and identification, the Pesach seder is it! Here lies a dangerous pitfall for the parent-educator. The leader of the seder is likely to concentrate on the text of the Haggadah without sufficiently taking into consideration the audience — the younger generation — and their level of interest. Absorbed with the sales-pitch, the salesperson often forgets the customer!

Prague, 1526

'The Four Parents:' Children Label Their Parents

IN THE DAYS of the patriarchal regime, we allowed ourselves to categorize our children harshly — accepting only one as positive — the wise one.

The simple, the wicked and the one who knows not how to ask questions had to swallow hard and hide their sense of being insulted . . .

Now in our days no child is identified as "the offspring of the parent" and often the parent is identified as "the parent of that child." We have arrived at an era not of partiarchy or matriarchy but the rule of children. In our age it is then miraculous that our dear, delightful children don't divide us up and categorize us. At the best, we would be rated "naive or simple minded parents" or "parents who don't know how to respond to a question."

(Israel Eldad, "The Victory of the Wise Son")

The Pitfalls of Labeling

I INSTINCTIVELY recoil from static stereotypes that label persons simplistically. Therefore, I choose to interpret the midrash of the four children as a diverse set of strategies for addressing four different facets of each and every child. Each personality combines these facets in different ways. For example, the wise and the rebellious facets can be combined for evil. Then the cunning mind is used to inflict pain on one's parents. Alternatively, the combination can produce a revolutionary chalutz (pioneer) seeking not just to undermine the traditional order but to create new frameworks of meaning. This requires an intelligence which is not conservative like the traditional "wise child" but which looks beyond the horizon, beyond the existing laws and their pat rationale.

(Yariv Ben Aharon, Kibbutz author)

The Four Children as a Screenplay

חָכָם וְרָשָׁע

1. *A simple reading* of the Haggadah's midrash of the four children can obscure the fact that it provides the script for a dialogue. Let each character in the dialogue be played by a different seder participant.

2. *The cast* is as follows: • Narrator
• Each of the four children
• Four parents who answer.

3. *The reading* goes as follows:

Kadesh
Urchatz
Karpas
Yachatz
Maggid

Four
Children

Narrator	**What does the wise child say?**
Wise or Thoughtful Child	"What are the testimonies, the statutes, and the laws which Adonai our God has commanded you?" *(Deuteronomy 6:20)*
Narrator	So, you teach the child all the laws of Pesach, till the last one:
First Parent	"We do not conclude the eating at the Pesach seder with the afikoman." *(Last Mishna in Pesachim, Chapter 10)*
Narrator	**What does the wicked child say?**
Wicked or Alienated Child	"Whatever does this service mean to *you*?" *(Exodus 12:26)*
Narrator	This child emphasizes "*you*" and not him or herself! Since the child excludes him or herself from the community and rejects a major principle of faith, you should set his or her teeth on edge and say:
Second Parent	"It is because of this, that Adonai did for *me* when *I* went free from Egypt." *(Exodus 13:8)*
Narrator	"*Me*" and not **that one over there**! Had that one been there, s/he would not have been redeemed.

חָכָם מַה הוּא אוֹמֵר?

"מָה הָעֵדֹת וְהַחֻקִּים וְהַמִּשְׁפָּטִים, אֲשֶׁר צִוָּה יי אֱלֹהֵינוּ אֶתְכֶם?" (דברים ו,כ)

וְאַף אַתָּה אֱמָר לוֹ כְּהִלְכוֹת הַפֶּסַח: "אֵין מַפְטִירִין אַחַר הַפֶּסַח אֲפִיקוֹמָן." (משנה, פסחים פרק י')

רָשָׁע מַה הוּא אוֹמֵר:

"מָה הָעֲבֹדָה הַזֹּאת לָכֶם?" (שמות יב,כו)

"לָכֶם" – וְלֹא לוֹ.

וּלְפִי שֶׁהוֹצִיא אֶת עַצְמוֹ מִן הַכְּלָל – כָּפַר בָּעִקָּר. אַף אַתָּה הַקְהֵה אֶת שִׁנָּיו, וֶאֱמָר לוֹ: "בַּעֲבוּר זֶה, עָשָׂה יי לִי, בְּצֵאתִי מִמִּצְרָיִם."

"לִי" – וְלֹא לוֹ. אִלּוּ הָיָה שָׁם, לֹא הָיָה נִגְאָל.

Otto Geismar, the Wise Child and the Wicked Child, 1927

Siegmund Forst, 1958

Beating the Bounds: Producing Wicked Children

THE PASSOVER CELEBRATION is aimed at the child in all of us, allowing us to open our imaginations, to rediscover the lost elements of wonder, pleasure, and hilarity that are captured in this event. Having children at the seder can help make this happen.

If we make our children unhappy, they will remember Passover, but not fondly. In the British Isles, there is a custom of taking sons out every year to "beat the bounds." Today they use the stick as the boundary markers, but they used to beat the boys at the site of those markers to ensure that they would remember the limits of ancestral property. Beating our ancient heritage into our children's psyches may make them remember, but it is probably the reason so many people remember ritual and ceremony as intrinsically unpleasant.

(Ira Steingroot, Keeping Passover)

'Who is truly Wise?'

THE WISE CHILD of the Haggadah is portrayed as a knowledgeable, believing and obedient child. This child formulates long complex questions, distinguishes multiple categories of laws, and accepts the God who commanded "us." But let's beware of this stereotyped, academic brainchild. Is this child truly wise?

- **Don Isaac Abrabanel, "The Smart Alec":** "This 'wise-guy' child is arrogant in his 'wisdom.' He shows off the distinctions he can make between types of mitzvot. *'But you teach him the subtleties down to the last detail in the Mishna.'* Let the 'smart-alec' who appears wise in his own eyes see that there is still much for him to learn.

   "There is twice as much wisdom in these laws as in the question. Let the wise grow in wisdom and in humility."

- **Israel Eldad, "To Know When to Ask":** "No! The wise child does not derive his title from the pretense to know-it-all. One who thinks he possesses wisdom already, does not ask at all. 'One who does not even know how to ask' has a negative trait, typical of the know-it-all. The truly wise child asks genuine questions, not cynically and mockingly like the rebellious child and not superficially like the simple child. He seeks the essence of things, *'What is the true nature of the laws, testimonies and statutes that God has commanded us?'*

- **The Chassidic Seer of Lublin:** "In my judgment, it is better to be a wicked person who knows he is wicked, than a righteous one who knows that he is righteous. Worst of all is to be a wicked person who thinks he is righteous."

(Menachem HaCohen, Haggadah of HaAm)

The Wicked Child — An Unfair Description?

The "wicked" child expresses a sense of alienation from our Jewish heritage. In this age of liberalism and democracy, of pluralistic tolerance for many cultural expressions, should a person who expresses such a feeling be condemned as "wicked" or "evil"?

- Hold a brief discussion on the topic. Would a different characterization be more appropriate to our contemporary sensibilities — such as "the rebellious one," "the skeptic," "the arrogant — chutzpadik?"

Is "setting his teeth on edge" the best strategy to deal with such a person?

- Role-Playing: try to "get inside" the personality of the so-called "wicked" children and their parents. Describe the feelings of each one in this tense confrontation described in the Haggadah.

Suggestion: Have the younger participants at the seder describe the feelings of the parent, and have those who are already parents describe the feelings of the child.

The Four Children Continued

Narrator — **What does the simple child ask?**

Simple or Naive Child — "What is this? *(Exodus 13:14)*

Narrator — And you shall say to that child:

Third Parent — "[Let me tell you an awesome tale.] With a mighty hand Adonai brought us out of Egypt, out of the house of bondage." *(Exodus 13:14)*

Narrator — **As for the child who does not know how to ask.** You should prompt the child. The Torah says: "You shall tell your child on that day."

[Don't wait for the child to take the initiative. Start the story, your story, and hopefully this silent child will listen, absorb and identify with you].

Fourth Parent — "It is because of this, that Adonai did for me when I went free from Egypt." *(Exodus 13:8)*

Kadesh
Urchatz
Karpas
Yachatz
Maggid

Four
Children

תָּם וְשָׁאֵינוֹ יוֹדֵעַ לִשְׁאוֹל

תָּם מַה הוּא אוֹמֵר?
"מַה זֹּאת?" (שמות יג,יד)
"וְאָמַרְתָּ אֵלָיו:
"בְּחֹזֶק יָד הוֹצִיאָנוּ יי מִמִּצְרַיִם, מִבֵּית עֲבָדִים."

וְשָׁאֵינוֹ יוֹדֵעַ לִשְׁאֹל?
אַתְּ פְּתַח לוֹ,
שֶׁנֶּאֱמַר: "וְהִגַּדְתָּ לְבִנְךָ בַּיּוֹם הַהוּא לֵאמֹר,
בַּעֲבוּר זֶה עָשָׂה יי לִי בְּצֵאתִי מִמִּצְרָיִם." (שמות יג,ח)

Otto Geismar, 1927

"You shall tell your child" *(Exodus 13:8)*

"You shall tell your child on that day: 'It is because of this, that Adonai did for me, when I went free from Egypt.'" *(Exodus 13:8)*

Could this verse mean that you should begin to tell the story at the beginning of the month of Nisan?

No, for the verse explicitly states "on that day" (of the Exodus).

Could that mean that we start when it is still daytime?

No, for the verse explicitly states: "because of this." **"This"** must refer to a time when matza and maror are laid before you [only on seder night]. *(Mekhilta)*

"This" implies that the parents must point at the matza and maror, using them as visual aids to tell the story. *(Rabbi Simcha of Vitri)*

וְהִגַּדְתָּ לְבִנְךָ

"וְהִגַּדְתָּ לְבִנְךָ" – יָכוֹל מֵרֹאשׁ חֹדֶשׁ?
תַּלְמוּד לוֹמַר "בַּיּוֹם הַהוּא." (שמות יג,ח)
אִי "בַּיּוֹם הַהוּא," יָכוֹל מִבְּעוֹד יוֹם?
תַּלְמוּד לוֹמַר "בַּעֲבוּר זֶה" –
"בַּעֲבוּר זֶה" לֹא אָמַרְתִּי, אֶלָּא בְּשָׁעָה
שֶׁיֵּשׁ מַצָּה וּמָרוֹר מֻנָּחִים לְפָנֶיךָ.

60

The Contemporary Four Children

Which famous person today would be the best representative of the "wise child," of the "wicked child," and so on? Suggest candidates and discuss their suitability.

A Child's Perspective

Ask the younger children to describe the behavior of "a bad child" at the seder.
- *What might be causing such behavior?*
- *Do they approve of the parent's response in the Haggadah?*
- *How would they handle the situation?*
- *Why do they think the "silent child" asks no questions?*
- *How might that child be coaxed into greater involvement?*

The Immigrant Family   Chicago Haggadah, 1879

Beyond Labels

I DO NOT VIEW labels as static pigeonholes. I believe in the power of the educational act to release locked up potentials. For example, **one who does not know how to ask** may be silenced by the rules of society. The silence may hide an exceptional, sensitive child whose questions are choked. A parent can "open the child up," remove the obstructions, enable personal growth and break stereotypes.

(Yariv Ben Aharon, Kibbutz author)

Bridging the Generation Gap

The inter-generational dialogues in the Torah explicitly refer to parents who participated in the Exodus addressing their children who have grown up in freedom in the Land of Israel. The parents have undergone an experience of slavery and redemption which is totally foreign to the reality of the younger generation. The gap in experience causes difficulties in the inter-generational dialogue.

Invite the seder participants to discuss the following:

What are the generational gaps among us, the participants of tonight's seder? Go around the table and have people relate a particular experience connected with their generation which might be difficult for a person of a different generation to comprehend.

The Art of the Four Children

1. **Compare and contrast** the artists' interpretations of each of the Four Children (page 56-71).

2. **Which portrayal** is most surprising? most disturbing? most appropriate?

3. **What conceptions** of Jewish values and society are implicit in the various depictions?

The Ideal Jewish Girl?
Tanya Zion, Israel, 1996

THE "BAD" CHILD הרשע

THE "WISE" CHILD החכם

THE "GOOD GIRL" SIMPLE החכמה התמה

THE ONE WHO DOES NOT ASK... שאינו יודע לשאול

CINDERELLA? DEBORA THE PROPHETESS? MADONNA? GOLDA MEIR? RABBI?

LAWYER? DOCTOR? MOTHER? WIFE? I.D.F. PILOT? SPORTSWOMAN? ACTRESS?

Kadesh
Urchatz
Karpas
Yachatz
Maggid
Four Children

Eastern European Types

Arthur Szyk,
Poland, 1939

63

בָּרוּךְ הַמָּקוֹם בָּרוּךְ הוּא

אַרְבָּעָה כְּנֶגֶד

וְאֶחָד רָשָׁע אֶחָד חָכָם

רָשָׁע

לָכֶם וְלֹא לוֹ. וּלְפִי שֶׁהוֹצִיא
אֶת עַצְמוֹ מִן הַכְּלָל כָּפַר בְּעִקָּר
אַף אַתָּה הַקְהֵה אֶת שִׁנָּיו וֶאֱ־
מֹר לוֹ: בַּעֲבוּר זֶה עָשָׂה יְיָ
לִי בְּצֵאתִי מִמִּצְרַיִם. לִי וְלֹא לוֹ.
אִלּוּ הָיָה שָׁם לֹא הָיָה נִגְאָל.

חָכָם

וְאַף אַתָּה אֱמֹר לוֹ כְּהִלְכוֹת
הַפֶּסַח אֵין מַפְטִירִין אַחַר הַ
פֶּסַח אֲפִיקוֹמָן.

The Blessing of Diversity

The artist and calligrapher David Moss explains his depiction of the Four Children:

EVERY CHILD is unique and the Torah embraces them all. The iconography that I've chosen here is based on playing cards. As in a game of chance, we have no control over the children dealt us. It is our task as parents, as educators, to play our hand based on the attributes of the children we are given. It is the child, not the parent, who must direct the process. This, I believe, is the intent of the midrash of the four children.

Each child's question appears on his card, and the Haggadah's answer appears below the card. The gold object in each picture denotes the suit of the card. The staves, swords, cups and coins used in Southern Europe developed parallel to the more familiar hearts, diamonds, clubs and spades of Northern Europe. The figures are likewise taken from archaic systems of playing cards which included king, knight, page, and joker or fool.

The king image here represents the wise child wearing the crown of Torah. The knight represents the wicked child. In almost all old haggadot the wicked child is shown as a soldier, sometimes mounted, sometimes on foot. The page is the simple child, and the joker or fool is the child who is not even capable of asking.

Every Child is a Blessing

I got the idea of representing the children as cards, by the way, from the tradition dating from the Middle Ages of depicting the simple child, or the child who doesn't know how to ask, as a jester or fool. I drew a book in each picture and positioned it to reflect each child's attitude to the tradition.

The text of the Haggadah introduces the four children with a short passage in which the word *baruch* (blessed) appears four times. I have designed these two pages to correlate each of these four "blessings" with one of the four children: every child is a blessing.

Diversity, how we deal with it, and how we can discover the blessing within it, is perhaps the theme of the midrash of the Four Children.

(David Moss, 20th C. artist, U.S.A. and Israel)

The Blessing of Diversity.
David Moss,
The Moss Haggadah © 1996

65

חָכָם מַה הוּא אוֹמֵר? מָה הָעֵדֹת וְהַחֻקִּים וְהַמִּשְׁפָּטִים, אֲשֶׁר צִוָּה יְיָ אֱלֹהֵינוּ אֶתְכֶם? וְאַף אַתָּה אֱמָר-לוֹ כְּהִלְכוֹת הַפֶּסַח: אֵין מַפְטִירִין אַחַר הַפֶּסַח אֲפִיקוֹמָן.

תָּם מַה הוּא אוֹמֵר? מַה זֹּאת? וְאָמַרְתָּ אֵלָיו: בְּחֹזֶק יָד הוֹצִיאָנוּ יְיָ מִמִּצְרַיִם מִבֵּית עֲבָדִים.

רָשָׁע מַה הוּא אוֹמֵר? מָה הָעֲבוֹדָה הַזֹּאת לָכֶם? לָכֶם וְלֹא לוֹ. וּלְפִי שֶׁהוֹצִיא אֶת עַצְמוֹ מִן הַכְּלָל, כָּפַר בָּעִקָּר. וְאַף אַתָּה הַקְהֵה אֶת שִׁנָּיו וֶאֱמָר-לוֹ: בַּעֲבוּר זֶה עָשָׂה יְיָ לִי בְּצֵאתִי מִמִּצְרַיִם. לִי וְלֹא לוֹ. אִלּוּ הָיָה שָׁם, לֹא הָיָה נִגְאָל.

וְשֶׁאֵינוֹ יוֹדֵעַ לִשְׁאֹל – אַתְּ פְּתַח לוֹ, שֶׁנֶּאֱמַר: וְהִגַּדְתָּ לְבִנְךָ בַּיּוֹם הַהוּא לֵאמֹר: בַּעֲבוּר זֶה עָשָׂה יְיָ לִי בְּצֵאתִי מִמִּצְרַיִם.

Four Attitudes to the Zionist Dream

Tzvi Livni, Israel, 1955 © Yavneh Publishers

Four Personalities   *Paul Freeman, U.S.A., 1960*

Clashing Cultures   *Sigmund Forst, Europe and U.S.A., 1959*

73/125

Shraga Weil '67

Four Children, Four Musicians

Shraga Weil, (CL 1963 Cat. S-3) © Safrai Gallery

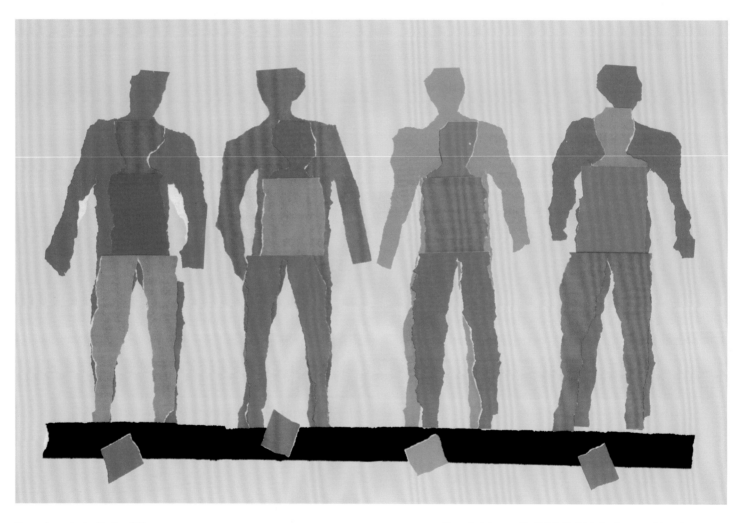

Four Aspects in Each of Us   *Dan Reisinger, © 1982, Rabbinical Assembly of America*

The Four Children as Four Books   *David Wander, The Haggadah in Memory of the Holocaust © 1988*

Clay Children   *Rony Oren, Animated Haggadah, © 1985 Jonathan Lubell, Scopus Films*

שֶׁאֵינוֹ
יוֹדֵעַ לִשְׁאוֹל   תָּם   רָשָׁע   חָכָם

Nota Koslowsky, U.S.A., 1944

Lola, U.S.A., 1920

Dick Codor © 1981

Jakob Steinhardt, Germany, 1923

Rav's Pesach Story
From Serving Idols to Spiritual Liberation

מִתְּחִלָּה עוֹבְדֵי עֲבוֹדָה זָרָה

1. *As we noted* above, the Haggadah offers two versions of the Exodus story. The Talmudic Rabbi, Shmuel, emphasized political enslavement ("We were slaves in Egypt"). Now we turn to his colleague, Rav, to hear about spiritual servitude.

2. *Rav's version* is drawn from Joshua's farewell speech to the nation of Israel. Joshua feared that the new Israelis might assimilate to the local pagan cultures. So he told them the story of Abraham's liberation from idolatry.

Kadesh
Urchatz
Karpas
Yachatz
Maggid

Spiritual
Slavery

IN THE BEGINNING our ancestors were idol worshippers. But now God has brought us near to serve Adonai.

The leader:

JOSHUA said to all the people: "Thus said Adonai, the God of Israel: Long ago your ancestors including Terach, father of Abraham and Nachor, lived beyond the Euphrates and worshipped other gods. But 1 took your father Abraham from beyond the Euphrates and led him through the whole land of Canaan and multiplied his offspring. I gave him Isaac, and to Isaac I gave Jacob and Esau . . . Then Jacob and his children went down to Egypt."

"Then I sent Moses and Aaron, and brought plagues on Egypt after which I freed you — I freed your ancestors — from Egypt. Now, therefore, serve Adonai with undivided loyalty . . . Or, if you are loath to serve Adonai, choose this day other gods to serve. But I and my family will serve Adonai."

All:

IN REPLY, the people declared, "Far be it from us to forsake Adonai and serve other gods! For it was Adonai our God who brought us and our ancestors up from the land of Egypt, the house of bondage, and who performed those wondrous signs before our very eyes . . . Now we too will serve Adonai, for Adonai is our God." *(Joshua 24:1-18)*

מִתְּחִלָּה עוֹבְדֵי עֲבוֹדָה זָרָה הָיוּ אֲבוֹתֵינוּ,
וְעַכְשָׁיו קֵרְבָנוּ הַמָּקוֹם לַעֲבֹדָתוֹ, שֶׁנֶּאֱמַר:

"וַיֹּאמֶר יְהוֹשֻׁעַ אֶל כָּל הָעָם:
כֹּה אָמַר יי אֱלֹהֵי יִשְׂרָאֵל –
בְּעֵבֶר הַנָּהָר יָשְׁבוּ אֲבוֹתֵיכֶם מֵעוֹלָם
– תֶּרַח אֲבִי אַבְרָהָם וַאֲבִי נָחוֹר –
וַיַּעַבְדוּ אֱלֹהִים אֲחֵרִים.
וָאֶקַּח אֶת אֲבִיכֶם, אֶת אַבְרָהָם, מֵעֵבֶר הַנָּהָר
וָאוֹלֵךְ אוֹתוֹ בְּכָל אֶרֶץ כְּנָעַן;
וָאַרְבֶּה אֶת זַרְעוֹ וָאֶתֶּן לוֹ אֶת יִצְחָק.
וָאֶתֵּן לְיִצְחָק אֶת יַעֲקֹב וְאֶת עֵשָׂו.
וָאֶתֵּן לְעֵשָׂו אֶת הַר שֵׂעִיר לָרֶשֶׁת אֹתוֹ,
וְיַעֲקֹב וּבָנָיו יָרְדוּ מִצְרָיִם."

Rav's Story of Spiritual Liberation

RAV'S STORY states that our ancestors were idol worshippers. Abraham's father was an idol worshipper, of course. But we wonder: "What are you talking about? Who needs to know on Pesach whether my ancestors were idol worshippers?" I always wonder to myself, "What fools! Who would want to worship sticks and stones." To make sense of Terach's faith and of Abraham's religious revolt, I have to tell my children about the appeal, the seduction of idolatry, *avodah zarah* (strange worship). They have to be told about their great grandfather who began in idolatry and who discovered a liberating worship. They must discover Abraham's childhood, and must grasp the lonely man of faith, Abraham *ha-ivri*. The midrash says that '*ivri*' ("Hebrew," also "side") means that the whole world was on one side and Abraham was on the other, alone. The child must learn the pain of loneliness that the convert has to bear. This is the story for Rav.

Abraham's conversion is an act of freedom. Jewish identity is saturated with freedom. Passover does not introduce a racist ethnic tribe; it brings to the fore a covenantal people of choice. "Are you prepared to listen how your grandfather was alone and struggled against false beliefs?" That is what the home has to say. After the child is told, then there can be a free embracing of who one is. That is the significance of singing Hallel on Passover night. Here is a singing towards personal identity. One rejoices at this self-definition: "I am a *ger*, a convert. I am who I am out of conviction. I am free and I choose to praise Adonai who liberated me."

(David Hartman, Jerusalem philosopher)

Alienation from Ourselves

THE DIFFERENCE between the slave and the free person is not merely one of social class, that the slave just happens to be enslaved to another, and the free person is not enslaved. One can find a cultured and learned slave whose spirit is filled with freedom, and conversely, a "free" person whose spirit is that of a slave. Real freedom is that **noble spirit** by which the individual and indeed the whole people are elevated to become loyal to their inner essential self, to the image of God within them. Through this characteristic they can perceive their lives as purposeful and worthy of value.

This is not true regarding people with the **spirit of a slave** — the content of their lives and their feelings are never attuned to the characteristics of their essential self, but rather to what is considered beautiful and good by the others. They are ruled by all sorts of constraints, whether they be formal or moral.

(Rav Avraham Yitzchak Kook, first Ashkenazi Chief Rabbi in Israel, 1921-1935)

Abraham the Iconoclast

ICONOCLAST IS A WORD which has come almost unchanged from the Greek *eikon* (image) and *klastes* (a breaker). Literally one who shatters sacred images, it has come to mean anyone who scoffs at our treasured beliefs.

The spiritual liberation from false gods begins, according to Rabbinic interpretation, with Abraham's critical search for truth. It culminates in a full scale rebellion against his own father, Terach the idol maker. The struggle for truth can threaten family solidarity and undermine tradition, yet it is still a value to be cherished, especially on Pesach.

Jews-by-Choice

Abraham and Sarah were Jews-by-choice who as mature adults made daring spiritual choices. Today many of us are really Jews-by-choice (whether as converts or as born Jews). For we continuously reflect on our life choices. To be a contemporary Jew requires a positive decision about what kind of a Jew to be and how central Judaism will be in our daily lives. Ask several people to share their personal journey as Jews. What choices and what ongoing hesitations shape their relationship to Judaism?

(continued from page 75)

I brought the food offering to them as usual. Then one god insisted: "Me, first." Another responded angrily: "No, me first!" Finally the biggest of them took his staff, smashed the rest and took the offering all for himself.

Terach stared at his first born Abram in disbelief and rage: "What kind of a joke is this? Don't mock me! None of these gods have the power you attributed to him."

Then Abram reasoned gently with his father: "Please, just let your ears hear what your mouth just said."

(Freely adapted from Philo, Maimonides, Nachmanides and Rabbinic midrashim)

A Debate: 'Is Abram a Wicked Child?'

After reading our adaptation of the Rabbinic story of young Abraham you may wish to stage a short debate. Divide the table down the middle into roughly equal constituencies, arbitrarily assigning the role of pro and con to debate the following proposition: **"Abraham is a rebellious son whose outrageous treatment of his parents' and his society's most cherished beliefs should be censured."** Begin with one short "pro" statement, then shift back and forth between pro and con sides of the table for 5 minutes.

At the end, put the question to a vote.

Kadesh
Urchatz
Karpas
Yachatz
Maggid
Terach's Idol Shop

Tanya Zion, 1995

Abraham Discovers God

A Rabbinic Children's Story

Long, long ago it was generally agreed that the gods were the heavenly lights — the sun, the moon, and the stars. For example, in the days of the Exodus Pharaoh believed in the sun god Ra and he bore the name Ra-meses — son of Ra. Idols of clay and wood were fashioned to embody the power of the heavenly lights. No one dared to disagree.

In those days in the city of Ur in Babylonia (today's Iraq) there lived a man named Terach, who was a skilled idol maker. His family prospered by selling these gods in the market.

Yet Terach's oldest son, Abram (later to be called Abraham), did not follow in his father's footsteps. From an early age Abram took nothing of his father's tradition for granted. Perhaps he was too inquisitive, too much an independent thinker. Terach considered Abram a rebellious son and worried that nothing good would come of him.

Once little Abram began to wonder: "Who really created the sky and the earth and me? Seeing the brilliance of the warm sun he worshipped it all day. But when the burning sun set in the west and the cool moon rose in the east surrounded by a thousand twinkling stars, he thought, "I must have been mistaken about the sun. It must be the moon with all its ministers — one for every nation on earth — that created the sky and the earth and me." All night long he worshipped the moon. However Abram was perplexed when next morning the cool moon set and all his servants disappeared and the burning sun rose again. "How" he wondered, "can either the sun or the moon be the supreme creator? Each is eclipsed in turn by the other!" Abram concluded that God was beyond all the physical forces, the Creator of all these processes. So he resolved in his heart to worship this invisible God alone.

The Idol Salesman

ONCE ABRAM'S FATHER, Terach, asked him to take over the idol shop in the market. Perhaps he hoped Abram would take an interest in the family business. An experienced soldier came to buy an idol to protect his new home.

Soldier: "Do you have a good idol?"

Abram: "What kind of god?"

Soldier: "Well, since I am a great soldier, give me a god like myself." Abram gave him the fiercest looking idol in the shop and the soldier paid full price.

Soldier: "By the way, are you sure this god is as fierce as I am?"

The lad could not contain himself.

Abram: "How old are you?"

Soldier: "I am fifty years of age, and have been a soldier for more than thirty years," was the answer.

Abram laughed: "You are fifty, whereas this idol was carved by my father only last week. And though you are a seasoned warrior, you seek protection from it!" Startled, the man took his money back and left the idol in the shop. An old woman entered next: "My house has been robbed, and my god was stolen from me. Sell me another," she said, putting the money on the counter.

Abram smiled: "Your idol could not protect even himself, yet you wish to buy another!" The woman retrieved her money and ran out angrily.

The Broken Idols

THE REST OF Terach's children ran to their father: "Abram will never make a salesperson. Let's make him a priest."

Abram asked: "What does a priest do?"

Terach's sons: "He stands before the gods serving them, washing them, and feeding them." Though doubtful, Abram agreed to try.

Abram prepared some tasty food and drink and told the gods: "Please help yourselves, take something to eat, take a drink, and please be good to the people who are giving you these gifts."

However, not one of the gods took any of his dinner. Abram began to make fun of the idols.

"They have mouths, but cannot speak, eyes but cannot see; they have ears, but cannot hear; noses, but cannot smell; they have hands, but cannot touch; feet, but cannot walk; they can make no sound in their throats. Those who fashion them, all who trust in them, shall become like them." (Psalm 115: 5-8)

Then he took a stick and smashed every idol except the largest one. Carefully he placed the stick, like a scepter, in the hand of the remaining idol and placed the food before him.

When Terach arrived he was shocked: "Who did this to our gods?"

Abram: "It was unbelieveable!

Keeping the Promise

בָּרוּךְ שׁוֹמֵר הַבְטָחָתוֹ

After recalling Abraham's spiritual journey to God (p. 72) and his **ascent** to Eretz Yisrael, the Haggadah will recount the **descent** of his great grandchildren to Egyptian slavery ("The

Wandering Aramean," p. 78). But first the Haggadah reassures us, as God did to Abraham, that there is a Divine pledge to Jewish continuity whatever the ups and downs of history.

The leader:

BLESSED is the One who keeps the Promise to Israel.

The Holy One calculated the end of our exile and acted just as promised to Abraham our Father at the Covenant between the Pieces. *(Genesis 15: 7-17)*

"And God said to Abram: You must know, that your seed will be strangers in a land not theirs; the people (of that land) will put them in servitude and afflict them for four hundred years. But as for the nation to which they are in servitude — I will bring judgment on them, and after that (your seed) will go out with great wealth." *(Genesis 15: 13-14)*

בָּרוּךְ שׁוֹמֵר הַבְטָחָתוֹ לְיִשְׂרָאֵל, בָּרוּךְ הוּא. שֶׁהַקָּדוֹשׁ בָּרוּךְ הוּא חִשֵּׁב אֶת הַקֵּץ, לַעֲשׂוֹת כְּמָה שֶׁאָמַר לְאַבְרָהָם אָבִינוּ בִּבְרִית בֵּין הַבְּתָרִים, שֶׁנֶּאֱמַר:
"וַיֹּאמֶר לְאַבְרָם: יָדֹעַ תֵּדַע, כִּי גֵר יִהְיֶה זַרְעֲךָ, בְּאֶרֶץ לֹא לָהֶם. וַעֲבָדוּם וְעִנּוּ אֹתָם – אַרְבַּע מֵאוֹת שָׁנָה. וְגַם אֶת הַגּוֹי, אֲשֶׁר יַעֲבֹדוּ, דָּן אָנֹכִי. וְאַחֲרֵי כֵן יֵצְאוּ בִּרְכֻשׁ גָּדוֹל."

(בראשית טו, יג-יד)

Kadesh
Urchatz
Karpas
Yachatz
Maggid

Keeping the Promise

Standing Up For Us

וְהִיא שֶׁעָמְדָה

1. Cover the matza, raise your cup and sing together, acknowledging God's commitment to our survival.

2. Afterwards, set the cup down and uncover the matza for the continuation of the Maggid.

❖ **THIS PROMISE** has stood for our parents and for us in good stead.
For not just one enemy has stood against us to wipe us out.
But in every generation there have been those who have stood against us to wipe us out.
Yet the Holy One keeps on saving us from their hands.

V'hee she-am-dah, la-a-vo-yei-nu v'la-nu.
She-lo eh-chad beel-vad,
amad alei-nu l'cha-lo-tei-nu.
Eh-la she-b'chol dor va-dor
om-deem a-lei-nu l'cha-lo-tei-nu.
V'ha-ka-dosh ba-ruch hu
ma-tzee-lei-nu mee-ya-dam.

וְהִיא שֶׁעָמְדָה לַאֲבוֹתֵינוּ וְלָנוּ.
שֶׁלֹּא אֶחָד בִּלְבַד,
עָמַד עָלֵינוּ לְכַלּוֹתֵנוּ.
אֶלָּא שֶׁבְּכָל דּוֹר וָדוֹר,
עוֹמְדִים עָלֵינוּ לְכַלּוֹתֵנוּ,
וְהַקָּדוֹשׁ בָּרוּךְ הוּא
מַצִּילֵנוּ מִיָּדָם.

RABBI JOACHIM PRINZ recalls that in Nazi Germany Jewish holidays assumed a new importance:

No longer were they perfunctory observances of the day. They became part of the context of danger, fear, death and hope in which we lived. Passover was now the great day of hope for delivery from our own Egypt. The whips which beat the naked bodies of Jewish slaves in Egypt were the very same that struck our bodies. Slavery was no longer an abstract term, foreign to the world of the twentieth century. We could now identify with the slaves for we, ourselves, were third-class citizens, and therefore slaves. Those people who had been taken from their homes and whom we no longer saw, but about whose fate we knew, illustrated the Haggadah in colors much more telling than those of the most graphic illustrations we had ever seen.

The Passover slogan, '*From slavery unto freedom*,' became the song of our lives. If the slaves of Egypt could be delivered from their fate, so would we. All the songs at the seder table were sung with new emphasis and new meaning and great religious fervor. When we read that *'in every generation one is obligated to see oneself as one who personally went out from Egypt'* and *'it was not only our ancestors whom God set free from slavery,'* the identification was complete. It was not historic memory. It was not history at all. It was the reality of every day and the hope of every person. Some day, we said, we shall be free.

Abraham's Descendents will be like the Stars (Genesis 15)

Ephraim Moses Lilien

But the greatest identification came when we read: *'Not merely one persecutor has stood up against us, but in every generation they persecuted us to destroy us, but The Holy One saved us from their hands.'* What more did we want? How much deeper could Jewish identification with the people go? Here it was. The persecution was upon us. But some day we would be saved.

I did not then know that I was later to sing *'We shall overcome some day'* with Martin Luther King. But when I did, I remembered the songs of the seder table under the Hitler regime.

'Arami Oved Avi'
The Wandering Jew

On Pesach each of us retells our story of wandering and homecoming, as did the farmer bringing the first fruits to

אֲרַמִּי אֹבֵד אָבִי

Jerusalem. Let the leader read the narrator's role and the others respond in unison as each Jew used to do in the Temple.

Kadesh
Urchatz
Karpas
Yachatz
Maggid

Wandering Jew

The Torah: A Tale of Persecution and Homecoming

Narrator:

When you enter the land that Adonai your God is giving you as an inheritance, and you possess it and settle on it, then you shall take some of every first fruit of the soil. Put it in a basket and go to the place where Adonai your God will choose to establish His Name. You will go before the *cohen* (priest) in charge at that time and say to him:

Prague, 1526

❖ I will tell Adonai today how I have come to the land Adonai swore to our ancestors to give to us: . . .
"MY ANCESTOR was a wandering Aramean. He descended to Egypt and resided there in small numbers. He became a nation — great, powerful and numerous. The Egyptians treated us badly. They persecuted us and put us under hard labor. We cried out to Adonai, the God of our ancestors. God heard our voice. God saw our persecution, our toil and our oppression. God took us out of Egypt with a strong hand and an outstretched arm, with awesome power, signs and wonders. God brought us to this place and gave us this land, a land of milk and honey. Now I have brought the first fruits of this soil, which you, God, gave me." *(Deut. 26:1-10)*

"אֲרַמִּי אֹבֵד אָבִי, וַיֵּרֶד מִצְרַיְמָה, וַיָּגָר שָׁם בִּמְתֵי מְעָט, וַיְהִי שָׁם לְגוֹי גָּדוֹל, עָצוּם וָרָב. וַיָּרֵעוּ אֹתָנוּ הַמִּצְרִים וַיְעַנּוּנוּ. וַיִּתְּנוּ עָלֵינוּ עֲבֹדָה קָשָׁה.

וַנִּצְעַק אֶל יי אֱלֹהֵי אֲבֹתֵינוּ, וַיִּשְׁמַע יי אֶת קֹלֵנוּ, וַיַּרְא אֶת עָנְיֵנוּ וְאֶת עֲמָלֵנוּ וְאֶת לַחֲצֵנוּ.

וַיּוֹצִאֵנוּ יי מִמִּצְרַיִם, בְּיָד חֲזָקָה, וּבִזְרֹעַ נְטוּיָה, וּבְמֹרָא גָּדֹל, וּבְאֹתוֹת וּבְמֹפְתִים. וַיְבִיאֵנוּ אֶל הַמָּקוֹם הַזֶּה, וַיִּתֶּן לָנוּ אֶת הָאָרֶץ הַזֹּאת, אֶרֶץ זָבַת חָלָב וּדְבָשׁ." (דברים כו, א-י)

May a Convert say: "God of my ancestors"?

QUESTION: I received a question from Ovadia, the wise and learned convert, may the God of Israel, under whose wings he sought cover, reward him for his work. You ask me if you, too, are allowed to say in the blessings and prayers: **"Our God and God of our ancestors," "You who have brought us out of the land of Egypt," "You who have worked miracles for our ancestors."**

RESPONSUM: Yes. In the same way as every Jew by birth says his blessings, you, too, shall pray . . . For Abraham our Father taught the people, opened their minds, and revealed to them the true faith and the unity of God; he rejected idols and abolished their adoration; he brought many children under the wings of the Divine Presence. *"For I have known (Abraham) to the end that he may command his children and his household after him, that they may keep the way of Adonai, to do righteousness and justice."* (Gen. 18:19). Ever since then whoever adopts Judaism and confesses the unity of the Divine Name is counted among the disciples of Abraham our Father.

Therefore, you shall pray, **"Our God and God of our ancestors,"** because Abraham is your father. **No difference exists between you and us,** and all miracles done to us have been done as it were to us and to you.

Torah and Midrash

On seder night we do not stick to the facts of the Biblical story. Taking our cue from the five rabbis of B'nai B'rak who went on all night, we are urged to expand on the Torah's version of the Exodus in the style of rabbinic commentary called midrash. The Mishna specifies the task at hand: *Expound the whole section of "My father was a wandering Aramean."* (Deut. 26:5-8; Mishna, Pesachim 10:4) This famous narrative recounts the story of a wandering people, exploited in Egypt, who finally came home to their own land in Israel. In the days of the Temple, beginning on Shavuot, the wanderers-turned-farmers would bring an offering of their first fruits balanced in a basket on their shoulders and recite their story of rags-to-riches, of wandering-to-rootedness in the land. Every Jew knew this narrative saga by heart.

This concise narrative is a jumping off point for midrashic commentary, associating the words of the Biblical text with larger themes. The Rabbis recommended that each family begin to expatiate on it, phrase by phrase. The Haggadah includes one classic version of this rabbinic art of interpretation, but the door is open to innovations. We have brought you a rich menu of Torah and Midrash organized thematically:

1. The Torah: Deuteronomy 26: 1-10,
2. The traditional Rabbinic Midrash of the Pesach Haggadah,
3. Our contemporary commentary on the issues raised by the Midrash.

Know that our ancestors, when they came out of Egypt, were mostly idolaters; they had mingled with the pagans in Egypt and imitated their way of life, until the Holy One sent Moses our Teacher, who brought us under the wings of the Divine Presence, us and all converts, and gave to all of us one Law. **Do not consider your origin as inferior.**

(A Letter from Moses Maimonides, 12th century, Egypt, philosopher, Talmudist, court physician, and head of the Jewish community)

The Classic Rabbinic Midrash on the Exodus

'The Wandering Aramean'

Read and study:

GO AND LEARN what (awful) plans Lavan the Aramean had for Jacob our Father:

(When Jacob migrated to Aram, he intended to stay with his uncle Lavan for only a few months. However, he fell in love with his cousin Rachel and was entrapped by his wily uncle Lavan the Aramean whose epithet also means "the cheat" — *ramai*. Jacob became his indentured servant and escaped with his wives and children only after 20 years of hard labor. Even then Lavan and his armed men pursued Jacob intending to do bodily harm, perhaps even to kill him but at least to enslave him again. Had God not appeared miraculously in a night vision to stay Lavan's hand, there would have been no people of Israel.)

THUS WHILE Pharaoh intended to kill only the boys, Lavan sought to uproot the whole of Jacob's family, the children of Israel.

THIS IS the hidden meaning of the verse, *"the wandering Aramean"* — the Aramean sought to exterminate my father — that is, Jacob.

צֵא וּלְמַד, מַה בִּקֵּשׁ לָבָן הָאֲרַמִּי לַעֲשׂוֹת לְיַעֲקֹב אָבִינוּ?

שֶׁפַּרְעֹה לֹא גָזַר אֶלָּא עַל הַזְּכָרִים, וְלָבָן בִּקֵּשׁ לַעֲקֹר אֶת־הַכֹּל, שֶׁנֶּאֱמַר:

"אֲרַמִּי אֹבֵד אָבִי." (דברים כו, ה-ז)

Kadesh

Urchatz

Karpas

Yachatz

Maggid

Rabbinic Symposium

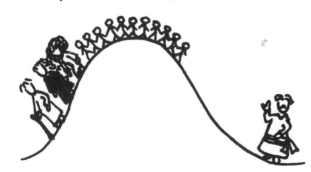

There is No Freedom Without First Fruits

WHY DOES the Pesach Haggadah's central midrash focus on the story of the first fruits, which is associated with Shavuot?

Perhaps the point is that Pesach is not only about the move from slavery to freedom, but from economic dependence to productivity, from the vulnerability of the alien to the security of the citizen.

The Aramean Who's Who

THE MIDRASH on Lavan the Aramean who was "worse than Pharaoh" is an outrageously forced reading of the Biblical text. However Rabbinic midrash felt no compunction about twisting the text to make an eyebrow-raising point. Perhaps they wanted to take a jab at their contemporary enemies — the Romans who destroyed Jerusalem (70 C.E.) and later forbade the teaching of Torah (135 C.E.). Coincidentally the name "Roman" (*Romi*) in Hebrew has the same consonants as Lavan the "Aramean" (*Arami*). For sermonic purposes the Rabbis typically exploit a Biblical text which itself is unclear.

The "wandering Aramean" of the Torah may also be **Abram** the Hebrew, who lived in Aram and crossed the Jordan. The name Hebrew (*ivri*) means the one who crossed over (*avar*). *(Rashbam)* Or perhaps he is **Jacob**, who wandered first to Aram and later to Egypt, where his grandchildren were enslaved. *(Ibn Ezra)*

Selecting a Topic for a Symposium

The Rabbinic treatment of the "Wandering Aramean" story raises several provocative themes for debate. You may wish to choose just one theme. Read the Rabbinic midrash and the contemporary sidebars and then open the topic to discussion.

1. Assimilation and Identity (see page 82)

Did the Jews succeed in resisting assimilation to Egyptian culture? How does a minority preserve its identity?

2. Anti-Semitism and Prejudice (see page 84)

How do antisemitic stereotypes function both in the minds of the oppressors and on the self-image of the Jews?

3. Ancient Egyptian Oppression (see page 86)

What was the historical nature of Egyptian slavery? How did the Rabbis conceive of spirit-crushing "harsh labor"?

4. From Resignation to Resistance (see page 88)

What is the turning point at which slaves wake up to their fate and begin to hope?

5. Sexuality and Liberation (see page 90)

How is sexual oppression related to the struggle for political liberation?

6. Suffering and its Lessons (see page 95)

Does suffering make us more empathetic to others? When does it make us vengeful or insensitive or apathetic?

Assimilation and Identity

"ISRAEL (JACOB) DESCENDED TO EGYPT, RESIDED THERE IN SMALL NUMBERS, AND BECAME THERE A NATION — GREAT, POWERFUL AND NUMEROUS." *(Deut. 26:5)*

"אֲרַמִּי אֹבֵד אָבִי, וַיֵּרֶד מִצְרַיְמָה, וַיָּגָר שָׁם בִּמְתֵי מְעָט. וַיְהִי שָׁם לְגוֹי גָּדוֹל, עָצוּם וָרָב."

"ISRAEL DESCENDED" compelled by the divine word, to fulfill the prophecy of God to Abraham that *"your descendants will be strangers in a land not their own, where they will be enslaved and persecuted . . . . "* *(Gen. 14-13)*

"וַיֵּרֶד מִצְרַיְמָה." אָנוּס עַל פִּי הַדִּבּוּר.

"ISRAEL RESIDED THERE" *(Deut. 26:5)* temporarily. Jacob our Father never intended to settle permanently in Egypt. Jacob's family made that clear from the onset. *"They said to the Pharaoh (who reigned in the days of Joseph): we have come (merely) to reside in this land, for there is no pasture for your servants' sheep. For the famine in the land of Canaan is very heavy. Therefore, please permit your servants to stay in the land of Goshen (within Egypt where grazing is good)."* *(Gen. 47:4)*

"וַיָּגָר שָׁם." מְלַמֵּד שֶׁלֹּא יָרַד יַעֲקֹב אָבִינוּ לְהִשְׁתַּקֵּעַ בְּמִצְרַיִם, אֶלָּא לָגוּר שָׁם, שֶׁנֶּאֱמַר (בראשית מ"ז, ד): "וַיֹּאמְרוּ אֶל פַּרְעֹה, לָגוּר בָּאָרֶץ בָּאנוּ, כִּי אֵין מִרְעֶה לַצֹּאן אֲשֶׁר לַעֲבָדֶיךָ, כִּי כָבֵד הָרָעָב בְּאֶרֶץ כְּנָעַן. וְעַתָּה, יֵשְׁבוּ נָא עֲבָדֶיךָ בְּאֶרֶץ גֹּשֶׁן."

"IN SMALL NUMBERS" *(Deut. 26:5)* Jacob arrived in Egypt. Moshe reminds us that: *"with only seventy persons, your ancestors descended to Egypt. Yet now Adonai, your God has made you as numerous as the stars of the sky."* *(Deut. 10:22)*

"בִּמְתֵי מְעָט." כְּמָה שֶׁנֶּאֱמַר (דברים י, כב): "בְּשִׁבְעִים נֶפֶשׁ, יָרְדוּ אֲבֹתֶיךָ מִצְרַיְמָה. וְעַתָּה, שָׂמְךָ יי אֱלֹהֶיךָ, כְּכוֹכְבֵי הַשָּׁמַיִם לָרֹב."

"THERE ISRAEL BECAME A NATION" *(Deut. 26:5)* — recognizable, distinctive, standing out from the others.

"וַיְהִי שָׁם לְגוֹי." מְלַמֵּד שֶׁהָיוּ יִשְׂרָאֵל מְצֻיָּנִים שָׁם.

Kadesh
Urchatz
Karpas
Yachatz
Maggid

Symposium: Assimilation

'In Small Numbers'

How Big is Israel?

Pharaoh's unfounded fears of the Jewish minority's power and size bring to mind the following incident. The Israeli Foreign Ministry sends high school juniors to represent Israel to their non-Jewish age-mates worldwide. In England in 1995 the presentation began with the following question: "How big would you say Israel is compared to England?" Most English high school students answered: "Oh, perhaps ten times as big but at least twice as big." They were shocked to learn that it was only one-tenth the size of Great Britain, equivalent to Wales. (Perhaps the inordinate press coverage devoted to Israel with 300 resident international journalists contributes to the exaggerated estimates).

When adults in England were asked for the percentage of Jews in their country, they guessed between 10-20%, even though the Jews comprise less than ½%. Worldwide the Jews were 250,000,000, they guessed, when in fact they are only 13,000,000 and shrinking towards 12,000,000 by 2020.

'Israel Resided There and Became There a Nation'

Did They Assimilate in Egypt?
Two Views

According to the Haggadah's midrash, Israel maintained its cultural distinctiveness in Egypt by holding on to some basic facets of their national identity:

"Israel was redeemed from Egypt through the merit of four things: they didn't change their names, they didn't forget their native language, they didn't reveal their secrets, and they didn't cease circumcision."
(Midrash Shocher Tov 114)

However, not all the Rabbis agreed on this point. According to another midrash, it was the very desire of the people of Israel to assimilate which aroused the anger of the native peoples. The midrash explains that when Joseph died *(Ex 1:6)*, Israel stopped circumcising their sons. They said, "Let's be like the Egyptians!" As soon as they did this, God allowed the affection with which the Egyptians had held Israel to turn into hatred, as it says: "He changed their hearts to hate His people." *(Ps. 105:25)* So Pharaoh acted as "one who did not know Joseph." *(Ex. 1:8; Ex. Rabbah)*

They Did Not Change Their Apparel

A HASSID of Rabbi David Moses of Chortkov came to the rabbi dressed in a short jacket and wearing a regular hat, unlike the custom of the Hassidim. The rabbi looked at him sharply and asked: "Why did you change your dress?"

The Hassid apologized: "I moved to one of the large cities of Western Europe, and there, among the non-Jews, who do not like Jews, it is very difficult to walk about with the traditional Hassidic garb."

The rabbi sat engrossed in thought for a time and finally exclaimed to the Hassid: "Nu, now that you have changed your clothes and you dress like one of them — do the non-Jews like you?" *(Menachem HaCohen)*

Captain Alfred Dreyfus, falsely accused of treason and exiled in 1895 to Devil's Island

'There Israel Became a Nation — Distinctive'

What's in a Name?

"They did not change their names." Rabbi Israel Baal Shem Tov, the founder of Hassidism, said: "A person's name is part of his spiritual essence. When one touches any part of a person's body, the entire body feels it. Similarly, when one calls out a person's name, even if he is asleep, he awakens. As the Jews did not change their names in Egypt, when they heard their original names being called, they immediately awakened and were ready to be redeemed." *(Menachem HaCohen)*

Antisemitism and Prejudice

"A NATION — GREAT AND POWERFUL" *(Deut. 26:5)* emerged at an incredible pace. *"The children of Israel were fruitful and swarmed, they multiplied and became very, very powerful. The whole land was filled with them."* *(Exodus 1:7)*

"A NUMEROUS NATION" *(Deut. 26:5)* also means "full-grown" *(rav)*. The prophet captures God's nurturing of Israel in Egypt with graphic imagery. *"I let you grow like the plants of the field. You continued to grow up until you attained womanhood, until your breasts became firm, and your hair flourished. Yet you were still naked (spiritually)."* *(Ezekiel 16:7)*

"THE EGYPTIANS TREATED US BADLY, THEY PERSECUTED US AND IMPOSED HARD LABOR ON US." *(Deut 26:6)*

"THE EGYPTIANS TREATED US BADLY" *(Deut. 26:6)* means they "bad-mouthed" our loyalty. Pharaoh set the ominous tone in speaking to his people: *"Let us outsmart them so that they may not increase. Otherwise, in the event of war, they will join our enemies, fight against us and expel us from the land."* *(Exodus 1:10)*

"גָּדוֹל עָצוּם." כְּמָה שֶׁנֶּאֱמַר (שמות א,ז) : "וּבְנֵי יִשְׂרָאֵל, פָּרוּ וַיִּשְׁרְצוּ, וַיִּרְבּוּ וַיַּעַצְמוּ, בִּמְאֹד מְאֹד, וַתִּמָּלֵא הָאָרֶץ אֹתָם."

"וָרָב." כְּמָה שֶׁנֶּאֱמַר (יחזקאל טז,ז) : "רְבָבָה כְּצֶמַח הַשָּׂדֶה נְתַתִּיךְ, וַתִּרְבִּי, וַתִּגְדְּלִי, וַתָּבֹאִי בַּעֲדִי עֲדָיִים. שָׁדַיִם נָכֹנוּ, וּשְׂעָרֵךְ צִמֵּחַ, וְאַתְּ עֵרֹם וְעֶרְיָה."

"וַיָּאֲבֹר עָלַיִךְ וָאֶרְאֵךְ מִתְבּוֹסֶסֶת בְּדָמָיִךְ וָאֹמַר לָךְ בְּדָמַיִךְ חֲיִי וָאֹמַר לָךְ בְּדָמַיִךְ חֲיִי."

"וַיָּרֵעוּ אֹתָנוּ הַמִּצְרִים." כְּמָה שֶׁנֶּאֱמַר (שמות א,י) : הָבָה נִתְחַכְּמָה לוֹ. פֶּן יִרְבֶּה, וְהָיָה כִּי תִקְרֶאנָה מִלְחָמָה, וְנוֹסַף גַּם הוּא עַל שֹׂנְאֵינוּ, וְנִלְחַם בָּנוּ וְעָלָה מִן הָאָרֶץ."

Kadesh
Urchatz
Karpas
Yachatz
Maggid

Symposium:
Antisemitism

Beware of the Fifth Column

ERNEST HEMINGWAY deserves credit for having established *"fifth column"* as a term for secret subversives working within a country. The phrase was first uttered by General Mola, who said, during the Spanish Civil War, that he was commanding five columns in the assault on Madrid, four converging on the city from various directions "and the fifth column within the city." But Hemingway made the phrase famous in a play called *The Fifth Column*.

The Egyptians 'Bad-mouthed' Our Loyalty

DON ISAAC ABRABANEL *(a Spanish and Portuguese statesman and later refugee from the Spanish Expulsion, 15th C.)* explained: "The Egyptians thought badly of us. They suspected us of being spies, and conspirators plotting a revolt against their rulers." Pharaoh himself created and manipulated this public image of Jews in the eyes of his own people. He outsmarted his own nation.

Prejudice and I

Recount a story in which you were involved in unjust discrimination whether as a victim, a witness or a perpetrator. How do these examples compare to Egyptian persecution of strangers?

Nazi caricature of a Jewish stockbroker

A Rabbi Combats the Nazi Image of the Jew

OUTSIDE THE SYNAGOGUE in the ghetto, that is, in the newspapers, on the radio, in the speeches of the government people, wherever Jews listened, on the propaganda placards of the Nazi regime, in the cartoons of the anti-Semitic papers, the Jews were depicted as non-persons — ugly, immoral, uncreative, cowardly, useless and inferior. I had to tell the Jews from the pulpit in every single sermon that to be a Jew is to be beautiful, great, noble, and that we have every right to feel superior. *(For this reason, Afro-Americans in the 1960's emphasized that "black is beautiful.")*

It was most important for me to demonstrate to the people that I was not afraid of anything. It is difficult to imagine now how important it was to Jews sitting in the pews to listen to someone expressing himself freely and often brutally against the Nazi regime, in spite of the fact that two Gestapo men were always sitting in the first row. I especially remember preaching a sermon against *Der Stuermer*, the most violent anti-Semitic paper whose editor Streicher was later hanged after the Nuremburg trials. I took a copy of the paper with me to the pulpit. I opened it to a page on which were printed some of the vicious caricatures of Jews, and I said in my sermon: "Is this what we really look like? Look at yourselves and look at each other. Is this the true picture of Jews?"

(Rabbi Joachim Prinz, Berlin 1933)

Ancient Egyptian Oppression

"THEY PERSECUTED US." *(Deut. 26:6)* *"They put task masters over Israel to conscript their labor in order to persecute them with their burdens. They built for Pharaoh the garrison cities of Pitom* (House of the god Atum) *and Ra-meses* (Domain of the Son of the Sun god)." *(Exodus 1:11)*

"וַיְעַנּוּנוּ." כְּמָה שֶׁנֶּאֱמַר (שמות א,יא) : "וַיָּשִׂימוּ עָלָיו שָׂרֵי מִסִּים, לְמַעַן עַנֹּתוֹ בְּסִבְלֹתָם. וַיִּבֶן עָרֵי מִסְכְּנוֹת לְפַרְעֹה, אֶת פִּתֹם וְאֶת רַעַמְסֵס."

"THEY IMPOSED HARD LABOR ON US." *(Deut. 26:6)* *"The Egyptians worked the children of Israel harshly (be-farech),"* *(Exodus 1:13)* degrading us with back-breaking and spirit-crushing labor.

"וַיִּתְּנוּ עָלֵינוּ עֲבֹדָה קָשָׁה." כְּמָה שֶׁנֶּאֱמַר (שמות א,יג) : "וַיַּעֲבִדוּ מִצְרַיִם אֶת בְּנֵי יִשְׂרָאֵל בְּפָרֶךְ."

Kadesh
Urchatz
Karpas
Yachatz
Maggid

Symposium:
Oppression

Egyptian slaves making mud bricks mixed with straw and water, dried in wooden frames　　　*Tomb of Rekhmire, 18th Century B.C.E.*

Rameses II (1290-1224 B.C.E.)

The Great Builder and the Greater Ego

Ruling the united kingdom of Egypt for 66 years was Rameses the Great, whose name means "born of *(meses)* the sun-god *(Ra)*." Using many Semitic laborers, he completed the temple of Karnak, and constructed the obelisks now located at the Place de la Concorde in Paris and in three squares in Rome.

The enormous statues of Rameses II which he constructed in Luxor epitomize in stone what the Egyptologists say of his character: "inordinately vain and ostentatious, the greatest of Egyptian boasters." Among his one hundred children, his thirteenth son, Merneptah (1224-1212 B.C.E.) later inscribed a stone stele, the first extra-Biblical evidence of the existence of the nation of Israel. There he boasts — prematurely it seems — that Israel has been conquered and wiped out forever.

(Moses and Egypt: Documentation for the movie The Ten Commandments, Henry Noerdlinger)

Midrash: Filling in the Gaps

WHILE THE BIBLE is short on concrete details, the Rabbinic midrash imaginatively reconstructs the daily pain and indignity of slavery from the hints in the text.

1. **Why** does the Torah use the rare term "**be-farech**" to describe the Egyptian harsh labor?

Rabbi Elazar explained: Don't read "*be-farech*" — "with harshness" but "*be-fe-rach*" — "with soft speech," with a silvery tongue. Pharaoh had already declared that the Egyptians must "outsmart" Israel. So he gathered all the children of Israel and gave them this "pitch:" "Please do me a favor today and give me a hand." Pharaoh took up a rake and a basket and began to make mud bricks. Everyone who saw him did likewise. Israel worked with him enthusiastically all day. When it grew dark, Pharaoh appointed task masters over them to count up their bricks. "That," he announced, "will be your daily quota!" *(Tanhuma Buber, BeHaalotcha)*

Rameses II (1290-1224 B.C.E.) with the snake crown and the royal scepter (Karnak, Egypt)

2. **What** does the Torah mean when it says, *"Moshe went out to his kinsfolk and saw their burdens"*? *(Ex. 2:11)*

Moshe saw a big burden on an old person and a small one on a young healthy person, a woman's task assigned to a man and a man's task assigned to a woman. He began to cry and say, "Oy! I feel so bad for them. I would give my life for them." So he would leave his royal retinue and go join his brothers and sisters. While pretending to be executing Pharaoh's orders, he rearranged the burdens, helping each and every slave.

Seeing they had no time to rest, he went to plead their cause before Pharaoh: "Any slave owner knows that if his slave doesn't rest one day a week, then he'll die." Pharaoh replied: "Go and take care of this problem!" So Moshe enacted for them a weekly day of rest — Shabbat.

3. **Why** did God choose Moses? Once, while Moses, our Teacher, was tending [his father-in-law] Yitro's sheep, one of the sheep ran away. Moses ran after it until it reached a small, shaded place. There, the lamb came across a pool and began to drink. As Moses approached the lamb, he said, "I did not know you ran away because you were thirsty. You are so exhausted!" He then put the lamb on his shoulders and carried him back. The Holy One said, "Since you tend the sheep of human beings with such overwhelming love — by your life, I swear you shall be the shepherd of My sheep, Israel."

(Exodus Rabba 2:2, [1:129])

From Resignation to Resistance

Ben Shahn, The Alphabet of Creation
© *Estate of Ben Shahn/Licensed by VAGA, NY, NY*

"וַנִּצְעַק אֶל יי אֱלֹהֵי אֲבֹתֵינוּ, וַיִּשְׁמַע יי אֶת קֹלֵנוּ,
וַיַּרְא אֶת עָנְיֵנוּ, וְאֶת עֲמָלֵנוּ, וְאֶת לַחֲצֵנוּ."

"וַנִּצְעַק אֶל יי אֱלֹהֵי אֲבֹתֵינוּ." כְּמָה שֶׁנֶּאֱמַר (שמות ב, כג) :
וַיְהִי בַיָּמִים הָרַבִּים הָהֵם, וַיָּמָת מֶלֶךְ מִצְרַיִם, וַיֵּאָנְחוּ
בְנֵי יִשְׂרָאֵל מִן הָעֲבֹדָה וַיִּזְעָקוּ. וַתַּעַל שַׁוְעָתָם אֶל
הָאֱלֹהִים מִן הָעֲבֹדָה."

"וַיִּשְׁמַע יי אֶת קֹלֵנוּ." כְּמָה שֶׁנֶּאֱמַר (שמות ב, כד) :
"וַיִּשְׁמַע אֱלֹהִים אֶת נַאֲקָתָם, וַיִּזְכֹּר אֱלֹהִים אֶת בְּרִיתוֹ,
אֶת אַבְרָהָם, אֶת יִצְחָק, וְאֶת יַעֲקֹב."

Kadesh
Urchatz
Karpas
Yachatz
Maggid

Symposium:
Resistance

**"WE CRIED OUT TO ADONAI, THE GOD OF OUR
FATHERS, GOD HEARD OUR VOICE, HE SAW OUR
PERSECUTION, OUR TOIL, AND OUR OPPRESSION."**

(Deut. 26:7)

"WE CRIED OUT TO ADONAI." *(Deut. 26:7)*

This was the turning point. *"After many, many days,
the king of Egypt died. The children of Israel groaned from
under the labor and cried out in protest. Their cry for help
rose up to God from their labor."* *(Ex. 2:23)*

"GOD HEARD OUR VOICE." *(Deut. 26:7)*

Just as it says in Exodus: *"God HEARD their moans and
God remembered the Divine covenant with Abraham and
Isaac and Jacob."* *(Exodus 2:24)*

'We Cried Out' — The Power of a Groan

THE HASSIDIC Rebbe of Gur says: The sigh, the groan and the crying out of the children of Israel from the slavery was the beginning of redemption. As long as they did not cry out against their exile they were neither worthy nor ready for redemption.

(Menachem HaCohen)

Hope is Saying 'No!'

PRESIDENT HAVEL of the Czech Republic (playwright and former prisoner in communist Czechoslovakia):

"Hope is saying 'no' to the world immediately experienced. Optimism is the belief that things will be different, will be better."

Internal Exile

THE MAGGID OF ZLOTSHOV said:

"When the Jews are in exile, the exile enters into them and they refuse to leave the exile and be redeemed. It was for this reason that the Holy One had to make Pharaoh a cruel king so that *'with a strong hand he would expel them from his country.'* (Ex. 6:1) This is what we say in the Haggadah: 'Had the Holy One not taken our fathers out of Egypt, we and our children, and our children's children would have been enslaved' — to this very day we would have been living by the fleshpots of Egypt."

'Our Oppression': Slavery and Patience

Waitings

The waitings which make up the life of a slave:

first he waits for a spokesman

and for plagues

to plead his cause,

then he waits for the waters

to open before him,

then he waits for the desert storms

to name themselves,

then (being a slave) he asks in his heart:

why did I wait for the parting of the waters?

why did I wait for all this uproar and these burnings?

then (being a slave) he waits for answers.

Stanley Chyet, Professor of American Jewish History, HUC

R. Hanoch-Henich of Alexander added: "This was the real meaning of the exile of Israel in Egypt: they learned to tolerate the evil decrees, and became accustomed to Pharaoh." *(Menachem HaCohen)*

Tears to Hide Our Tears

ONE OF THE TROUBLES in Egypt was that we could not cry and complain, for we were surrounded with enemies looking for an excuse to harm us. But when the king of Egypt died and everyone lamented his death in processions all over the city, then we could safely cry over our own troubles. We groaned and wept with the Egyptians. While they thought we were mourning the death of the king, no one could accuse us of wrongdoing. Yet God knew the true reason of our tears. *(Mei-am Loez)*

Sexuality and Liberation

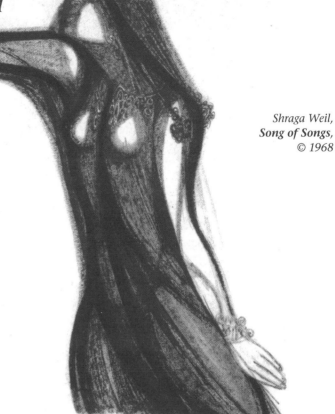

Shraga Weil,
Song of Songs,
© 1968

Kadesh
Urchatz
Karpas
Yachatz
Maggid

Symposium:
Sexual
Liberation

"GOD SAW OUR PERSECUTION." *(Deut. 26:7)*
The root *"oni"* (persecution) is similar to *"ona"* (marital intimacy), thus hinting at Pharaoh's policy of enforced abstention from *"ona"* (sexual intercourse). Perhaps that is delicately intimated when it says *(Ex 2:25)* that: *"God saw the children of Israel, and God **knew**"* (their marital suffering, for knowledge has sexual overtones as in *"Adam **knew** his wife Eve."* *[Gen. 4:1]*)

"OUR TOIL" *(Deut. 26:7)* refers to the sons — the lost fruits of our "labor" who were drowned in Egypt. Pharaoh proclaimed: *"Every son who is born shall be cast into the Nile, while every daughter shall live."* *(Ex. 1:22)*

"OUR OPPRESSION" *(Deut. 26:7)* refers to *"the pressure which the Egyptians applied to them."* *(Ex. 3:9)*

"וַיַּרְא אֶת עָנְיֵנוּ." זוֹ פְּרִישׁוּת דֶּרֶךְ אֶרֶץ. כְּמָה שֶׁנֶּאֱמַר
(שמות ב, כה): "וַיַּרְא אֱלֹהִים אֶת בְּנֵי יִשְׂרָאֵל. וַיֵּדַע
אֱלֹהִים."

"וְאֶת עֲמָלֵנוּ." אֵלּוּ הַבָּנִים. כְּמָה שֶׁנֶּאֱמַר (שמות א, כב):
"כָּל הַבֵּן הַיִּלּוֹד הַיְאֹרָה תַּשְׁלִיכֻהוּ, וְכָל הַבַּת תְּחַיּוּן."

"וְאֶת לַחֲצֵנוּ." זֶה הַדֹּחַק. כְּמָה שֶׁנֶּאֱמַר (שמות ג, ט):
"וְגַם רָאִיתִי אֶת הַלַּחַץ, אֲשֶׁר מִצְרַיִם לֹחֲצִים אֹתָם."

ZPG — Zero Population Growth

THE MIDRASH COMMENTS that Pharaoh's decree — throwing the male babies into the Nile — demoralized the Jewish leadership. Amram, future father of Moses, leader of his generation, divorced his wife Yocheved, and declared that all couples should now refrain from marriage because there was no point any more in bearing children. The midrash says that Amram was opposed by his young daughter Miriam. We give here a free adaptation of their midrashic dialogue:

Miriam: Where are you going with those leaflets?

Amram: We're holding the founding meeting of the Jewish ZPG society. All Jews must stop having babies.

Miriam: But you always said you wanted a big family? Look how much we all love my baby brother Aaron!

Amram: That was before Pharaoh issued these horrible decrees. He says that all baby boys must be thrown into the Nile. I'm not going to bring a baby into the world to suffer such a horrible fate! Even if he somehow escapes — what kind of life does this world offer him other than endless slavery and indignity?

Miriam: But you're worse than Pharaoh!

Amram: How dare you make such an accusation!

Miriam: But it's true! Pharaoh has only decreed against the male children. If your efforts are successful, not even female babies will be born!

Amram: But what good are females without the males?

Miriam: That's what you and that stupid chauvinist Pharaoh think! But in God's eyes all represent the image of God. Perhaps through the merit of righteous women we will be redeemed. At any rate we have to keep on making Jewish babies no matter how dark the prospects — and leave the rest up to God.

Amram: You know, that makes sense. I'm going to call off the meeting. Go tell Mommy we'll be drinking our best wine at dinner tonight.

Sexuality and Liberation

THE EGYPTIANS' express purpose in enslaving Israel was to drastically cut their birth rate. The hard labor in the fields exhausted the slaves physically and spiritually. According to a Rabbinic midrash, it was the women who resisted the intent of the decree. They used their sexuality to arouse their husbands, and so re-ignite the fundamental will to life:

"When Israel performed hard labor in Egypt, Pharaoh decreed that the men must not sleep in their homes, so that they would not engage in sexual relations. Rabbi Shimon bar Halafta said: What did the daughters of Israel do? They went down to draw water from the Nile and God would bring little fish into their jars. They cooked some of the fish and sold the rest, buying wine with the proceeds. Then they went out to the fields and fed their husbands. After eating and drinking, the women would take out bronze mirrors and look at them with their husbands. The wife would say "I'm prettier than you," and the husband would reply, "I'm more beautiful than you." Thus they would arouse themselves to desire and they would then "be fruitful and multiply."

Years later, when God told Moses to build a tabernacle in the desert, all Israel came to volunteer beautiful things. Some brought gold and silver. The women said, "What do we have to donate to the tabernacle?" They took their bronze mirrors and brought them to Moses.

At first, Moses became angry and refused to accept the mirrors since their function is to arouse jealousy and sexual desire. God said to Moses: "Moses, do you dare scorn these mirrors? They are more precious to Me than all the other donations, because through these mirrors the women gave birth in Egypt to all these multitudes. Take them and make them into the bronze basin, with which the priests will purify themselves."
(Tanhuma Pikudei 9)

The Bedrooms of Israel

PHARAOH HAD ENTERED the bedrooms of Israel. The birthing beds of Hebrews were matters of state. The Hebrew womb had fallen under the heel of Pharaoh.
(Moses, Man of the Mountain, by Zora Neale Hurston, Afro-American novelist, 1920's)

Discrimination

Discuss: Are women still oppressed in contemporary society? What should liberation mean today?

The Ten Plagues
God's Strong Hand, His Outstretched Arm, and His Little Finger

עֶשֶׂר מַכּוֹת

1. **The main ceremony** of removing ten drops of wine for the Ten Plagues is on page 98. *(Some may wish to skip directly to that climax of the lengthy Rabbinic discussion of the Ten Plagues).*

2. **The Rabbis** debated about the Ten Plagues: On the one hand, they were a necessary instrument of liberation and a just punishment for Egyptian cruelty. Yet, on the other, they involved the suffering of fellow human beings. The meaning of suffering and its lessons for the victim and the oppressor are explored here.

Kadesh
Urchatz
Karpas
Yachatz
Maggid

Symposium: Ten Plagues

"GOD TOOK US OUT OF EGYPT WITH A STRONG HAND, AND AN OUTSTRETCHED ARM, WITH AWESOME POWER, SIGNS AND WONDERS." *(Deut. 26:8)*

"וַיּוֹצִאֵנוּ יי מִמִּצְרַיִם, בְּיָד חֲזָקָה, וּבִזְרֹעַ נְטוּיָה, וּבְמֹרָא גָּדֹל וּבְאֹתוֹת וּבְמֹפְתִים."

"GOD TOOK US OUT" *(Deut. 26:8)* — **Not** by the hands of an angel, **Not** by the hands of a seraph, **Not** by the hands of a messenger, **But** The Holy One Himself in His own Glory. Just as it says, *"I will pass through the land of Egypt, and I will strike down every first born in Egypt, both human and beast, I will execute judgment on all the gods of Egypt, I am God."* *(Ex. 12:12)*

"וַיּוֹצִאֵנוּ יי מִמִּצְרַיִם." לֹא עַל יְדֵי מַלְאָךְ, וְלֹא עַל יְדֵי שָׂרָף, וְלֹא עַל יְדֵי שָׁלִיחַ. אֶלָּא הַקָּדוֹשׁ בָּרוּךְ הוּא בִּכְבוֹדוֹ וּבְעַצְמוֹ. שֶׁנֶּאֱמַר (שמות יב,יב):
"וְעָבַרְתִּי בְאֶרֶץ מִצְרַיִם בַּלַּיְלָה הַזֶּה, וְהִכֵּיתִי כָל בְּכוֹר בְּאֶרֶץ מִצְרַיִם, מֵאָדָם וְעַד בְּהֵמָה, וּבְכָל אֱלֹהֵי מִצְרַיִם אֶעֱשֶׂה שְׁפָטִים אֲנִי יי."

"וְעָבַרְתִּי בְאֶרֶץ מִצְרַיִם בַּלַּיְלָה הַזֶּה" – אֲנִי וְלֹא מַלְאָךְ. "וְהִכֵּיתִי כָל בְּכוֹר בְּאֶרֶץ מִצְרַיִם" – אֲנִי וְלֹא שָׂרָף. "וּבְכָל אֱלֹהֵי מִצְרַיִם אֶעֱשֶׂה שְׁפָטִים" – אֲנִי וְלֹא הַשָּׁלִיחַ. "אֲנִי יי." – אֲנִי הוּא וְלֹא אַחֵר.

"WITH A STRONG HAND" refers to an epidemic of animal disease *(dever)* — the fifth plague. *"The **hand** of Adonai will strike your livestock in the fields — the horses, the donkeys, the camels, the cattle, and the sheep — with a very severe disease."* *(Ex. 9:3)*

"בְּיָד חֲזָקָה." זוֹ הַדֶּבֶר. כְּמָה שֶׁנֶּאֱמַר (שמות ט,ג):
"הִנֵּה יַד יי הוֹיָה, בְּמִקְנְךָ אֲשֶׁר בַּשָּׂדֶה, בַּסּוּסִים בַּחֲמֹרִים בַּגְּמַלִּים, בַּבָּקָר וּבַצֹּאן, דֶּבֶר כָּבֵד מְאֹד."

A Pacifist Interprets the Midnight Plague

Rabbi Aaron Samuel Tamares
(Lithuanian Orthodox rabbi, early Zionist and pacifist, 1869-1931)

"For I will go through the land of Egypt in that night" (Ex. 12:12) — *"I and not an intermediary."* Now obviously the Holy One could have given the children of Israel the power to avenge themselves upon the Egyptians, but He did not want to sanction the use of their fists for self-defense even at that time. At that moment they might merely have defended themselves against evil-doers, but **in the end defenders become aggressors.**

"It came to pass at midnight." (Ex. 12:29) The Holy One took great pains to remove Israel completely from any participation in the vengeance upon the evil-doers, to such an extent that they were not permitted even to see the events. For that reason **midnight**, the darkest hour, was designated as the time for the deeds of vengeance, and the children of Israel were warned not to step outside their houses at that hour.

". . . None of you shall go out of the door of their house until the morning . . . that there not be in your midst the plague of the destroyer." (Ex. 12:22-23) The language itself is very precise. Your abstention from any participation in the vengeance upon Egypt will prevent the plague of vengeance from stirring the power of the **destroyer** which is in you yourselves.

The Tenth Plague   Leon Baxter

Egyptology and the 'gods'

"I will punish all the gods of Egypt, I am Adonai." (Ex. 12:12)

By attacking the gods of Egypt and disrupting the cosmic order established on earth by the god **Ra**, the ten plagues delegitimized Pharaoh, who claimed to be the divine king bearing the name "Son of Ra." Pharaoh's query — *"Who is Adonai, that I should heed his voice"* (Ex. 5:2) — is answered pointedly by the "hand of God," an idiom meaning in ancient Egyptian, "a plague." Many of the plagues strike at the domains particular to Egyptian deities.

One Rabbinic midrash exemplifies this idea: "Why did the first plague turn the Nile into blood? For Pharaoh and the Egyptians worshipped the Nile. So God said: Go and strike their god until he bleeds." (Tanchuma, Shmot Rabbah 9) **Hapi** was the Egyptian god of the Nile. The second plague struck at **Heket** the god who took the shape of a frog. The fifth plague, cattle disease, attacked the gods **Hathor** (cow) and **Apis** (bull). The ninth plague, darkness, triumphed over the sun god **Ra**. Finally, the tenth showed the vulnerability of Pharaoh himself, the son of the Sun god. The Torah puns on the name of Egypt's supreme god "Ra" and calls him "*ra'a*," the source of evil. (Ex. 10:10)

An Outstretched Arm

According to an Afghani Jewish custom, the leader of the seder raises the bone (**zeroa**) from the seder plate as a symbol of God's outstretched arm (**zeroa**).

"WITH AN OUTSTRETCHED ARM" *(zeroa)* — refers to God's sword (as a metaphor for the plague of the first born) just as it does elsewhere: *"David woke up and saw the angel of Adonai standing between heaven and earth, with a drawn sword in his hand, **outstretched** against Jerusalem."* *(I Chronicles 21:16)*

(David had sinned and his realm was punished with a plague of death. The verse describes the moment when the plague stopped, and the spot was then consecrated as the site for the future Temple.)

"WITH AWESOME POWER" refers to the revelation of God's power to our very eyes. That is just what Moshe tells Israel: *"Did a God ever before attempt to come and extract one nation for himself from the midst of another nation by prodigious acts, by signs and wonders, by war, by a strong hand, an outstretched arm **and awesome power**, as Adonai your God did for you in Egypt before your very eyes?"* *(Deut. 4:34)*

"WITH SIGNS" refers to the staff, as God told Moshe: *"Take the staff in your hand to do **signs** with it."* *(Ex. 4:17)*

וּבְזְרֹעַ נְטוּיָה

"וּבִזְרֹעַ נְטוּיָה." זוֹ הַחֶרֶב. כְּמָה שֶׁנֶּאֱמַר (דה"א כא, טז) : "וְחַרְבּוֹ שְׁלוּפָה בְּיָדוֹ, נְטוּיָה עַל יְרוּשָׁלָיִם."

"וּבְמֹרָא גָּדוֹל." זֶה גִּלּוּי שְׁכִינָה. כְּמָה שֶׁנֶּאֱמַר (דברים ד, לד) : "אוֹ הֲנִסָּה אֱלֹהִים, לָבוֹא לָקַחַת לוֹ גוֹי מִקֶּרֶב גּוֹי, בְּמַסֹּת בְּאֹתֹת וּבְמוֹפְתִים וּבְמִלְחָמָה, וּבְיָד חֲזָקָה וּבִזְרֹעַ נְטוּיָה, וּבְמוֹרָאִים גְּדֹלִים. כְּכֹל אֲשֶׁר עָשָׂה לָכֶם יי אֱלֹהֵיכֶם בְּמִצְרַיִם, לְעֵינֶיךָ."

"וּבְאֹתוֹת." זֶה הַמַּטֶּה, כְּמָה שֶׁנֶּאֱמַר (שמות ד, יז) : "וְאֶת הַמַּטֶּה הַזֶּה תִּקַּח בְּיָדֶךָ. אֲשֶׁר תַּעֲשֶׂה בּוֹ אֶת הָאֹתֹת."

Kadesh
Urchatz
Karpas
Yachatz
Maggid

Ten
Plagues

94

Giving a Helping Hand

Just as God showed compassion to the Jews when they were strangers in Egypt, so all of us are commanded to imitate God's active concern for the poor, the persecuted and the outsider.

Ask the participants to describe examples of how people have helped refugees, the mistreated and the "other" in society.

Otto Geismar, 1927

'Even Harsher'

Ask someone to name a very harsh task and explain why it is so difficult especially for him. Ask the next one to name an even harsher, more embittering, more humiliating task and explain the choice . . . If you were a slave, what would you hate most?

Suffering and its Lessons

When we dwell on being victims, then those memories may either corrupt us or help us grow in empathy for others. Consider the negative effects of suffering: self-pity, dreams of vengeance, self-righteousness and self-blame. Often one loses the ability to feel for others since "I suffered much worse."

Yet the Torah seeks to extract positive lessons from our persecution in Egypt: activism, hope, solidarity among victims and empathy for the other, *"for you were strangers in the land of Egypt."*

Compare and contrast Pharaoh's and God's advice to their children below:

Pharaoh's Advice

HEARKEN TO THAT which I say to you . . .
Harden yourself against all subordinates.
The people give heed to him who terrorizes them.
Approach them not alone.
Fill not your heart with a brother.
Know not a friend,
Nor make for yourself intimates,
Wherein there is no end.
When you sleep,
Guard for yourself your own heart,
For a man has no people.
In the day of evil,
I gave to the beggar.
I nourished the orphan.
I admitted the insignificant,
As well as him who was of great account.
But he who ate my food made insurrection.
He to whom I gave my land, aroused fear therein. *(Pharaoh Amenemhet, 1780 B.C.E)*

God's Advice

WHEN A STRANGER resides with you in your land, you shall not wrong him.
The stranger who resides with you shall be to you as one of your citizens.
You shall love him as yourself, for you were strangers in the land of Egypt.
I, Adonai, am your God who freed you from the land of Egypt. *(Leviticus 19:33-36)*
You shall not subvert the rights of your needy in their disputes. *(Ex. 23:6)*
You shall have one law for all of you. The same for both stranger and citizen for I, Adonai, am your God. *(Lev. 24.22)*
When you reap the produce of your land, you must not harvest the corners of your field nor gather the fallen sheaves. Leave them for the poor and the stranger.
I, Adonai, am your God. *(Lev. 23.22)*
You shall not oppress a stranger, for you know the feelings of the stranger, having yourselves been strangers. *(Ex. 22.9)*

God's Fingers and the Sixteen Drops

אֶצְבַּע אֱלֹהִים

It is a medieval custom to dip one's finger in the seder's second cup of wine and to remove sixteen drops of wine. As each plague is recited we decrease our own joy, drop by drop, as we recall the enemy's pain. **Besides the ten plagues, the** extra six drops correspond to the three prophetic plagues mentioned by the prophet Joel — **blood, fire and smoke** — and the three word abbreviation of the ten plagues invented by Rabbi Yehuda — **d'tzach, adash, b'achab.**

Kadesh
Urchatz
Karpas
Yachatz
Maggid

Ten
Plagues

"**WITH WONDERS**" refers to the plagues of blood, fire and smoke that are recalled by the prophet Joel: "Before the great and terrible day of Adonai comes, I will set wonders in the sky and on earth . . . ***blood, fire, pillars of smoke! Da-am*** (drop of wine) ***va-eish*** (drop) ***v'teemrot ashan*** (drop)! The sun shall turn to darkness and the moon into blood." *(Joel 3:3)*

"וּבְמוֹפְתִים." זֶה הַדָּם. כְּמָה שֶׁנֶּאֱמַר (יואל ג, ג) :
"וְנָתַתִּי מוֹפְתִים, בַּשָּׁמַיִם וּבָאָרֶץ."

דָּם. וָאֵשׁ. וְתִימְרוֹת עָשָׁן.

Alluding to Ten:

The Rabbis offer an additional midrash on the verse from Deuteronomy 26:8: *"God took us out of Egypt with a strong hand, and an outstretched arm, with awesome power; signs and wonders."* This midrash allowed them to find allusions to all of the ten plagues:

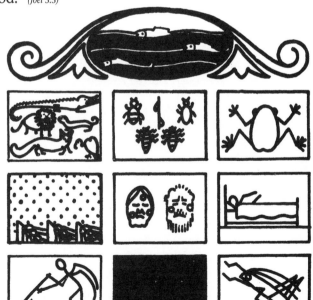

"**WITH A** strong hand" — two!
"with an outstretched arm"— two!
"with awesome power" — two!
"with signs" — two!
"with wonders" — two!
That equals ten.

דָּבָר אַחֵר. "בְּיָד חֲזָקָה" – שְׁתַּיִם.
"וּבִזְרֹעַ נְטוּיָה" – שְׁתַּיִם.
"וּבְמוֹרָא גָדוֹל" – שְׁתַּיִם.
"וּבְאֹתוֹת" – שְׁתַּיִם.
"וּבְמֹפְתִים" – שְׁתַּיִם.

Otto Geismar, 1927

96

The Little Finger and the Itchy Lice

THE FINGER USED to remove the wine recalls the metaphor used by Pharaoh's magicians who could not rid themselves of the plague of lice. Unable to alleviate the third plague with all their incantations, they acknowledged: *"This must be the Finger of God."* (Ex. 8:15)

Games of the Ten Plagues

1. Pantomime

Prepare cards with the name or picture of one of the ten plagues. Let ten participants at the seder choose a card out of a hat and present a pantomime of the plague while the others try to guess the name of the plague. (Try using its Hebrew name). You may let the children do the pantomime and the adults guess.

2. "The Yukkiest Plague"

Divide the children into three groups. Each group will be given as a theme either blood, frogs, or wild animals (the first, second, and fourth plague). They have five to ten minutes to prepare a short play. The adults may judge and award an Oscar (or better a "Moses") for the most vivid, original, and devastating presentation.

The Ecology of Plagues

R. YEHUDA HALEVI, the 12th C. Spanish physician and poet, explained the division of plagues into twos:

Two plagues from the water (blood and frogs from the Nile);

Two plagues from the earth (lice and wild animals);

Two plagues from air-carried infections (plague and boils);

Two plagues from air-carried damages (hailstorms and locusts);

Two plagues from supernatural acts (darkness caused by an eclipse and the plague of the first born).

Recount the Plagues

Recount the plagues that have struck this year and for each remove a drop of wine from one's cup of joy. Some families recount ecological plagues at this point.

The Ten Plagues

❖ The Holy One brought **ten plagues** on the Egyptians in Egypt. These are the ten:

1. *D'am* (drop of wine) — Blood
2. *Tz'far-dei-ah* (drop) — Frogs
3. *Kee-neem* (drop) — Lice
4. *Ah-rov* (drop) — Wild beasts (or insects)
5. *Deh-ver* (drop) — Cattle Plague
6. *Sh'cheen* (drop) — Boils
7. *Ba-rad* (drop) — Hail
8. *Ar-beh* (drop) — Locust
9. *Cho-shech* (drop) — Darkness
10. *Ma-kat B'cho-rot* (drop) — Death of the Firstborn

Rabbi Yehuda used to abbreviate them as an acrostic:

D-Tza-Kh (drop) — (Da-am/Tzefar-dei-ah/**Kee**-neem)
A-Da-Sh (drop) — (**A**h-rov/**D**eh-ver/**Sh'**cheen)
B'-A-Cha-B (drop) — (**Ba**-rad/**A**r-beh/**Cho**-shech/Makat B'chorot)

עֶשֶׂר מַכּוֹת

אֵלּוּ עֶשֶׂר מַכּוֹת שֶׁהֵבִיא הַקָּדוֹשׁ בָּרוּךְ הוּא עַל הַמִּצְרִים בְּמִצְרַיִם, וְאֵלּוּ הֵן:

1. דָּם
2. צְפַרְדֵּעַ
3. כִּנִּים
4. עָרוֹב
5. דֶּבֶר
6. שְׁחִין
7. בָּרָד
8. אַרְבֶּה
9. חֹשֶׁךְ
10. מַכַּת בְּכוֹרוֹת

רַבִּי יְהוּדָה הָיָה נוֹתֵן בָּהֶם סִמָּנִים:
דְּצַ"ךְ
עַדַ"שׁ
בְּאַחַ"ב.

Kadesh
Urchatz
Karpas
Yachatz
Maggid

Ten Plagues

'Let My People Go'

An African-American Spiritual

Sing:

When Israel was in Egypt's land,
"Let My people go." *(Ex. 5:1)*
Oppressed so hard they could not stand,
"Let My people go."

Go down, Moses, way down in Egypt's land,
Tell old Pharaoh: "Let My people go."

Thus said the Lord, bold Moses said,
"Let My people go."
If not, I'll smite your first-born dead,
"Let My people go."

Go down, Moses, way down in Egypt's land,
Tell old Pharaoh: "Let My people go."

No more shall they in bondage toil,
"Let My people go. "
Let them come out with Egypt's spoil,
"Let My people go."

Go down, Moses, way down in Egypt's land.
Tell old Pharaoh: "Let my people go."

'Black Moses'

HARRIET TUBMAN escaped in 1849 from her plantation in Maryland with the help of the "Underground Railroad." Soon she became a major "conductor" bringing more than 300 slaves to freedom. Despite the high price on her head, her faith in God gave her the courage to persist and earn the nickname "Moses of her people."

Tanya Zion 1996

Should We Feel Joy at the Downfall of Our Enemies?

בַּאֲבֹד רְשָׁעִים רִנָּה

Kadesh
Urchatz
Karpas
Yachatz
Maggid

Ten Plagues

1. *The spilling* of the sixteen drops has been understood traditionally in opposite ways. Either it signifies sympathy for the enemy Egyptians who suffered as a result of the painful process of liberating the Jews from Egyptian tyranny; or it reaffirms the righteous vengeance of God's sword exercising judgment against a relentless, cruel and stubborn oppressor.

2. *We have arrayed* contrasting views: on the right, the joys of just punishment and on the left, the need for restraint on vengeful feelings. You may wish to read responsively the contrasting speeches of Shylock (#5) and Yitzchak Rabin (#5).

3. *Discuss* to what extent these statements reflect your feelings about Muslim terrorists, contemporary Egyptians, Nazis, or criminals in general.

On the One Hand: The Joys of Justice

1. "When the wicked perish,
There are shouts of joy!" *(Proverbs 11:10)*

2. The Song of the Red Sea

"Israel saw the Egyptians dead on the shore of the sea . . . Then Moshe and Israel sang to Adonai: . . . Your right hand, Adonai, shatters the Foe. The Foe said: 'I will pursue, I will overtake, I will divide the spoil. My desire shall have its fill of them. I will bare my sword' . . . But You, God, made your wind blow, the sea covered them." *(Ex. 14:31, 15:1,9-10)*

3. President Abraham Lincoln

"If every drop of blood drawn by the lash must be paid by one drawn by the sword, still must it be said, 'The judgments of the Lord are true and righteous altogether.'"

(Psalm 19; Second Inaugural Address, 1865)

Rabbi Jacob Halevi Moulin
(15th C. Germany, an era of pogroms and expulsions)
"The **sixteen drops** refer to the **sixteen facets** of God's avenging sword."

4. Rabbi Shalom from Noitch

On the seventh day of Pesach (the anniversary of the crossing of the Red Sea), one should be sure to add the phrase "the day of our joy" *(simchatenu)* to the Kiddush, for the Egyptians were drowned in the sea.

5. Shylock

"My Revenge! He hath disgraced me, and hind'red me half a million; laughed at my losses, mocked at my gains, scorned my nation, thwarted my bargains, cooled my friends, heated mine enemies — and what's his reason? I am a Jew. Hath not a Jew eyes? Hath not a Jew hands, organs, dimensions, senses, affections, passions?

Fed with the same food, hurt with the same weapons, subject to the same diseases, healed by the same means, warmed and cooled by the same winter and summer as a Christian is? If you prick us, do we not bleed? If you tickle us, do we not laugh? If you poison us, do we not die? **And if you wrong us, shall we not revenge?** If we are like you in the rest, we will resemble you in that. If a Jew wrong a Christian, what is his humility? **Revenge.** If a Christian wrong a Jew, What should his sufferance be by Christian example? Why, **revenge!** The villainy you teach me I will execute, and it shall go hard but I will better the instruction."

(William Shakespeare, "The Merchant of Venice," 1597)

On the Other Hand: Restraints on Revenge

1. "If your enemy falls.
Do not celebrate.
If he trips,
Let not your heart rejoice."
(Proverbs 24:17)

2. Rabbi Yochanan

"God is not happy at the downfall of the wicked . . . When the angels tried to sing songs of praise to God at the Red Sea, God silenced them: **'My handiwork, my human creatures, are drowning in the sea and you want to sing a song of praise?'"** *(T.B. Megillah 10b)*

3. Don Isaac Abrabanel
(refugee of the Expulsion from Spain, 1492)

"By spilling a drop of wine, from the Pesach cup for each plague, we acknowledge that our own joy is lessened and incomplete. For our redemption had to come by means of the punishment of other human beings. Even though these are just punishments for evil acts, it says **'Do not rejoice at the fall of your enemy.'"** *(Proverbs 24:17)*

בִּנְפֹל אוֹיִבְךָ,
אַל תִּשְׂמָח'

4. Rabbi Simcha Cohen from Divinsk
(Lithuanian Talmudist)

"The Torah never mentions 'joy' in relation to the holiday of Pesach as it does for Shavuot and Sukkot. On Pesach — unlike the other pilgrimage holidays — we do not recite all the Psalms of Hallel (except on the first day) because as Shmuel quotes from Proverbs: *In the downfall of your enemy, do not rejoice.* **We celebrate the Exodus from Egypt, not the downfall of the Egyptians.**"

5. Chief of Staff, General Yitzhak Rabin, Six Day War, June 1967
(later Prime Minister of the State of Israel, 1974-77, 1992-95)

"War is harsh and cruel, filled with blood and tears. While the joy of victory seized the whole people, among the community of fighters themselves there is a strange phenomenon: they cannot celebrate wholeheartedly. There is a large measure of sadness, of shock, mixed into their festivities. Some fighters cannot celebrate at all. The frontline soldiers saw with their own eyes — not only the glory of victory, but also its price — their fellow fighters fell at their sides in pools of blood. I know that the price paid by the enemy also touched a deep place in the hearts of many. **Perhaps the Jewish people has never been educated and never become accustomed to the joy of the conqueror. Therefore, our victory is received with mixed feelings.**"

Bruria and the Hoodlums

A GANG OF HOODLUMS lived in Rabbi Meir's neighborhood and they used to torment him endlessly. Rabbi Meir prayed for their death. His wife Bruria said to him: "How did you reach such a decision?" He replied: "The Bible says, *'Let sins be obliterated from the earth.'"* *(Psalms 104:35)* She answered: "Is it written 'sinners?' The verse says 'sins.' Look further to the end of the verse: *'. . . And the wicked will be no more.' (Psalms 104:35)* Since all sins will be obliterated, then of course *'the wicked will be no more.'* Therefore, pray that these hoodlums repent and then they will not be 'wicked' anymore."

Rabbi Meir prayed for them and they indeed mended their ways.
(2nd C. Eretz Yisrael, Babylonian Talmud, Berachot 10a)

Reflections on Vengeance

"You shall not take vengeance nor bear a grudge against your people. Rather you shall love your neighbor as yourself, I am Adonai." *(Leviticus 19:18-19)*

"Whoever takes vengeance destroys his own house." *(R. Papa, T.B. Sanhedrin 102b)*

"Don't say, since I have been humiliated; let my neighbor be humiliated also. Know! It is the image of God in your neighbor, you would be humiliating." *(Ben Azzai, Tanhuma Gen. R. 24:7)*

"This shall be our revenge! We shall revive what they kill, and raise what they topple . . . This is the banner of our vengeance and its name is Jerusalem." *(Peretz Smolenskin, Zionist, 1882)*

Midrashic Supplement
Multiplying the Ten Plagues: Three Numerical Riddles

1. RABBI YOSSI the Galilean posed the riddle: "How do you know that God struck the Egyptians with only **10 blows** in Egypt, while God struck them with **50 blows** at the Red Sea?"

Solution: In Egypt God used **1 finger** just as *"the Egyptian magicians said to Pharaoh: This (plague) is the finger of God."* *(Ex. 8:15)* But at the Red Sea, God used the **whole hand**. *"Israel saw the* ***great hand*** *that God used against Egypt."* *(Ex. 14:31)* Logically, if **1 finger** produced 10 plagues in Egypt, then a whole hand (5 fingers) produced 50 plagues at the Red Sea.

2. RABBI ELIEZER posed the riddle: "How do you know that each of the 10 plagues in Egypt was really **4 plagues** rolled into one?"

Solution: In Psalms 78:49 God's burning anger at the Egyptians is described with **4 extra synonyms:** (1) *"wrath;"* (2) *"indignation;"* (3) *"trouble;"* and (4) *"a band of deadly messengers."* Each of the plagues must have four dimensions. Logically, God struck **40** blows (4 x 10) in Egypt (using just one finger) and **200** blows (4 x 10 x 5) at the Sea (using his whole hand).

3. RABBI AKIBA posed the riddle: "How do you know that each of the 10 plagues in Egypt was really **5 plagues** rolled into one?"

Solution: In Psalms 78:49 we must figure 5 synonyms for anger expressed in each plague: *"(God) inflicted: (1) His burning anger upon them; (2) wrath; (3) indignation; (4) trouble; and (5) a band of deadly messengers."* Logically, God struck 50 blows (5 x 10) in Egypt (using just one finger) and 250 blows (using his whole hand).

250 מַכּוֹת

Kadesh
Urchatz
Karpas
Yachatz
Maggid

250
Plagues

רַבִּי יוֹסֵי הַגְּלִילִי אוֹמֵר: מִנַּיִן אַתָּה אוֹמֵר, שֶׁלָּקוּ הַמִּצְרִים בְּמִצְרַיִם עֶשֶׂר מַכּוֹת, וְעַל הַיָּם, לָקוּ חֲמִשִּׁים מַכּוֹת?

בְּמִצְרַיִם מָה הוּא אוֹמֵר? "וַיֹּאמְרוּ הַחַרְטֻמִּם אֶל פַּרְעֹה, אֶצְבַּע אֱלֹהִים הוּא." (שמות ח,טו)

וְעַל הַיָּם מָה הוּא אוֹמֵר? "וַיַּרְא יִשְׂרָאֵל אֶת הַיָּד הַגְּדֹלָה, אֲשֶׁר עָשָׂה יי בְּמִצְרַיִם, וַיִּירְאוּ הָעָם אֶת יי. וַיַּאֲמִינוּ בַּיי, וּבְמֹשֶׁה עַבְדּוֹ." (שמות יד,לא) כַּמָּה לָקוּ בְּאֶצְבַּע – עֶשֶׂר מַכּוֹת. אֱמֹר מֵעַתָּה, בְּמִצְרַיִם לָקוּ עֶשֶׂר מַכּוֹת, וְעַל־הַיָּם, לָקוּ חֲמִשִּׁים מַכּוֹת.

רַבִּי אֱלִיעֶזֶר אוֹמֵר: מִנַּיִן שֶׁכָּל מַכָּה וּמַכָּה, שֶׁהֵבִיא הַקָּדוֹשׁ בָּרוּךְ הוּא עַל הַמִּצְרִים בְּמִצְרַיִם, הָיְתָה שֶׁל אַרְבַּע מַכּוֹת?

שֶׁנֶּאֱמַר (תהילים עח,מט): "יְשַׁלַּח בָּם חֲרוֹן אַפּוֹ, עֶבְרָה וָזַעַם וְצָרָה. מִשְׁלַחַת מַלְאֲכֵי רָעִים." עֶבְרָה אַחַת. וָזַעַם שְׁתַּיִם. וְצָרָה שָׁלֹשׁ. מִשְׁלַחַת מַלְאֲכֵי רָעִים אַרְבַּע. אֱמֹר מֵעַתָּה, בְּמִצְרַיִם לָקוּ אַרְבָּעִים מַכּוֹת, וְעַל הַיָּם לָקוּ מָאתַיִם מַכּוֹת.

רַבִּי עֲקִיבָא אוֹמֵר: מִנַּיִן שֶׁכָּל מַכָּה וּמַכָּה, שֶׁהֵבִיא הַקָּדוֹשׁ בָּרוּךְ הוּא עַל הַמִּצְרִים בְּמִצְרַיִם, הָיְתָה שֶׁל חָמֵשׁ מַכּוֹת?

שֶׁנֶּאֱמַר: "יְשַׁלַּח בָּם חֲרוֹן אַפּוֹ, עֶבְרָה וָזַעַם וְצָרָה. מִשְׁלַחַת מַלְאֲכֵי רָעִים." חֲרוֹן אַפּוֹ, אַחַת. עֶבְרָה, שְׁתַּיִם. וָזַעַם, שָׁלֹשׁ. וְצָרָה, אַרְבַּע. מִשְׁלַחַת מַלְאֲכֵי רָעִים, חָמֵשׁ. אֱמֹר מֵעַתָּה, בְּמִצְרַיִם לָקוּ חֲמִשִּׁים מַכּוֹת, וְעַל הַיָּם לָקוּ חֲמִשִּׁים וּמָאתַיִם מַכּוֹת.

So Many Plagues?

SINCE GOD could have removed Israel from Egypt in one swift act of liberation, what was the point of prolonging the process — ten plagues and then trapping the Egyptians in the Red Sea?

God answers this query in the Torah. *"I could have stretched forth My hand and stricken you (Pharaoh) and your people . . . and you would have been effaced from the earth. Nevertheless, I have spared you for this purpose."* (Ex. 9:15-16) *"I will multiply My signs and marvels in the land of Egypt . . . and the Egyptians will know that I am Adonai."* (Ex. 7:3,5) **God's goal is not merely the physical liberation of slaves, but the spiritual liberation of Pharaoh from his illusions of total power.** To know deep down that Egypt has no right to enslave others means to dispel the religious foundation of Pharaoh's idolatrous self-deification. God's battle for recognition in the eyes of ancient Egyptian civilization is achievable only by a long series of blows to its self-esteem that gradually chip away at their self-evident preeminence as one of the longest lasting empires in human history.

Wanted: Pharaoh's Heart

SEFORNO (*Italian Renaissance, 16th C.*) explains that God hardened Pharaoh's heart so that he wouldn't submit simply out of a pragmatic desire to end the pain of the plagues. The plagues were a call to a "change of heart," not only of policy. God was anxious to accept true repentance.

Splitting the Red Sea

Joseph Horna, Mexico, 1946

Dayeinu
'It Would Have Been Enough'

Dayeinu commemorates a long list of miraculous things God did for us, any one of which would have been pretty amazing just by itself. For example, "Had God only taken us out of Egypt but not punished the Egyptians — it would have been enough." **Dayeinu**, translated liberally, means, "Thank you, God, for overdoing it." (See the English on page 108.)

Kadesh
Urchatz
Karpas
Yachatz
Maggid

Dayeinu

❖ כַּמָּה מַעֲלוֹת טוֹבוֹת לַמָּקוֹם עָלֵינוּ:

אִלּוּ הוֹצִיאָנוּ מִמִּצְרַיִם,
וְלֹא עָשָׂה בָהֶם שְׁפָטִים, דַּיֵּנוּ!

אִלּוּ עָשָׂה בָהֶם שְׁפָטִים,
וְלֹא עָשָׂה בֵאלֹהֵיהֶם, דַּיֵּנוּ!

אִלּוּ עָשָׂה בֵאלֹהֵיהֶם,
וְלֹא הָרַג אֶת בְּכוֹרֵיהֶם, דַּיֵּנוּ!

אִלּוּ הָרַג אֶת בְּכוֹרֵיהֶם,
וְלֹא נָתַן לָנוּ אֶת מָמוֹנָם, דַּיֵּנוּ!

אִלּוּ נָתַן לָנוּ אֶת מָמוֹנָם,
וְלֹא קָרַע לָנוּ אֶת הַיָּם, דַּיֵּנוּ!

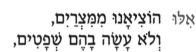

Ee-lu ho-tzee-anu mee-Meetz-ra-yim,
v'lo asa va-hem sh'fa-teem,   **Da-yeinu**

Ee-lu asa va-hem sh'fa-teem,
v'lo asa vei-lo-hei-hem,   **Da-yeinu**

Ee-lu asa vei-lo-hei-hem,
v'lo ha-rag et b'cho-rei-hem,   **Da-yeinu**

Ee-lu ha-rag et b'cho-rei-hem,
v'lo natan la-nu et ma-mo-nam,   **Da-yeinu**

Ee-lu natan la-nu et ma-mo-nam,
v'lo kara la-nu et ha-yam,   **Da-yeinu**

Dayeinu continued

אִלּוּ קָרַע לָנוּ אֶת הַיָּם,
וְלֹא הֶעֱבִירָנוּ בְּתוֹכוֹ בֶּחָרָבָה,   דַּיֵּנוּ!

אִלּוּ הֶעֱבִירָנוּ בְּתוֹכוֹ בֶּחָרָבָה,
וְלֹא שִׁקַּע צָרֵינוּ בְּתוֹכוֹ,   דַּיֵּנוּ!

אִלּוּ שִׁקַּע צָרֵינוּ בְּתוֹכוֹ,
וְלֹא סִפֵּק צָרְכֵּנוּ בַּמִּדְבָּר אַרְבָּעִים שָׁנָה,   דַּיֵּנוּ!

אִלּוּ סִפֵּק צָרְכֵּנוּ בַּמִּדְבָּר אַרְבָּעִים שָׁנָה,
וְלֹא הֶאֱכִילָנוּ אֶת הַמָּן,   דַּיֵּנוּ!

אִלּוּ הֶאֱכִילָנוּ אֶת הַמָּן,
וְלֹא נָתַן לָנוּ אֶת הַשַּׁבָּת,   דַּיֵּנוּ!

Ee-lu ka-ra la-nu et ha-yam,
  v'lo he-eh-vee-ra-nu
  v'to-cho beh-cha-ra-va,   **Da-yeinu**

Ee-lu he-eh-vee-ra-nu
  b'to-cho beh-cha-ra-va,
  v'lo shee-ka et tza-rei-nu b'to-cho,   **Da-yeinu**

Ee-lu shee-ka et tza-rei-nu b'to-cho,
  v'lo see-peik tzor-kei-nu ba-meed-bar
  ar-ba-eem shana,   **Da-yeinu**

Ee-lu see-peik tzor-kei-nu ba-meed-bar
  ar-ba-eem sha-na,
  v'lo he-eh-chee-la-nu et ha-man,   **Da-yeinu**

Ee-lu he-eh-chee-la-nu et ha-man,
  v'lo na-tan la-nu et ha-Shabbat,   **Da-yeinu**

Dayeinu continued

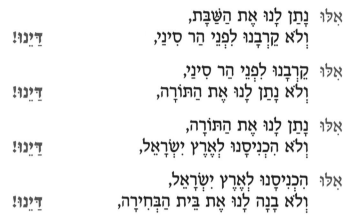

אִלּוּ נָתַן לָנוּ אֶת הַשַּׁבָּת,
וְלֹא קֵרְבָנוּ לִפְנֵי הַר סִינַי, **דַּיֵּנוּ!**

אִלּוּ קֵרְבָנוּ לִפְנֵי הַר סִינַי,
וְלֹא נָתַן לָנוּ אֶת הַתּוֹרָה, **דַּיֵּנוּ!**

אִלּוּ נָתַן לָנוּ אֶת הַתּוֹרָה,
וְלֹא הִכְנִיסָנוּ לְאֶרֶץ יִשְׂרָאֵל, **דַּיֵּנוּ!**

אִלּוּ הִכְנִיסָנוּ לְאֶרֶץ יִשְׂרָאֵל,
וְלֹא בָנָה לָנוּ אֶת בֵּית הַבְּחִירָה, **דַּיֵּנוּ!**

Kadesh
Urchatz
Karpas
Yachatz
Maggid

Dayeinu

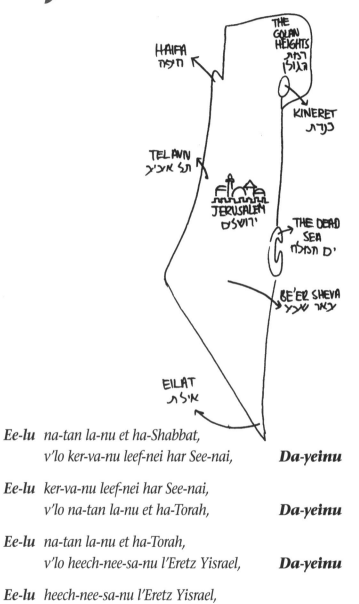

Ee-lu na-tan la-nu et ha-Shabbat,
  v'lo ker-va-nu leef-nei har See-nai, **Da-yeinu**

Ee-lu ker-va-nu leef-nei har See-nai,
  v'lo na-tan la-nu et ha-Torah, **Da-yeinu**

Ee-lu na-tan la-nu et ha-Torah,
  v'lo heech-nee-sa-nu l'Eretz Yisrael, **Da-yeinu**

Ee-lu heech-nee-sa-nu l'Eretz Yisrael,
  v'lo va-na la-nu et beit ha-b'chee-ra, **Da-yeinu**

The Afghani Onion Free-for-All

If things at your seder are slowing down and people seem drowsy, try the Afghani custom of distributing green onions.

Beginning with the ninth stanza, *"Even if You had supplied our needs in the desert for 40 years, but not fed us manna from heaven,"* the participants hit each other (gently?) with the green onion stalks, everytime they sing the refrain *"Da-yeinu."*

Perhaps this custom is tied to the biblical story of the Jews who complained about the manna God had given them and recalled with longing the onions in Egypt. *"We remember the fish that we used to eat in Egypt, the cucumbers, the melons, the leeks, the ONIONS and the garlic. Now our gullets are shrivelled. There is nothing at all. Nothing but this manna to look at."* (Numbers 11:5-6) **By beating each other with onions we admonish ourselves not to yearn for the fleshpots of Egypt and not to forget the Egyptian bondage.**

Is It Ever Enough?

"**Had God but split the sea, and not passed us through it on dry land — it would have been enough.**" How could it have been enough? Had Israel not escaped through the Red Sea, they would have been slaughtered by the Egyptians!

The point of the poem is to express gratitude for every facet of God's miraculous deliverance. There is a sense that the Exodus, which reached its fulfillment in the entry into the Land and the building of the Temple (a process of over 400 years!) unfolded in many steps, each constituting a miracle in itself. The poet feels the living power of each gesture of divine favor, irrespective of the total result. Had You only done this and no more — it would have been enough for me to feel Your divine love. The principle of "dayeinu," of giving thanks even for the partial and incomplete, is crucial for living in this uncertain world in which few dreams ever come to total fruition. We thank God every day for the miracle of being alive. In learning gratitude to God we also learn to show gratitude to parents, teachers, loved ones and friends, even when their efforts fall short of completeness.

Counting and Recounting Our Own Blessings: An Update

Dayeinu establishes a pattern of enumerating our blessings one at a time but it ends with the building of the Temple circa 1000 B.C.E. Suggest another ten national or family events deserving thanks since then. For example, the Six Day War (1967), or the airlift of Ethiopian Jews to Israel (1991). You may wish to use Rabbi Steve Greenberg's contemporary Dayeinu *(see page 109).*

Dayeinu continued

EACH ONE of these good things would have been enough to earn our thanks. Dayeinu!

GOD took us out of Egypt, punished the oppressors, and humiliated their gods, exposing their futility.

GOD killed their first born (when the Egyptians refused to release Israel, God's first born) and gave us some of the Egyptians' wealth, just compensation for our labor.

GOD divided the Red Sea for us, bringing us across on dry land, while drowning our pursuers in the sea.

GOD supplied our needs for forty years in the desert — feeding us manna.

GOD granted us the Shabbat and brought us to Mount Sinai to receive the Torah.

GOD ushered us into Eretz Yisrael and later built us a Temple, the chosen place to atone for our crimes and misdemeanors.

עַל אַחַת כַּמָּה וְכַמָּה

עַל אַחַת כַּמָּה וְכַמָּה טוֹבָה כְפוּלָה
וּמְכֻפֶּלֶת לַמָּקוֹם עָלֵינוּ:

שֶׁהוֹצִיאָנוּ מִמִּצְרַיִם, וְעָשָׂה בָהֶם שְׁפָטִים,
וְעָשָׂה בֵאלֹהֵיהֶם,

וְהָרַג אֶת בְּכוֹרֵיהֶם,
וְנָתַן לָנוּ אֶת מָמוֹנָם,

וְקָרַע לָנוּ אֶת הַיָּם,
וְהֶעֱבִירָנוּ בְתוֹכוֹ בֶּחָרָבָה, וְשִׁקַּע צָרֵינוּ בְּתוֹכוֹ,

וְסִפֵּק צָרְכֵּנוּ בַּמִּדְבָּר אַרְבָּעִים שָׁנָה,
וְהֶאֱכִילָנוּ אֶת הַמָּן,

וְנָתַן לָנוּ אֶת הַשַּׁבָּת,
וְקֵרְבָנוּ לִפְנֵי הַר סִינַי, וְנָתַן לָנוּ אֶת־הַתּוֹרָה,

וְהִכְנִיסָנוּ לְאֶרֶץ יִשְׂרָאֵל,
וּבָנָה לָנוּ אֶת בֵּית הַבְּחִירָה,
לְכַפֵּר עַל כָּל עֲוֹנוֹתֵינוּ.

Kadesh
Urchatz
Karpas
Yachatz
Maggid

Dayeinu

Otto Geismar, 1927

108

Is It Ever Enough?

created in honor of the anniversary of the birth of the State of Israel by Rabbi Steven Greenberg and Rabbi David Nelson

"It Would Have Been Enough . . . "

Had God upheld us throughout 2,000 years of Dispersion,
But not preserved our hope for return   **Dayeinu!**

   Had God preserved our hope for return,
But not sent us leaders to make the dream a reality   **Dayeinu!**

   Had God sent us leaders to make the dream a reality,
But not given us success in the U.N. vote in 1947   **Dayeinu!**

   Had God given us success in the U.N. vote,
But not defeated our attackers in 1948   **Dayeinu!**

   Had God defeated our attackers in 1948,
But not unified Jerusalem   **Dayeinu!**

   Had God unified Jerusalem,
But not led us towards peace with Egypt and Jordan   **Dayeinu!**

   Had God returned us to the land of our ancestors,
But not filled it with our children   **Dayeinu!**

   Had God filled it with our children,
But not caused the desert to bloom   **Dayeinu!**

   Had God caused the desert to bloom,
But not built for us cities and towns   **Dayeinu!**

   Had God rescued our remnants from the Holocaust,
But not brought our brothers from Arab lands   **Dayeinu!**

   Had God brought our brothers from Arab lands,
But not opened the gate for Russia's Jews   **Dayeinu!**

   Had God opened the gate for Russia's Jews,
But not redeemed our people from Ethiopia   **Dayeinu!**

   Had God redeemed our people from Ethiopia,
But not strengthened the State of Israel   **Dayeinu!**

   Had God strengthened the State of Israel,
But not planted in our hearts a covenant of one people   **Dayeinu!**

   Had God planted in our hearts a covenant of one people,
But not sustained in our souls a vision of a perfected world   **Dayeinu!**

Pesach, Matza and Maror

פֶּסַח, מַצָּה, וּמָרוֹר

1. **The Maggid section** (devoted to storytelling and explanations) is almost complete. Before eating the seder's edible symbols, the Haggadah brings us **Rabban Gamliel's checklist** on the three essential foods, whose significance must be understood by all the participants in the seder.

Why these three? The Pesach lamb, matza and maror constituted the original menu in the Egyptian seder. "They shall eat the meat (of the lamb) . . . roasted over the fire, with matza and with maror." *(Ex. 12:8)*

2. **As in a three** act play Rabban Gamliel identifies these foods with three progressive historical moments in the Exodus:

(1) **Maror** captures the bitterness of the enslavement;

(2) The **Pesach lamb**, represented today by the roasted bone (zeroa), recalls the blood on the doorposts and the terror and anticipation of the night of the plague of the first born;

(3) **Matza** stands for the following morning, when Israel was rushed out of Egypt with no time to let their dough rise.

Kadesh
Urchatz
Karpas
Yachatz
Maggid

Rabban Gamliel

❖ **RABBAN GAMLIEL** used to say: "All who have not explained the significance of three things during the Pesach seder have not yet fulfilled their duty. The three are: the **Pesach lamb**, the **matza** and the **maror**."

רַבָּן גַּמְלִיאֵל הָיָה אוֹמֵר: כָּל שֶׁלֹּא אָמַר שְׁלֹשָׁה דְבָרִים אֵלּוּ בַּפֶּסַח, לֹא יָצָא יְדֵי חוֹבָתוֹ, וְאֵלּוּ הֵן: פֶּסַח. מַצָּה וּמָרוֹר.

❖ **WHY THE PESACH LAMB?**

Leader points at (but does not raise) the roasted bone:

"Pesach Al Shum Ma?" — The Passover lamb (that our ancestors ate in the days of the Temple) — why did we used to eat it?

All:

TO REMIND ourselves that God **passed over** our ancestors' houses in Egypt (at this very hour on this very date). Moshe has already instructed us: *"When your children ask you, 'What do you mean by this ceremony?' you shall say: 'It is the **Passover** offering to Adonai, because God **passed over** the houses of Israel in Egypt when God struck the Egyptians, but saved our houses . . . .'"* *(Ex. 12:26-27)*

פֶּסַח שֶׁהָיוּ אֲבוֹתֵינוּ אוֹכְלִים, בִּזְמַן שֶׁבֵּית הַמִּקְדָּשׁ הָיָה קַיָּם, עַל שׁוּם מָה?

עַל שׁוּם שֶׁפָּסַח הַקָּדוֹשׁ בָּרוּךְ הוּא, עַל בָּתֵּי אֲבוֹתֵינוּ בְּמִצְרַיִם, שֶׁנֶּאֱמַר (שמות יב,כז) : "וַאֲמַרְתֶּם זֶבַח פֶּסַח הוּא לַיָי, אֲשֶׁר פָּסַח עַל בָּתֵּי בְנֵי יִשְׂרָאֵל בְּמִצְרַיִם, בְּנָגְפּוֹ אֶת מִצְרַיִם וְאֶת בָּתֵּינוּ הִצִּיל, וַיִּקֹד הָעָם וַיִּשְׁתַּחֲווּ."

Pesach — A Night of Fear and Liberation

"IN THE MIDDLE of the night Adonai struck down all the first-born in the land of Egypt. Pharaoh arose in the night, because there was a loud cry in Egypt; for there was no house where there was not someone dead. He summoned Moses and Aaron in the night and said, 'Up, depart from among my people, you and the Israelites with you! Go, worship Adonai as you said! Take also your flocks and your herds, and begone! May you bring a blessing upon me also!'

The Egyptians urged the people on, impatient to have them leave the country, for they said, 'We shall all be dead.' So the people took their dough before it was leavened, their kneading bowls wrapped in cloaks upon their shoulders.

The length of time that Israel lived in Egypt was 430 years. At the end of the 430th year, to the very day, all the ranks of Adonai departed from the land of Egypt . . . about six hundred thousand people on foot, aside from children." *(Ex. 12)*

'When I left Egypt. I took with me . . . '

Try this children's memory game. Go around the table asking everyone to fill in the blank: "When I left Egypt, I took with me my most treasured possession _____." The participants in turn must repeat the objects mentioned and add their own.

The Lasting Souvenirs

"Just as one sends a letter from place to place, one may send, to one's self or others, **letters through time**. Photographs, mementos and journal entries are letters we send into the future; and by writing or speaking about events gone by, we can communicate to some extent with the past. To do this regularly and intelligently is to expand our being in time." *(Robert Grudin, Time and the Art of Living)*

Rabban Gamliel identifies the Pesach meat, the matza and the maror as the three essential mementos from the Exodus experience that are to be sent on into the future and revisited annually on seder night. Similarly, each of us keeps **heirlooms of our personal past**, that one sends into the future for oneself and one's children, aspects of oneself which ought not to be lost.

Try the following exercise: select one item that somehow represents your personal Jewish identity, or that preserves some pivotal memories. Explain your choice. If possible, bring those mementos to the seder table and share their explanation with others.

Arye Allweil, 1949 first Israeli army Haggadah

Why This Matza?

Everyone holds up matza.

 Leader:

"Matza Al Shum Ma?" — This matza! Why do we eat it?

מַצָּה זוֹ שֶׁאָנוּ אוֹכְלִים, עַל שׁוּם מָה?

All:

TO REMIND ourselves that even before the dough of our ancestors in Egypt had time to rise and become leavened, the King of kings, the Holy One revealed Himself and redeemed them.

The Torah says: *"They baked unleavened cakes of the dough that they had taken out of Egypt, for it was not leavened, since they had been driven out of Egypt and could not delay; nor had they prepared any provisions for themselves."* (Ex. 12:39)

עַל שׁוּם שֶׁלֹא הִסְפִּיק בְּצֵקָם שֶׁל אֲבוֹתֵינוּ לְהַחֲמִיץ, עַד שֶׁנִּגְלָה עֲלֵיהֶם מֶלֶךְ מַלְכֵי הַמְּלָכִים, הַקָּדוֹשׁ בָּרוּךְ הוּא, וּגְאָלָם, שֶׁנֶּאֱמַר (שמות יב,לט): "וַיֹּאפוּ אֶת הַבָּצֵק, אֲשֶׁר הוֹצִיאוּ מִמִּצְרַיִם, עֻגֹת מַצּוֹת, כִּי לֹא חָמֵץ. כִּי גֹרְשׁוּ מִמִּצְרַיִם, וְלֹא יָכְלוּ לְהִתְמַהְמֵהַּ, וְגַם צֵדָה לֹא עָשׂוּ לָהֶם."

Kadesh
Urchatz
Karpas
Yachatz
Maggid

Rabban
Gamliel

Why This Maror?

Everyone raises maror from the seder plate.

 Leader:

"Maror Al Shum Ma?" — This maror! Why do we eat it?

מָרוֹר זֶה שֶׁאָנוּ אוֹכְלִים, עַל שׁוּם מָה?

All:

TO REMIND ourselves that the Egyptians embittered our ancestors' lives: *"They embittered their lives with hard labor, with mortar and bricks (construction) and with all sorts of field labor (agriculture). Whatever the task, they worked them ruthlessly."* (Ex 1:14)

עַל שׁוּם שֶׁמֵּרְרוּ הַמִּצְרִים אֶת חַיֵּי אֲבוֹתֵינוּ בְּמִצְרַיִם, שֶׁנֶּאֱמַר (שמות א,יד): "וַיְמָרְרוּ אֶת חַיֵּיהֶם בַּעֲבֹדָה קָשָׁה, בְּחֹמֶר וּבִלְבֵנִים, וּבְכָל עֲבֹדָה בַּשָּׂדֶה. אֵת כָּל עֲבֹדָתָם, אֲשֶׁר עָבְדוּ בָהֶם בְּפָרֶךְ."

Maror — 'All Is Not Well That Begins Well!'

THE RABBIS recommended [Romaine] lettuce over all other forms of maror, though horseradish is far more bitter. R. Shmuel bar Nachman said: "How is Egypt similar to maror? Just as maror when it first grows is gentle, but it turns harsh and bitter, so the exile in Egypt began gently, but ended harshly." *(T.B. Pesachim 39)*

Union Soldiers

ONE OF THE MOST literal yet inventive representations of charoset was conceived during the American Civil War, when a group of Jewish Union soldiers made a seder for themselves in the wilderness of West Virginia. They had none of the ingredients for traditional charoset handy, so they put a real brick in its place on the seder tray. *(Ira Steingroot)*

'Charoset Taste Test'

Though neither the Torah nor Rabban Gamliel lists charoset with the essential "big three" — Pesach, matza and maror, it is still a mitzvah to eat charoset with the maror. In fact the rabbis were very explicit about its ingredients and their rationales.

Taste and compare two traditional recipes for charoset. Identify as many ingredients as possible.

Why This Charoset

Why must charoset be so thick? Why must it be made from pungent fruits, like apples? The rabbis offered two explanations — one drawn from the construction industry and one from the realm of romance:

1. Egyptian Bricks

Charoset mixed with cinnamon sticks simulates Egyptian mud bricks reinforced with straw or papyrus stalks. These sun-dried bricks produced on the Nile river banks constituted the chief building material of Egypt used by the Hebrew slaves. Their "employer" — Rameses II — was the greatest builder Pharaoh since the era of the pyramids, built a thousand years before the Exodus.

2. A Taste of the Song of Songs

Though its texture may be like mortar, the taste of charoset is sweet like a fruit ambrosia from the Garden of Eden. It reminds us of the apple orchards of Egypt. According to the rabbinic midrash, the Jewish women were heroines in the battle against Pharaoh's attempt to stop the Jews from having children. The women took the initiative to arouse their husbands to procreate. In the Song of Songs the Rabbis detected allusions to this heroic love-making in the woman's open invitations to her lover to come to the garden of fruits and nuts:

"Come, my beloved
Let us go into the open
. . . Under the apple tree I roused you
It was there your mother conceived you.

I went down to the nut grove . . .
The pomegranates were in bloom . . .
the figs . . . the almonds . . . the dates . . .
all choice fruits." (Song of Songs 7:12-14, 5:11)

Shraga Weil, Song of Songs © 1968

In Every Generation

בְּכָל דּוֹר וָדוֹר

Identifying with the Exodus

"The Exodus from Egypt occurs in every human being, in every era, in every year and even on every day," said the Hassidic Rabbi Nachman of Bratslav. *At the seder we must try to empathize with that original liberation and to discover its relevance throughout the generations.*

Kadesh
Urchatz
Karpas
Yachatz
Maggid

In Every
Generation

 IN EVERY generation one is obligated to see oneself as one who personally went out from Egypt. Just as it says: *"You shall tell your child on that very day: 'It's because of this that God did for* **me** *when* **I went out from Egypt.'"** *(Ex. 13:8)*

NOT ONLY were our ancestors redeemed by the Holy One, but even *we* were redeemed with them. Just as it says: *"God took* **us** *out from there in order to bring* **us** *and to give* **us** *the land God swore to our ancestors."* *(Deut. 6:23)*

בְּכָל דּוֹר וָדוֹר חַיָּב אָדָם לִרְאוֹת אֶת עַצְמוֹ,
כְּאִלּוּ הוּא יָצָא מִמִּצְרָיִם.
שֶׁנֶּאֱמַר (שמות יג,ח) : "וְהִגַּדְתָּ לְבִנְךָ בַּיּוֹם הַהוּא לֵאמֹר:
בַּעֲבוּר זֶה עָשָׂה יי לִי, בְּצֵאתִי מִמִּצְרָיִם."

לֹא אֶת אֲבוֹתֵינוּ בִּלְבָד, גָּאַל הַקָּדוֹשׁ בָּרוּךְ הוּא, אֶלָּא אַף
אוֹתָנוּ גָּאַל עִמָּהֶם, שֶׁנֶּאֱמַר (דברים ו,כג) : "וְאוֹתָנוּ הוֹצִיא
מִשָּׁם, לְמַעַן הָבִיא אֹתָנוּ, לָתֶת לָנוּ אֶת הָאָרֶץ אֲשֶׁר
נִשְׁבַּע לַאֲבֹתֵינוּ."

Tanya Zion, 1995

Life Passages

"The Exodus from Egypt occurs in every human being, in every era, in every year, and even in every day." *(Rabbi Nachman of Bratslav)*

Think of the many "exoduses" throughout our lives — whether emerging from one geographical place to another or from an experience of "slavery" to one of greater freedom.

How might you fill in the "Pass-over Pass-port" below? A few people might be asked to share their most important personal "exoduses." They might even bring their old passports or photographs to illustrate their journey from port to port.

My Invisible Identity Card

Kibbutz Ein Harod's Haggadah

Q: On every Pesach one must ask oneself: When was I born? Where was I born? . . . What is the historical memory I bear?

A: I look at my identity card and read what is engraved in invisible script: "My parents were born as slaves in Egypt, when the king of that Egyptian Empire ordered the first planned national genocide in our history. I too was there with them."

'When I Went Out'

The Exodus of Three Refuseniks, Three Prisoners of Zion

NATAN SHARANSKY (formerly Anatoly Sharansky and later Cabinet Minister in Israel) writes:

"I, as practically all Soviet Jews, was absolutely assimilated. I knew nothing about our language, about our history about our religion. But the pride of being a Jew, the pride for our State of Israel after the Six Day War, made me feel free. And, after I turned to Jewish identification, I felt myself really free from that big Soviet prison. I was free even before the very last day of my leaving the Soviet Union."

VLADIMIR SLEPAK described his first Israeli morning: "It is like being reborn. Until I die, I'll never forget this morning when I woke up and looked out at the sun rising over the Judean Hills, and the Old City in front of me."

IDA NUDEL said upon arrival at Ben Gurion Airport: "A few hours ago I was almost a slave in Moscow. Now I'm a free woman in my own country. It is the most important moment of my life. I am at home at the soul of the Jewish people. I am a free person among my own people." *(from the CLAL Soviet Jewry Haggadah)*

Body Language

Acting the Part

Maimonides changes one letter in the traditional formula: "In every generation one is obligated to SEE oneself as one who personally went out of Egypt." He inserts "SHOW" ("להראות") instead of "SEE" ("לראות"). One's posture must show the stature of a liberated person. Freedom speaks a special body language reinforcing feeling with actions. On seder night one must act out the part for all to see and to learn. *(Mishne Torah, Chametz-u-Matza 7:6-7)*

The Torah reports that Israel emerged from Egypt with arms raised high. That phrase has become an idiom for triumph — "to gain the upper hand." The "high five" or the V-sign can also express the sense of personal elation as "I" emerged from slavery.

THE PASSOVER PASSPORT

English Name:

Hebrew Name:

Date of Birth (Hebrew, Civil Calendar):

Parents/Grandparents:

Addresses (past, present, future):

Religion:

Nationality (past, present, future):

Ports Through Which I Have Passed:

BORDER CONTROL
TANIS EGYPT
10 TISHRI-1422 BCE
ENTRANCE STAMP

GOSHEN EGYPT
BORDER CONTROL
15 NISAN-1222 BCE
8
EXIT VISA

A New Song — Hallel-u-jah

לְפִיכָךְ

After covering all the matza at the table, everyone raises
their second cup of wine in a toast to God and sings Hallel.

The Toast

Leader:

❖ WE HAVE just completed the Maggid, the story that
begins with slavery and ends with liberation.
We have retold it as our own personal story.
Now it is only fitting that we thank God
by singing a new song.

THEREFORE we owe it to God: to thank, to sing,
to praise and honor, to glorify and bless,
to raise up and acclaim the One who has done
all these wonders for our ancestors and for us.

God took us from **slavery to freedom**,
> from **sorrow to joy**,
> from **mourning to festivity**,
> from **thick darkness to a great light**,
> from **enslavement to redemption**!

Let us sing before God, a new song.
> HALLELUJAH!

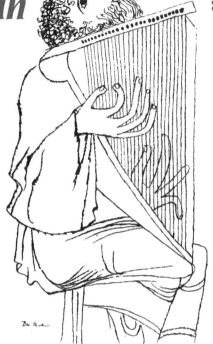

Ben Shahn, Hallelujah Suite,
© 1996, Ben Shahn Estate/Licensed by Vaga, NY, NY

לְפִיכָךְ אֲנַחְנוּ חַיָּבִים לְהוֹדוֹת, לְהַלֵּל, לְשַׁבֵּחַ,
לְפָאֵר, לְרוֹמֵם, לְהַדֵּר, לְבָרֵךְ, לְעַלֵּה וּלְקַלֵּס,
לְמִי שֶׁעָשָׂה לַאֲבוֹתֵינוּ וְלָנוּ אֶת כָּל הַנִּסִּים הָאֵלוּ.

הוֹצִיאָנוּ מֵעַבְדוּת לְחֵרוּת, מִיָּגוֹן לְשִׂמְחָה,
וּמֵאֵבֶל לְיוֹם טוֹב, וּמֵאֲפֵלָה לְאוֹר גָּדוֹל,
וּמִשִּׁעְבּוּד לִגְאֻלָּה.
וְנֹאמַר לְפָנָיו שִׁירָה חֲדָשָׁה. הַלְלוּיָה.

Kadesh
Urchatz
Karpas
Yachatz
Maggid
Hallel
Begins

The body language of liberation is standing up ("an uprising") and stretching. Every morning the Rabbis celebrate the loosening of our stiff muscles by reciting the blessing for the "God who unties the bound up." These are the same words used to celebrate the "release of prisoners who are bound up."

Perhaps after sitting at the seder for so long, everyone may wish to stand up, stretch out arms and legs and recite the blessing for liberation of muscles/prisoners:

Blessed are You who releases the bound up.

בָּרוּךְ מַתִּיר אֲסוּרִים

Blessed are You who made me free.

בָּרוּךְ שֶׁעָשַׂנִי בֶּן חוֹרִין

You release the prisoners...

...מַתִּיר אֲסוּרִים

A Toast to Freedom

E **ach cup we raise this night** is an act of memory and of reverence. The story we tell, this year as every year, is not yet done. It begins with them, then; it continues with us, now. We remember not out of curiosity or nostalgia, but because it is our turn to add to the story.

Our challenge this year, as every year, is to feel the Exodus,
to open the gates of time and become one with those
who crossed the Red Sea from slavery to freedom.

Our challenge this year, as every year, is to know the Exodus,
to behold all those in every land who have yet to make the crossing.

Our challenge this day, as every day, is to reach out
our hands to them and help them cross to freedomland.

We know some things that others do not always know — how arduous is the struggle, how very deep the waters to be crossed and how treacherous their tides, how filled with irony and contradiction and suffering are the crossing and then the wandering.

We know such things because we ourselves wandered in the desert for forty years. Have not those forty years been followed by thirty-two centuries of struggle and of quest? Heirs to those who struggled and quested, we are old-timers at disappointment, veterans at sorrow, but always, always, prisoners of hope. The hope is the anthem of our people *(Hatikvah)*, and the way of our people.

For all the reversals and all the stumbling-blocks, for all the blood and all the hurt, hope still dances within us. That is who we are, and that is what this seder is about. For the slaves do become free, and the tyrants are destroyed. Once, it was by miracles; today, it is by defiance and devotion.

(Leonard Fein, American social activist)

Hallel: Psalm 113

The first part of Hallel (Psalms 113-114) begins here before the meal and the rest is completed after eating.

The verses which we have printed in bold stand out as particularly relevant to the Exodus when recited on Passover.

HALLELUJAH.

> **O servants of Adonai,** give praise;
> praise the name of Adonai.

Let the name of Adonai be blessed now and forever.

From east to west the name of Adonai is praised.

> Adonai is exalted above all nations;
> God's glory is above the heavens.

Who is like Adonai our God,

who, enthroned on high,

sees what is below, in heaven and on earth?

> **God raises the poor from the dust,**
> **lifts up the needy from the refuse heap**
> to place them with the great men of God's people.

God places the childless woman among her household

as a happy mother of children.

HALLELUJAH.

הַלְלוּיָהּ.
הַלְלוּ עַבְדֵי יי. הַלְלוּ אֶת שֵׁם יי.
יְהִי שֵׁם יי מְבֹרָךְ מֵעַתָּה וְעַד עוֹלָם.
מִמִּזְרַח שֶׁמֶשׁ עַד מְבוֹאוֹ. מְהֻלָּל שֵׁם יי.
רָם עַל כָּל גּוֹיִם יי. עַל הַשָּׁמַיִם כְּבוֹדוֹ.
מִי כַּיי אֱלֹהֵינוּ. הַמַּגְבִּיהִי לָשָׁבֶת.
הַמַּשְׁפִּילִי לִרְאוֹת בַּשָּׁמַיִם וּבָאָרֶץ.
מְקִימִי מֵעָפָר דָּל. מֵאַשְׁפֹּת יָרִים אֶבְיוֹן.
לְהוֹשִׁיבִי עִם נְדִיבִים. עִם נְדִיבֵי עַמּוֹ.
מוֹשִׁיבִי עֲקֶרֶת הַבַּיִת אֵם הַבָּנִים שְׂמֵחָה.
הַלְלוּיָהּ.

Kadesh
Urchatz
Karpas
Yachatz
Maggid

Hallel
Begins

During the later years of Ben's life there was a certain resurgence of religious imagery in his work. It seemed to me that, since he had rather emphatically cast off his religious ties and traditions during his youth, he could now return to them freely with a fresh eye, and without the sense of moral burden and entrapment that they once held for him. He rediscovered myth and story and a holy spirit that had once offended him but that now held a tremendous charm, and even amusement, and that he could now depict with a light touch and affectionate tenderness.
— *Bernarda Bryson Shahn*

Ben Shahn, Hallelujah Suite,

Otto Geismar, 1927

My Narrow Prison

The Hebrew word for Egypt, "Meetzrayim," means a tight spot or a narrow strait where we feel "boxed in."

One day, a few days after the liberation, I walked through the country past flowering meadows, for miles and miles, toward the market town near the camp. Larks rose to the sky and I could hear their joyous song. There was no one to be seen for miles around; there was nothing but the wide earth and sky and the larks' jubilation and the **freedom of space**. I stopped, looked around, and up to the sky — and then I went down on my knees. At that moment there was very little I knew of myself or of the world — I had but one sentence in mind — always the same: *"I called to Adonai from my narrow prison and God answered me in the freedom of space."* (Psalm 118:5)

How long I knelt there and repeated this sentence, memory can no longer recall. But I know that on that day, in that hour, my new life started. Step for step I progressed, until I again became a human being.

(Viktor Frankl, Man's Search for Meaning, lessons from a concentration camp)

Freedom Songs

If I Had a Hammer

IF I HAD A HAMMER
I'd hammer in the morning
I'd hammer in the evening
All over this land.
I'd hammer out danger
I'd hammer out warning
I'd hammer out love between
My brothers and my sisters
All over this land.

IF I HAD A BELL
I'd ring it in the morning
I'd ring it in the evening
All over this land.
I'd ring out danger
I'd ring out warning
I'd ring out love between
My brothers and my sisters
All over this land.

IF I HAD A SONG
I'd sing it in the morning
I'd sing it in the evening
All over this land.
I'd sing out danger
I'd sing out warning
I'd sing out love between
My brothers and my sisters
All over this land.

WELL, I GOT A HAMMER
And I've got a bell
And I've got a song to sing
All over this land.
It's the hammer of justice!
It's the bell of freedom!
It's the song about love between
My brothers and my sisters
All over this land.

(by Pete Seeger and Lee Hays)

Oh Freedom!

OH FREEDOM, oh freedom,
Oh freedom over me
And before I'll be a slave,
I'll be buried in my grave
And go home to my Lord and be free.

We Shall Overcome

WE SHALL OVERCOME (3)
some day.
Oh, deep in my heart,
I do believe
We shall overcome, some day.

(Gospel song adapted from Louise Shropshire, 1942)

The Battle Hymn of the Republic

(The Union's spiritual anthem during the American Civil War)

Oh, mine eyes have seen the glory
of the coming of the LORD.
He is trampling out the vintage
where the grapes of wrath are stored.
He hath loosed the faithful lightning
of his terrible swift sword.
His truth is marching on!

Refrain:
Glory, glory, hallelujah (3)
His truth is marching on!

(by Julia Ward Howe, 1861)

Hallel: Psalm 114

❖ WHEN ISRAEL went forth from Egypt,
The house of Jacob from a people of strange speech,
> Judah became God's holy one,
> Israel, God's dominion.

The sea saw them and fled,
The Jordan ran backward,
> Mountains skipped like rams,
> Hills like sheep.

What alarmed you, sea, that you fled,
Jordan, that you ran backward,
> Mountains, that you skipped like rams,
> Hills, like sheep?

Tremble, earth,
at the presence of Adonai,
at the presence of
the God of Jacob,
> **Who turned the rock**
> **into a pool of water,**
> **The flinty rock**
> **into a fountain.**

Ben Shahn, Hallelujah Suite

בְּצֵאת יִשְׂרָאֵל

בְּצֵאת יִשְׂרָאֵל מִמִּצְרַיִם   בֵּית יַעֲקֹב מֵעַם לֹעֵז.
הָיְתָה יְהוּדָה לְקָדְשׁוֹ   יִשְׂרָאֵל מַמְשְׁלוֹתָיו.
הַיָּם רָאָה וַיָּנֹס   הַיַּרְדֵּן יִסֹּב לְאָחוֹר.
הֶהָרִים רָקְדוּ כְאֵילִים   גְּבָעוֹת כִּבְנֵי צֹאן.
מַה לְּךָ הַיָּם כִּי תָנוּס   הַיַּרְדֵּן תִּסֹּב לְאָחוֹר.
הֶהָרִים תִּרְקְדוּ כְאֵילִים   גְּבָעוֹת כִּבְנֵי צֹאן.
מִלִּפְנֵי אָדוֹן חוּלִי אָרֶץ   מִלִּפְנֵי אֱלוֹהַּ יַעֲקֹב.
הַהֹפְכִי הַצּוּר אֲגַם מָיִם   חַלָּמִישׁ לְמַעְיְנוֹ מָיִם.

Kadesh
Urchatz
Karpas
Yachatz
Maggid

Hallel
Begins

B'tzeit Yis-ra-el, mee-Meetz-rai-eem,
Hai-ta Ye-hu-da l'kod-sho,
Ha-yam ra-a va-ya-nos,
Heh-ha-reem rak-du ch'ei-leem,
Ma-l'cha ha-yam, kee-ta-noos,
Heh-ha-reem, teer-k'du ch'ei-leem,
Mee-leef-nei A-don, chu-lee aretz,
Ha-chof-chee ha-tzur, agam ma-yeem,

Beit Ya-a-kov, mei-am lo-eiz:
Yisra-el mam-sh'lo-tav.
Ha-Yar-den yee-sov l'a-chor.
G'va-ot keev-nei tzon.
Ha-Yar-den, tee-sov l'achor.
G'va-ot keev-nei tzon.
Mee-leef-nei, Elo-ha Ya-a-kov.
Cha-la-meesh, l'mai-no ma-yeem.

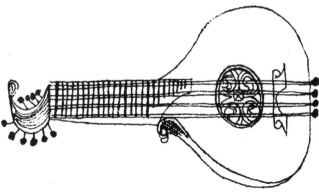

Splitting the Mediterranean

The Original Proposal

On July 4, 1776, Benjamin Franklin, Thomas Jefferson and John Adams were given the task of designing the American seal. Jefferson suggested the children of Israel in the wilderness led by a cloud by day and a pillar of fire by night. Franklin's design included Moses "standing on the shore and extending his hand over the Sea, thereby causing the same to overwhelm Pharaoh who is sitting in an open Chariot, a crown on his Head and a Sword in his Hand. Rays from a Pillar of Fire in the Clouds reach to Moses to express that he acts by command of the Deity."

The seal's proposed motto was "Rebellion to Tyrants is Obedience to God," coined by Oliver Cromwell, leader of the Puritan revolution in England.

The Fiftieth Anniversary of the S.S. Exodus 1947

After World War II the Jewish Agency purchased a former luxury liner from Chesapeake Bay (the S.S. President Warfield, 1928). It had served the military in the invasion of Nazi Europe at Normandy (1944). After refitting in Baltimore, the newly named "Exodus 1947" boarded 4,554 Jewish refugees from Displaced Persons Camps in Europe. However, the British intercepted this Hagana ship and deported it from Haifa back to Germany as the world media played up the fate of these victims of Nazi Germany denied a safe haven in the Jewish homeland.

"In my opinion, no single action, either political or military had as much impact as 'illegal immigration' on the decision of the British to relinquish Palestine. The picture of these refugees on the deck of the Exodus became ingrained in the consciousness of people everywhere." (Teddy Kollek, Mayor of Jerusalem, 1965-1994)

On November 29, 1947, the UN voted to end the British Mandate and to establish an independent Jewish State (May 15, 1948). Soon the State of Israel passed the "Law of Return" guaranteeing all Jews free entry and automatic citizenship upon returning to their homeland.

In 1957, the Baltimorean Leon Uris wrote his best-selling novel *Exodus*. Its movie version (1960), starring Paul Newman, impacted on the West. When illegally published *(samizdat)* in the USSR, the novel inspired the "refuseniks" who led the Soviet Jewry movement to another Exodus of over 1,000,000 Jews to Israel.

The Cup of Redemption

כּוֹס שֵׁנִי

1. **We conclude** the long Maggid section (storytelling) by drinking the second cup of wine, the Cup of Redemption.

2. **Recline** on a pillow to the left and drink at least half the second cup of wine.

HERE I AM, ready to perform the mitzvah of the second of the four cups, the cup of redemption.

הִנְנִי מוּכָן וּמְזֻמָּן לְקַיֵּם מִצְוַת כּוֹס שֵׁנִי שֶׁל אַרְבַּע כּוֹסוֹת.

❖ BLESSED ARE YOU, Adonai our God, Sovereign of the Universe, who redeemed us and redeemed our ancestors from Egypt, and who brought us to this night to eat matza and maror. Adonai, our God and God of our ancestors, may You bring us in peace to future holidays. May we celebrate them in your rebuilt city, and may we be able to eat the Pesach lamb and the other sacrifices offered on the altar. We will thank you for our redemption. BLESSED ARE YOU, the Redeemer of Israel.

בָּרוּךְ אַתָּה יי, אֱלֹהֵינוּ מֶלֶךְ הָעוֹלָם, אֲשֶׁר גְּאָלָנוּ וְגָאַל אֶת אֲבוֹתֵינוּ מִמִּצְרַיִם, וְהִגִּיעָנוּ לַלַּיְלָה הַזֶּה, לֶאֱכָל בּוֹ מַצָּה וּמָרוֹר. כֵּן, יי אֱלֹהֵינוּ וֵאלֹהֵי אֲבוֹתֵינוּ, יַגִּיעֵנוּ לְמוֹעֲדִים וְלִרְגָלִים אֲחֵרִים, הַבָּאִים לִקְרָאתֵנוּ לְשָׁלוֹם. שְׂמֵחִים בְּבִנְיַן עִירָךְ, וְשָׂשִׂים בַּעֲבוֹדָתֶךָ, וְנֹאכַל שָׁם מִן הַזְּבָחִים וּמִן הַפְּסָחִים, אֲשֶׁר יַגִּיעַ דָּמָם, עַל קִיר מִזְבַּחֲךָ לְרָצוֹן, וְנוֹדֶה לְךָ שִׁיר חָדָשׁ עַל גְּאֻלָּתֵנוּ, וְעַל פְּדוּת נַפְשֵׁנוּ.

בָּרוּךְ אַתָּה יי, גָּאַל יִשְׂרָאֵל.

BLESSED ARE YOU, Adonai our God, Sovereign of the Universe, Creator of the Fruit of the Vine.

Ba-rukh ata Adonai Elo-hei-nu me-lech ha-olam, bo-rei pree ha-gafen.

בָּרוּךְ אַתָּה יי, אֱלֹהֵינוּ מֶלֶךְ הָעוֹלָם, בּוֹרֵא פְּרִי הַגָּפֶן.

Miriam's Cup

Many contemporary women pour water into a large decorative cup in honor of Miriam the heroine and poet/prophet, the singer and dancer, who not only saved baby Moshe from the Nile but led the celebration of redemption at the Red Sea. The water in her cup recalls the Rabbis' identification of Miriam with the legendary "wandering well" that nourished Israel in the desert with its waters of life but it also symbolizes the rebirth of freedom. Sometimes each guest is asked to pour a little water into the Cup of Miriam and to express their wishes for healing and rejuvenation.

Kadesh
Urchatz
Karpas
Yachatz
Maggid
Second Cup

Nachshon at the Red Sea

WHAT WAS IT LIKE at the Red Sea? Rabbi Meir said: When God ordered the tribes to "move out" into the water even before the sea was parted, each of the tribes competed: "I will go first;" "No, I will go first."

But Rabbi Yehuda replied: It was not like that at all. Each tribe said: "I am not going into the water first." During the endless debates, Nachshon from the tribe of Judah jumped into the sea. He was almost drowned when God suddenly divided the waters. *(T.B. Sotah 36)*

Can you recall a case in which someone acted like Nachshon?

'God will surely help'

MORRIS was a God-fearing man. When the warning was sounded that a flood was coming, he had complete trust; God would protect him. So he remained in his home even while others fled. The local police came to his door and offered to help him evacuate, but he assured them: "Don't worry, God will help." The rains came and the waters began to rise. The emergency rescue team came to his house in a boat and urged him to leave, but Morris refused to go with them, saying, "I'm not worried. God will help." As the flood worsened, Morris finally moved onto the roof of his house to escape the water. A military helicopter flew over to him; but Morris turned them down, insisting, "I trust in God. He will provide a miracle." Unfortunately,

the storm continued unabated. Morris was carried off and drowned.

When he arrived in heaven, Morris was enraged. He approached the holy throne: "God, how could you abandon me when I put all my trust in You?" Quickly a response came: "Morris, I tried to help you. I sent you three miracles: the police in a car, the rescue workers in a boat, and then the army in a helicopter. What were you waiting for?"

The God of Surprise

Central to the Pesach seder is the recounting of the ten plagues. As moderns educated in natural science, the story strikes us as childish, as primitive, as mythological. Yet we may be missing the point of these extraordinary events if we understand it as ancient superstition. Instead, the miracle is a symbol of spontaneity in history, a faith in the changeability of oppressive regimes. What appears as historical necessity, a small people subject to a great empire, is revealed as an illusion. God's miraculous intervention in Egypt presents history as an open-textured drama. There is an unpredictable Power present in the universe, the God of surprise.

Belief in miracle is the basis of the "hope model" of Judaism. **Exodus becomes a call to revolutionary hope regardless of the conditions of history.** Out of this memory of redemption, they can defy the given conditions. **The act of protest against their environment can occur because the Jews possess a memory of the impossible that became possible.** The order that people observe in the cosmos and in history is not irreversible. **Tomorrow will not necessarily be like today.**

(David Hartman, Jerusalem Philosopher)

Nachshon at the Red Sea

Rachtza
Washing Before Eating Matza

רׇחְצָה

1. **Finally** we begin the Passover meal, the third section or "third cup" of the seder. Storytelling leads into communal eating, because on Passover, "Jews eat history."

2. **On Passover** the traditional handwashing is often done seated, while volunteers bring around a pitcher, a towel and a basin to each participant. After pouring water over each hand, say the blessing.

❖ BLESSED ARE YOU, Adonai our God, Sovereign of the Universe, who sanctified us with Divine mitzvot and commanded us on the washing of the hands.

Ba-ruch ata Adonai,
Elo-hei-nu me-lech ha-olam,
asher kee-d'shanu b'meetz-vo-tav
v'tzee-va-nu al n'teelat ya-da-yeem.

בָּרוּךְ אַתָּה יי
אֱלֹהֵינוּ מֶלֶךְ הָעוֹלָם,
אֲשֶׁר קִדְּשָׁנוּ בְּמִצְוֹתָיו,
וְצִוָּנוּ עַל נְטִילַת יָדָיִם.

Motzi/Matza
Eating the Matza

מוֹצִיא מַצָּה

1. **This is the one time** during Pesach in which one is obligated to eat matza. It must be plain matza without eggs or other ingredients that might enrich this bread of poverty.
  Take the three matzot in hand. Make sure the middle one is broken and the others are still whole. Recite the usual blessing for all forms of bread — the "motzi" — and the special blessing for matza — "al acheelat matza."

2. **Take and eat** from the top and middle matza, while reclining (left). Save the third matza for the Hillel sandwich.
  You may dip the matza in salt or charoset.
  One should eat an amount equivalent to at least ⅓-⅔ of a standard machine-made matza.

HERE I AM, ready to perform the mitzvah of eating matza.

הִנְנִי מוּכָן וּמְזֻמָּן לְקַיֵּם מִצְוַת אֲכִילַת מַצָּה.

❖ BLESSED ARE YOU, Adonai our God, Sovereign of the Universe, who extracts bread from the earth.

Ba-ruch ata Adonai,
Elo-hei-nu me-lech ha-olam,
ha-mo-tzee le-chem meen ha-aretz.

בָּרוּךְ אַתָּה יי,
אֱלֹהֵינוּ מֶלֶךְ הָעוֹלָם,
הַמּוֹצִיא לֶחֶם מִן הָאָרֶץ.

❖ BLESSED ARE YOU, Adonai our God, Sovereign of the Universe, who sanctified us by commanding us to eat matza.

Ba-ruch ata Adonai, Elo-hei-nu me-lech
ha-olam, asher kee-d'shanu b'meetz-vo-tav
v'tzee-va-nu al achee-lat matza.

בָּרוּךְ אַתָּה יי, אֱלֹהֵינוּ מֶלֶךְ
הָעוֹלָם, אֲשֶׁר קִדְּשָׁנוּ בְּמִצְוֹתָיו
וְצִוָּנוּ עַל אֲכִילַת מַצָּה.

Kadesh
Urchatz
Karpas
Yachatz
Maggid
Rachtza
Motzi
Matza

Washing Hands and Eating Matza

With or Without Salt

RABBI YOSEF KARO, author of the Shulchan Aruch *(16th C., Safed, Israel)*, requires that the matza be dipped in **salt**, just as challah is dipped in salt, to make it tastier, as befits food consumed in a ritual context. Our table is like God's altar and our bread is like a royal offering to God. Therefore, just as each sacrificial offering must be salted *(Leviticus 2:1-3)*, so should we salt the matza of the holiday of liberation. *(Aruch Hashulchan O.H. 475:5)*

But other rabbis protested that matza is the bread of poverty and should be eaten plain without any seasoning.

Obviously, those on a salt-free diet are obligated to eat their matza plain, since the Torah was given for life, not for death.

With or Without Charoset?

RAV AMRAM GAON *(9th C., Babylonia)* and Maimonides *(12th C., Egypt)* require that matza be dipped in charoset just as maror and karpas should be. **Charoset** (a symbol of mortar) is appropriately mixed both with matza (the bread of poverty) and with maror (the taste of bitter slavery). But Rabbi Avraham Hayarchi *(French Talmudist, 12th C.)* never heard of such a strange custom. Why, he asks, dip the matza (the bread of liberation eaten during the Exodus) in charoset (the reminder of slavery)? Rabbi Joel Sirkis replied that for Maimonides the matza dipped in charoset stands for the experience of emergence from slavery

Sefer HaMinhagim, Amsterdam

to freedom. The contrast of matza and charoset makes us aware of the meaning of freedom.

The Blessing Over Chametz: Bergen-Belsen

BEFORE EATING CHAMETZ in the concentration camp seder, Jews recited a special prayer:

"Our Father in Heaven! It is well-known to you that we desire to follow your will and celebrate Pesach with matza — strictly avoiding chametz. Yet our hearts are pained that the enslavement prevents us from doing so for our lives are in danger. We are here, ready to observe the positive commandment of **'living by your laws'** *(Lev. 18:5)* — not dying by them. We must take care not to violate the negative commandment, **'beware and guard yourself well,'** lest we endanger our lives. Therefore, our prayer to You is to preserve our lives and redeem us quickly, so that we may observe Your will and serve You wholeheartedly. Amen."

Maror

מָרוֹר

1. Take out an ounce of raw maror, *preferably romaine lettuce, but almost equally good is horseradish ("chrein") which was popular in wintry northern Europe when lettuce was unavailable. Maror embodies the taste of slavery.*

2. Dip it in charoset *(but not so much that it eradicates the bitter taste). Recite the blessing, eat and savor the maror but* **do not recline!** *Reclining is a custom of the free, while maror and charoset remind us of persecution.*

Kadesh
Urchatz
Karpas
Yachatz
Maggid
Rachtza
Motzi
Matza
Maror
Eating
Bitter
Herbs

HERE I AM, ready to perform the mitzvah of eating maror.

הִנְנִי מוּכָן וּמְזֻמָּן לְקַיֵּם מִצְוַת אֲכִילַת מרוֹר.

BLESSED ARE YOU, Adonai
our God, Sovereign of the Universe,
who sanctified us
by commanding us to eat maror.

Ba-ruch ata Adonai,
Elo-hei-nu me-lech ha-olam,
asher kee-d'shanu b'meetz-vo-tav
v'tzee-va-nu al achee-lat maror.

בָּרוּךְ אַתָּה יי,
אֱלֹהֵינוּ מֶלֶךְ הָעוֹלָם,
אֲשֶׁר קִדְּשָׁנוּ בְּמִצְוֹתָיו
וְצִוָּנוּ עַל אֲכִילַת מָרוֹר.

A Meditation on Maror

PERSONALLY, I cannot imagine Passover without horseradish. Its combination of intense pleasure and pain makes a good analog for the bittersweet nature of our memories at Passover: We remember good times with family and friends, often with those who are no longer with us or are far away. We give our brief lives added dimension by linking them to the pain and triumph of Jewish history.

As the Irish fiddler Seamus Connolly once said in the name of his mother, **"We're never so happy as when we're crying."** We never enjoy the horseradish so much as when it **brings tears to our eyes.** *(Ira Steingroot)*

Weeping Man

Ben Shahn
© Ben Shahn Estate/
Licensed by Vaga, NY, NY, 1996

Maror and the Salad Bar

Question: Which species should be used for maror (bitter herbs)?

Responsum: For the benefit of the public I think it is useful to let everyone know that the **chazeret** mentioned in the Mishnah as the preferred species for maror is the plant known in German as *Salat*. Its Hebrew name **chasa** also means "to protect" just as God protected our homes from the plague.

Since in the cold climate of Germany and Poland, lettuce is not available at the time of Passover, people use **chrein**, horseradish. This substitution has had detrimental results, because many people eat less than the required minimum of a *kazayit* (an olive's size) due to the pungent flavor of the horseradish. Thus many neglect the mitzvah of maror. Meticulously observant Jews who do eat a full dosage of the horseradish are endangering their health. Therefore whoever is God-fearing should buy *latuga-Salat* (**romaine lettuce**) for maror, even if it is costly.

(Rabbi Tzvi Ashkenazi, 1660-1718, Greece and Germany; from Asher Finkel, Responsa Anthology)

Matza and Maror as Silverware

ALL THIS DIPPING can be quite messy. Yet seen from a historical perspective, bread and fresh vegetables have always been used to spoon up sauces and dips in the era before forks and spoons became common utensils *(16th-17th C.)*.

"Our Way" Passover brochure in sign language for the Jewish deaf (National Conference of Synagogue Youth of the Union of Orthodox Jewish Congregations of America)

Korech
Hillel's Sandwich at the Temple

Take the third, *bottom matza, and prepare a sandwich of matza, maror and charoset. Eat it while reclining to the left.*

❖ *Leader:*

WE have just eaten matza and maror separately. However, in the days of the Temple, Hillel, the head of the Sanhedrin, used to bind into one sandwich: Pesach lamb, matza and maror. He ate them all together in order to observe the law: *"You shall eat it (the Pesach sacrifice) on matzot and maror."* (Numbers 9:11)

Eating the sandwich tonight reminds us of the Temple sacrifice in Jerusalem as performed according to Hillel.

All:

IN MEMORY of Pesach in the Temple as Hillel used to celebrate it.

זֵכֶר לַמִּקְדָּשׁ כְּהִלֵּל.
כֵּן עָשָׂה הִלֵּל בִּזְמַן שֶׁבֵּית הַמִּקְדָּשׁ הָיָה קַיָם.
הָיָה כּוֹרֵךְ פֶּסַח מַצָּה וּמָרוֹר וְאוֹכֵל בְּיַחַד.
לְקַיֵם מַה שֶׁנֶּאֱמַר (במדבר ט,יא): "עַל מַצּוֹת
וּמְרוֹרִים יֹאכְלֻהוּ."

A Soviet Sandwich

WE HELD THE SEDER in a hurry, as in the time of the Exodus from Egypt, since the camp authorities prohibited the holding of a seder. Instead of *maror*, we ate slices of onion, and for *zeroa* (roasted bone symbolizing the Passover sacrifice), we used burnt soup cubes. We read from one Haggadah, the only copy we had, and when we reached *korech*, we had nothing to put between the matzot. Then Joseph Mendelevich said, **"We do not need a symbol of our suffering. We have real suffering and we shall put that between the matzot."**

(Shimon Grillius, a prisoner in a Soviet labor camp, whose crime was his desire to make aliyah)

An English Sandwich

BRITISH NOBILITY gave us the word *"sandwich"* invented by John Montague, nicknamed "Jemmy Twitcher," an inveterate gambler in the court of George III. Famous for his round-the-clock sessions at the gaming tables, "Jemmy" used to order his servant to bring him pieces of meat between slices of bread, so that he could continue gambling without loss of time. Soon the bread-and-meat combination was called the sandwich. "Jemmy," you see, was more formally known as the fourth **Earl of Sandwich**.

Sandwiches both during the Exodus in the 13th century B.C.E. and in 18th century C.E. England were **"fast foods."**

In the twentieth century the revivers of the Hebrew language sat down to invent a term for the sandwich. They first suggested it be called a *"Hilleleet,"* named after Hillel, head of the Sanhedrin, just as the English "sandwich" was named after an illustrious personage. Later they settled for *"kareech"* from the verb that describes Hillel's original sandwich — "Korech." Today most Israelis call it a *"sandwich,"* a term borrowed from the English.

Kadesh
Urchatz
Karpas
Yachatz
Maggid
Rachtza
Motzi
Matza
Maror
Korech
Shulchan Orech

Hillel's Sandwich and the Family Meal

Shulchan Orech
The Pesach Family Meal

שֻׁלְחָן עוֹרֵךְ

The Dutch Family Seder

Bernard Picart, 1725

Eating the Hidden Afikoman

צָפוּן

1. **The Afikoman**, the other half of the middle matza which was hidden at the beginning of the seder, must now be eaten. Its taste lingers as the last food eaten at the seder.

2. **At this point** the leaders of the seder "discover to their dismay" that the afikoman has been "stolen" by the children. Knowing that it must be eaten at the end of the meal, the leaders must bargain for its return.

3. **It is recommended** that Jewish prizes be offered (a book, a game), as well as the promise of some money. Some families ask the children to give 10% of their afikoman prize to a tzedaka of their choice and to announce the beneficiary at this point. The adults may be solicited for matching gifts.

4. **After everyone has finished dessert**, distribute a piece of afikoman combined with additional matza (altogether the equivalent of ½ a machine made matza). Though the participants may be quite full, it is important to end the seder with the taste of matza, eaten while reclining (left).

5. **Since matza** has already been eaten at the beginning of the seder, the significance of the afikoman is its role as a stand-in for the Pesach lamb that was once consumed at the end of the seder after one had eaten one's fill.

6. **After finishing** the afikoman there is no more eating or drinking except for the third and fourth cups of wine.

Kadesh
Urchatz
Karpas
Yachatz
Maggid
Rachtza
Motzi
Matza
Maror
Korech
Shulchan Orech
Tzafun
Afikoman

Find the hidden Pesach Fours: 4 matzot, 4 presents, 4 "?", 4 cups!

Tanya Zion

הִנְנִי מוּכָן וּמְזֻמָּן לְקַיֵּם מִצְוַת אֲכִילַת אֲפִיקוֹמָן זֵכֶר לְקָרְבַּן פֶּסַח הַנֶּאֱכָל עַל הַשּׂוֹבַע.

❖ HERE I AM, ready to fulfill the mitzvah of eating the afikoman. This matza is a reminder of the Pesach sacrifice which was eaten on a full stomach in the days of the Temple!

130

SOLOMON THE KING excelled in the glory of treasure and magnificent buildings, of shipping and navigation, of service and attendance, of fame and renown, yet he makes no claim to any of those glories, but only to the glory of inquisition of truth; for so he says expressly, *"The glory of God is to conceal a thing, but the glory of the king is to find it out."* (Proverbs 25:2) It is like the innocent play of children; the Divine Majesty took delight to hide His works, to the end to have them found out. It is as if kings could not obtain a greater honor than to be **God's play-fellows** in that game.

(Francis Bacon, The Advancement of Learning, 1605)

Afikoman — 'It's Greek to me!'

 επι κωμον

The Mishna explicitly forbids "completing the Pesach seder with an afikoman." (Pesachim 10:8) But in today's parlance we always consummate the seder meal with the eating of what we call "the afikoman" — a piece of matza. How on earth can we explain this? What does the Greek term *"afikoman"* mean?

To the Talmudist Rav it was clear: **"Afikoman" is the Greek custom of going around from house to house on the night of a celebration.** This procession (*"komon"*) held after (*"epi"*) the formal symposium, involved dropping in at friends' homes and probably joining them for dessert.

Personal Meditation: Seeking Our Lost Other Half

Pesach is a holiday celebrating our reunion with the lost parts of ourselves. Often hiding and separation are essential stages in our life. In the Biblical story of the Exodus both Moshe and God played "hide-and-go-seek." Moshe was hidden for three months from Pharaoh until he was adopted by Pharaoh's daughter. Then the grown Moshe went out to seek his brothers. The Divine face too was hidden for hundreds of years of servitude until God's revelation to Moshe at the burning bush. Initially Moshe hid his face, but eventually he helped all Israel to encounter God face to face at Mount Sinai. On seder night we hide and then seek the afikoman, reuniting the two parts separated at the beginning of the seder. May we learn to discover the lost parts of ourselves, to become reconciled with relatives who have become distant and to find wholeness in a Jewish tradition from which we have become alienated.

However, on seder night in the days of the Temple one was allowed to eat only with one's pre-arranged dinner partners (havurah) who had subscribed to the sacrifice of that Pesach lamb in advance. The lamb was offered in their name and no one could join their dinner gathering as an afterthought.

Therefore, on Pesach the Rabbis forbade the Greek practice of a post-symposium procession from group to group — an *"afikoman"* that might lead people to eat from a Pesach sacrifice not meant for them.

So how, we may ask, did the Greek *"epikomon"* become today's matza? The Talmudists Shmuel and Rabbi Yochanan understood the word "afikoman" to mean "dessert." They read the Mishna this way: **"It is forbidden to eat afikoman (i.e. dessert) after eating the Pesach lamb"** since that is the last and most important item on the menu, and its aftertaste should remain in our mouth all night.

Later the term afikoman was applied to the special dessert that was mandated at the seder. Now it refers to the matza eaten in lieu of the bite of Pesach lamb which used to conclude the meal in Temple times.

Birkat Hamazon — Barech
The Blessing after the Meal

1. **After the meal** we thank God not only for the food but for all the Divine gifts we have received. These blessings are recited over the third cup of wine which we pour now and drink at the end of Barech.

2. **Usually a guest** is chosen to lead the blessing, so that one can thank the hosts and God simultaneously. For three or more adults (post bar-mitzvah) the **invitation** is said (p. 133). For ten or more, add to the invitation the word "Eloheinu," our God, since God's presence dwells in community.

HERE I AM, ready to perform the mitzvah of thanking God for the food we have eaten. Just as it says, *"You shall eat and be satisfied and bless Adonai, your God, for the good land God gave you."* (Deut. 8:10)

הִנְנִי מוּכָן וּמְזֻמָּן לְקַיֵּם מִצְוַת עֲשֵׂה כְּמוֹ שֶׁכָּתוּב בַּתּוֹרָה: "וְאָכַלְתָּ וְשָׂבַעְתָּ וּבֵרַכְתָּ."

A SONG OF ASCENTS
The Dream of the Return from Exile

they who sow in tears... הַזֹּרְעִים בְּדִמְעָה

שִׁיר הַמַּעֲלוֹת

WHEN ADONAI restores the fortunes of Zion
— we see it as in a dream —
our mouths shall be filled with laughter,
our tongues, with songs of joy.
> Then shall they say among the nations,
> "Adonai has done great things for them!"
> Adonai will do great things for us
> and we shall rejoice.
Restore our fortunes, Adonai,
like watercourses in the Negev.
> They who sow in tears
> shall reap with songs of joy.
Though he goes along weeping,
carrying the seed-bag, he shall come back with
songs of joy, carrying his sheaves. *(Psalm 126)*

Sheer ha-ma-alot.
B'shuv Adonai et sheev-at Tzion,
ha-yeenu k'chol-meem.
Az y'ma-lei s'chok pee-nu
u'l-sho-nei-nu reena.
Az yo-m'ru va-goyim
heeg-deel Adonai la-asot eem eleh.
Heeg-deel Adonai la-asot eemanu
ha-yee-nu s'mei-cheem.
Shuva Adonai, et sh'vee-tei-nu
ka-afee-keem ba-negev.
Ha-zor-eem b'deem-ah, b'reena yeek-tzo-ru.
Ha-loch yei-lech u-va-cho
no-sei me-shech hazara,
Bo yavo v'ree-na, no-sei alu-mo-tav.

שִׁיר הַמַּעֲלוֹת.
בְּשׁוּב יי אֶת שִׁיבַת צִיּוֹן
הָיִינוּ כְּחֹלְמִים.
אָז יִמָּלֵא שְׂחוֹק פִּינוּ
וּלְשׁוֹנֵנוּ רִנָּה.
אָז יֹאמְרוּ בַגּוֹיִם
הִגְדִּיל יי לַעֲשׂוֹת עִם אֵלֶּה.
הִגְדִּיל יי לַעֲשׂוֹת עִמָּנוּ
הָיִינוּ שְׂמֵחִים.
שׁוּבָה יי אֶת שְׁבִיתֵנוּ
כַּאֲפִיקִים בַּנֶּגֶב.
הַזֹּרְעִים בְּדִמְעָה בְּרִנָּה יִקְצֹרוּ.
הָלוֹךְ יֵלֵךְ וּבָכֹה
נֹשֵׂא מֶשֶׁךְ הַזָּרַע
בֹּא יָבֹא בְרִנָּה נֹשֵׂא אֲלֻמֹּתָיו.

132

THE INVITATION

בִּרְכַּת הַמָּזוֹן

Leader (raises the cup and begins): My friends, let us bless God for the meal.

Cha-vei-rai n'va-rech.

חֲבֵרַי נְבָרֵךְ!

All: "May Adonai's name be blessed from now and forever." *(Psalm 113:2)*

Y'hee sheim Adonai m'vo-rach mei-ata v'ad olam.

יְהִי שֵׁם יי מְבֹרָךְ מֵעַתָּה וְעַד עוֹלָם.

Leader (repeats): "May Adonai's name be blessed from now and forever."

Y'hee sheim Adonai m'vo-rach mei-ata v'ad olam.

יְהִי שֵׁם יי מְבֹרָךְ מֵעַתָּה וְעַד עוֹלָם.

Leader (adds words in parenthesis when there is a minyan): With your permission, let us bless (our God) from whose food we have eaten.

Beer-shut, n'va-rech (Eloheinu) she-achal-nu mee-shelo.

בִּרְשׁוּת, נְבָרֵךְ (אֱלֹהֵינוּ) שֶׁאָכַלְנוּ מִשֶּׁלוֹ.

All: Blessed be (our God) from whose food we have eaten.

Ba-ruch (Eloheinu) she-achal-nu mee-shelo, uv'tu-vo cha-yeenu.

בָּרוּךְ (אֱלֹהֵינוּ) שֶׁאָכַלְנוּ מִשֶּׁלוֹ וּבְטוּבוֹ חָיִינוּ.

Leader (repeats): Blessed be (our God) from whose food we have eaten.

Ba-ruch (Eloheinu) she-achal-nu mee-shelo, uv'tu-vo cha-yeenu.

בָּרוּךְ (אֱלֹהֵינוּ) שֶׁאָכַלְנוּ מִשֶּׁלוֹ וּבְטוּבוֹ חָיִינוּ.

All: Blessed be God, Blessed be the Divine Name.

Ba-ruch hu u-varuch sh'mo.

בָּרוּךְ הוּא וּבָרוּךְ שְׁמוֹ.

FIRST BLESSING: FOR THE FOOD
(traditionally attributed to Moshe)

 BLESSED ARE YOU, Adonai our God, Sovereign of the universe, who nourishes the whole world. Your kindness endures forever. May we never be in want of food, for God provides for all the creatures which God has created. **Blessed are You, Adonai, who feeds all.**

Ba-ruch ata Adonai
Elo-hei-nu me-lech ha-olam,
Ha-zan et ha-olam ku-lo b'tuvo,
b'chein, b'chesed, u-v'ra-cha-meem.
Hu no-ten le-chem l'chol ba-sar,
kee l'olam chas-do.
Uv-tu-vo ha-gadol, ta-meed lo chasar lanu,
v'al yech-sar lanu ma-zon, l'olam va-ed.
Ba-avur sh'mo ha-gadol,
kee hu Eil zan um-far-neis la-kol
U-mei-teev la-kol, u-mei-cheen ma-zon
l'chol bree-yo-tav asher ba-ra,
Baruch ata Adonai, ha-zan et ha-kol.

בָּרוּךְ אַתָּה יי,
אֱלֹהֵינוּ מֶלֶךְ הָעוֹלָם,
הַזָּן אֶת הָעוֹלָם כֻּלּוֹ בְּטוּבוֹ
בְּחֵן בְּחֶסֶד וּבְרַחֲמִים.
הוּא נוֹתֵן לֶחֶם לְכָל בָּשָׂר
כִּי לְעוֹלָם חַסְדוֹ.
וּבְטוּבוֹ הַגָּדוֹל תָּמִיד לֹא חָסַר לָנוּ,
וְאַל יֶחְסַר לָנוּ מָזוֹן לְעוֹלָם וָעֶד.
בַּעֲבוּר שְׁמוֹ הַגָּדוֹל,
כִּי הוּא אֵל זָן וּמְפַרְנֵס לַכֹּל
וּמֵטִיב לַכֹּל, וּמֵכִין מָזוֹן
לְכֹל בְּרִיּוֹתָיו אֲשֶׁר בָּרָא.
בָּרוּךְ אַתָּה יי, הַזָּן אֶת הַכֹּל.

...will reap with joy!
...בְּרִנָּה יִקְצֹרוּ!

SECOND BLESSING: FOR THE LAND AND THE FOOD
(attributed to Joshua)

WE THANK YOU, Adonai our God, for having given us a beautiful, good, and spacious land; for having taken us out of Egypt and redeemed us from the house of slavery; for your covenant which You sealed in our flesh; for your Torah which You have taught us; for the life, grace and kindness You have granted us; and for the food which sustains us at all times.

THE TORAH says: *"After you have eaten and are satisfied, you shall bless Adonai your God for the good land God has given you."* (Deut. 8:10) **Blessed are You, Adonai, for the land and for the food.**

Ka-ka-tuv v'achal-ta, v'sa-vata u-vei-rach-ta, et Adonai Elo-he-cha, al ha-aretz ha-tova asher natan lach. Ba-ruch ata Adonai, al ha-aretz v'al ha-mazon.

נוֹדֶה לְּךָ יי אֱלֹהֵינוּ עַל שֶׁהִנְחַלְתָּ לַאֲבוֹתֵינוּ, אֶרֶץ חֶמְדָּה טוֹבָה וּרְחָבָה, וְעַל שֶׁהוֹצֵאתָנוּ יי אֱלֹהֵינוּ מֵאֶרֶץ מִצְרַיִם, וּפְדִיתָנוּ, מִבֵּית עֲבָדִים, וְעַל בְּרִיתְךָ שֶׁחָתַמְתָּ בִּבְשָׂרֵנוּ, וְעַל תּוֹרָתְךָ שֶׁלִּמַּדְתָּנוּ, וְעַל חֻקֶּיךָ שֶׁהוֹדַעְתָּנוּ וְעַל חַיִּים חֵן וָחֶסֶד שֶׁחוֹנַנְתָּנוּ, וְעַל אֲכִילַת מָזוֹן שָׁאַתָּה זָן וּמְפַרְנֵס אוֹתָנוּ תָּמִיד, בְּכָל יוֹם וּבְכָל עֵת וּבְכָל שָׁעָה.

וְעַל הַכֹּל יי אֱלֹהֵינוּ אֲנַחְנוּ מוֹדִים לָךְ, וּמְבָרְכִים אוֹתָךְ, יִתְבָּרַךְ שִׁמְךָ בְּפִי כָּל חַי תָּמִיד לְעוֹלָם וָעֶד.

כַּכָּתוּב: "וְאָכַלְתָּ וְשָׂבָעְתָּ, וּבֵרַכְתָּ אֶת יי אֱלֹהֶיךָ עַל הָאָרֶץ הַטֹּבָה אֲשֶׁר נָתַן לָךְ." **בָּרוּךְ אַתָּה יי, עַל הָאָרֶץ וְעַל הַמָּזוֹן.**

THIRD BLESSING: FOR JERUSALEM
(attributed to David)

HAVE MERCY, Adonai our God, on Israel your people, on Jerusalem your city, on Zion Your dwelling place, on the house of David your anointed Messiah, and on the holy Temple that bears your name. Our Divine Parent, take care of us and support us, grant us relief from all our troubles, release us from reliance on the gifts and loans of human beings, that we may never be put to shame and disgrace. Let us be dependent only on your open-handed generosity.

רַחֵם נָא יי אֱלֹהֵינוּ, עַל יִשְׂרָאֵל עַמֶּךָ, וְעַל יְרוּשָׁלַיִם עִירֶךָ, וְעַל צִיּוֹן מִשְׁכַּן כְּבוֹדֶךָ, וְעַל מַלְכוּת בֵּית דָּוִד מְשִׁיחֶךָ, וְעַל הַבַּיִת הַגָּדוֹל וְהַקָּדוֹשׁ שֶׁנִּקְרָא שִׁמְךָ עָלָיו. אֱלֹהֵינוּ, אָבִינוּ, רְעֵנוּ, זוּנֵנוּ, פַּרְנְסֵנוּ, וְכַלְכְּלֵנוּ, וְהַרְוִיחֵנוּ, וְהַרְוַח לָנוּ יי אֱלֹהֵינוּ מְהֵרָה מִכָּל צָרוֹתֵינוּ, וְנָא, אַל תַּצְרִיכֵנוּ יי אֱלֹהֵינוּ, לֹא לִידֵי מַתְּנַת בָּשָׂר וָדָם, וְלֹא לִידֵי הַלְוָאָתָם. כִּי אִם לְיָדְךָ הַמְּלֵאָה, הַפְּתוּחָה, הַקְּדוֹשָׁה וְהָרְחָבָה, שֶׁלֹּא נֵבוֹשׁ וְלֹא נִכָּלֵם לְעוֹלָם וָעֶד.

[On Shabbat add]:
[On this great and holy Shabbat, we abstain from work and we rest according to your will. Grant us tranquility so that there be no sorrow and grief on our day of rest. Let us live to see Jerusalem your holy city rebuilt, for You are Master of all redemption and comfort.]

רְצֵה וְהַחֲלִיצֵנוּ יי אֱלֹהֵינוּ בְּמִצְוֹתֶיךָ וּבְמִצְוַת יוֹם הַשְּׁבִיעִי הַשַּׁבָּת הַגָּדוֹל וְהַקָּדוֹשׁ הַזֶּה. כִּי יוֹם זֶה גָּדוֹל וְקָדוֹשׁ הוּא לְפָנֶיךָ, לִשְׁבָּת בּוֹ וְלָנוּחַ בּוֹ בְּאַהֲבָה כְּמִצְוַת רְצוֹנֶךָ וּבִרְצוֹנְךָ הָנִיחַ לָנוּ יי אֱלֹהֵינוּ, שֶׁלֹּא תְהֵא צָרָה וְיָגוֹן וַאֲנָחָה בְּיוֹם מְנוּחָתֵנוּ. וְהַרְאֵנוּ יי אֱלֹהֵינוּ בְּנֶחָמַת צִיּוֹן עִירֶךָ, וּבְבִנְיַן יְרוּשָׁלַיִם עִיר קָדְשֶׁךָ, כִּי אַתָּה הוּא בַּעַל הַיְשׁוּעוֹת וּבַעַל הַנֶּחָמוֹת.

Kadesh
Urchatz
Karpas
Yachatz
Maggid
Rachtza
Motzi
Matza
Maror
Korech
Shulchan Orech
Tzafun
Barech
Blessing after Eating

GOD, may your memories of us, of our ancestors, of the son of David your servant, of Jerusalem your holy city, and of all your people the house of Israel, ascend and be acceptable before you, for life and peace. On this day of the **Feast of Matzot**, remember us, Adonai our God, for goodness; consider us for blessing; save us for life for we look to you, for you are a gracious and merciful God and Sovereign.

אֱלֹהֵינוּ וֵאלֹהֵי אֲבוֹתֵינוּ, **יַעֲלֶה וְיָבֹא**, וְיַגִּיעַ, וְיֵרָאֶה, וְיֵרָצֶה, וְיִשָּׁמַע, וְיִפָּקֵד, וְיִזָּכֵר זִכְרוֹנֵנוּ וּפִקְדוֹנֵנוּ, וְזִכְרוֹן אֲבוֹתֵינוּ, וְזִכְרוֹן מָשִׁיחַ בֶּן דָּוִד עַבְדֶּךָ, וְזִכְרוֹן יְרוּשָׁלַיִם עִיר קָדְשֶׁךָ, וְזִכְרוֹן כָּל עַמְּךָ בֵּית יִשְׂרָאֵל לְפָנֶיךָ, לִפְלֵיטָה לְטוֹבָה לְחֵן וּלְחֶסֶד וּלְרַחֲמִים, לְחַיִּים וּלְשָׁלוֹם **בְּיוֹם חַג הַמַּצּוֹת הַזֶּה**. זָכְרֵנוּ יי אֱלֹהֵינוּ בּוֹ לְטוֹבָה. וּפָקְדֵנוּ בוֹ לִבְרָכָה. וְהוֹשִׁיעֵנוּ בוֹ לְחַיִּים, וּבִדְבַר יְשׁוּעָה וְרַחֲמִים, חוּס וְחָנֵּנוּ, וְרַחֵם עָלֵינוּ וְהוֹשִׁיעֵנוּ, כִּי אֵלֶיךָ עֵינֵינוּ, כִּי אֵל מֶלֶךְ חַנּוּן וְרַחוּם אָתָּה.

REBUILD JERUSALEM the holy city quickly in our days. **Blessed are You, Adonai, who rebuilds Jerusalem in mercy. Amen.**

*U-v'nei Yeru-sha-layeem eer ha-kodesh
beem-hei-ra b'ya-meinu.
Ba-ruch ata Adonai,
Bo-neh v'ra-cha-mav, Yeru-sha-layeem, Amen.*

וּבְנֵה יְרוּשָׁלַיִם עִיר הַקֹּדֶשׁ בִּמְהֵרָה בְּיָמֵינוּ. בָּרוּךְ אַתָּה יי, בּוֹנֵה בְרַחֲמָיו יְרוּשָׁלַיִם. אָמֵן.

FOURTH BLESSING: FOR DIVINE GOODNESS
(written after the defeat of the Bar Kochba Revolt 135 C.E.)

BLESSED ARE YOU, Adonai our God, Sovereign of the universe. You are our Parent, our Sovereign, our Creator, and our Redeemer, the Shepherd of Israel. You grant favors to us constantly. You lavish us with kindness and mercy, success and blessing, comfort and support, life and peace. May You never deprive us of any good thing.

בָּרוּךְ אַתָּה יי אֱלֹהֵינוּ מֶלֶךְ הָעוֹלָם, הָאֵל אָבִינוּ, מַלְכֵּנוּ, אַדִּירֵנוּ בּוֹרְאֵנוּ, גּוֹאֲלֵנוּ, יוֹצְרֵנוּ, קְדוֹשֵׁנוּ קְדוֹשׁ יַעֲקֹב, רוֹעֵנוּ רוֹעֵה יִשְׂרָאֵל. הַמֶּלֶךְ הַטּוֹב, וְהַמֵּטִיב לַכֹּל, שֶׁבְּכָל יוֹם וָיוֹם הוּא הֵטִיב, הוּא מֵטִיב, הוּא יֵיטִיב לָנוּ. הוּא גְמָלָנוּ, הוּא גוֹמְלֵנוּ, הוּא יִגְמְלֵנוּ לָעַד לְחֵן וּלְחֶסֶד וּלְרַחֲמִים וּלְרֶוַח הַצָּלָה וְהַצְלָחָה בְּרָכָה וִישׁוּעָה, נֶחָמָה, פַּרְנָסָה וְכַלְכָּלָה, וְרַחֲמִים, וְחַיִּים וְשָׁלוֹם, וְכָל טוֹב, וּמִכָּל טוּב לְעוֹלָם אַל יְחַסְּרֵנוּ.

MAY the Merciful One reign over us forever.
MAY the Merciful One grant us an honorable livelihood.
MAY the Merciful One break the yoke from our neck, and lead us upright into our land.
MAY the Merciful One send ample blessing into this house and upon this table at which we have eaten.
MAY the Merciful One send us Elijah the prophet who will bring us good tidings of consolation and comfort.

הָרַחֲמָן, הוּא יִמְלוֹךְ עָלֵינוּ לְעוֹלָם וָעֶד.
הָרַחֲמָן, הוּא יִתְבָּרַךְ בַּשָּׁמַיִם וּבָאָרֶץ.
הָרַחֲמָן, הוּא יִשְׁתַּבַּח לְדוֹר דּוֹרִים, וְיִתְפָּאַר בָּנוּ לָעַד וּלְנֵצַח נְצָחִים, וְיִתְהַדַּר בָּנוּ לָעַד וּלְעוֹלְמֵי עוֹלָמִים.
הָרַחֲמָן, הוּא יְפַרְנְסֵנוּ בְּכָבוֹד.
הָרַחֲמָן, הוּא יִשְׁבּוֹר עֻלֵּנוּ מֵעַל צַוָּארֵנוּ וְהוּא יוֹלִיכֵנוּ קוֹמְמִיּוּת לְאַרְצֵנוּ.
הָרַחֲמָן, הוּא יִשְׁלַח לָנוּ בְּרָכָה מְרֻבָּה בַּבַּיִת הַזֶּה, וְעַל שֻׁלְחָן זֶה שֶׁאָכַלְנוּ עָלָיו.
הָרַחֲמָן, הוּא יִשְׁלַח לָנוּ

*HaRa-cha-man, hu yee-sh'lach lanu,
et Ei-lee-ya-hu ha-na-vee, za-chur la-tov,
vee-vaser lanu, b'sorot to-vot,
y'shu-ot v'ne-chamot.*

אֶת אֵלִיָּהוּ הַנָּבִיא זָכוּר לַטּוֹב, וִיבַשֶּׂר לָנוּ בְּשׂוֹרוֹת טוֹבוֹת יְשׁוּעוֹת וְנֶחָמוֹת.

MAY GOD BLESS (the hosts or my guests, my father, my mother, my grandparents, my spouse, my children, my grandchildren, my uncles and aunts, my cousins) myself and everyone gathered here, just as you blessed our ancestors with a complete blessing.

(You may wish to add personalized good wishes in Hebrew or English such as mazal tov for a newly married couple.)

הָרַחֲמָן, הוּא יְבָרֵךְ אֶת כָּל הַמְסֻבִּין כָּאן, אוֹתָנוּ וְאֶת כָּל אֲשֶׁר לָנוּ, כְּמוֹ שֶׁנִּתְבָּרְכוּ אֲבוֹתֵינוּ, אַבְרָהָם יִצְחָק וְיַעֲקֹב. בַּכֹּל, מִכֹּל, כֹּל, כֵּן יְבָרֵךְ אוֹתָנוּ כֻּלָּנוּ יַחַד. בִּבְרָכָה שְׁלֵמָה, וְנֹאמַר אָמֵן.

MAY HEAVEN find merit in us. May we find favor and good sense in the eyes of God and human beings.

Ba-ma-rom y'lamdu alei-hem v'alei-nu
z'chut she-t'hei l'meesh-meret shalom,
v'neesa v'racha mei-eit Adonai
u-tzedaka mei-Elohei yeesh-einu
v'neemtza chein v'seichel tov
b'einei Eloheem v'Adam.

בַּמָּרוֹם יְלַמְּדוּ עֲלֵיהֶם וְעָלֵינוּ זְכוּת, שֶׁתְּהֵא לְמִשְׁמֶרֶת שָׁלוֹם, וְנִשָּׂא בְרָכָה מֵאֵת יי וּצְדָקָה מֵאלֹהֵי יִשְׁעֵנוּ, וְנִמְצָא חֵן וְשֵׂכֶל טוֹב בְּעֵינֵי אֱלֹהִים וְאָדָם.

[On Shabbat]:
[May the Merciful One let us inherit the day which will be an era of perfect Shabbat rest, a time of eternal life.]

הָרַחֲמָן, הוּא יַנְחִילֵנוּ יוֹם שֶׁכֻּלּוֹ שַׁבָּת וּמְנוּחָה לְחַיֵּי הָעוֹלָמִים.

MAY the Merciful One let us inherit the day of total goodness.

הָרַחֲמָן, הוּא יַנְחִילֵנוּ יוֹם שֶׁכֻּלּוֹ טוֹב.

MAY the Merciful One bless the State of Israel.

הָרַחֲמָן, הוּא יְבָרֵךְ אֶת מְדִינַת יִשְׂרָאֵל.

MAY the Merciful One grant peace between the children of Jacob and the children of Ishmael.

הָרַחֲמָן, הוּא יַשְׁכִּין שָׁלוֹם בֵּין בְּנֵי יַעֲקֹב וּבְנֵי יִשְׁרָאֵל.

MAY the Merciful One enable us to live in the days of the Messiah and earn the world to come.

הָרַחֲמָן, הוּא יְזַכֵּנוּ לִימוֹת הַמָּשִׁיחַ וּלְחַיֵּי הָעוֹלָם הַבָּא.

GOD IS A TOWER OF STRENGTH, who shows kindness to David and his offspring forever.

GOD WHO CREATES PEACE in the heavenly heights, may You grant peace for us and for all Israel; and say, Amen.

Meegdol y'shu-ot mal-ko,
v'oseh chesed leem-shee-cho,
l'-David u-l'zaro ad olam.
Oseh shalom beem-romav,
hu ya-aseh shalom, aleinu
v'al kol yisrael v'eemru Amen.

מִגְדּוֹל יְשׁוּעוֹת מַלְכּוֹ, וְעֹשֶׂה חֶסֶד לִמְשִׁיחוֹ לְדָוִד וּלְזַרְעוֹ עַד עוֹלָם. עֹשֶׂה שָׁלוֹם בִּמְרוֹמָיו, הוּא יַעֲשֶׂה שָׁלוֹם, עָלֵינוּ וְעַל כָּל יִשְׂרָאֵל, וְאִמְרוּ אָמֵן.

Kadesh
Urchatz
Karpas
Yachatz
Maggid
Rachtza
Motzi
Matza
Maror
Korech
Shulchan Orech
Tzafun
Barech

Blessing after Eating and Third Cup

"GIVE THANKS to Adonai, for God is good; God's kindness endures forever." *(Psalm 118:1)* "You open your hand and satisfy the desire of every living thing." *(Psalm 145:16)* "Blessed is the one who trusts in Adonai, and for whom Adonai provides security." *(Jeremiah 17:7)*

"יִרְאוּ אֶת יי קְדֹשָׁיו, כִּי אֵין מַחְסוֹר לִירֵאָיו.
כְּפִירִים רָשׁוּ וְרָעֵבוּ, וְדוֹרְשֵׁי יי לֹא יַחְסְרוּ כָל טוֹב.
הוֹדוּ לַיי כִּי טוֹב, כִּי לְעוֹלָם חַסְדּוֹ.
פּוֹתֵחַ אֶת יָדֶךָ, וּמַשְׂבִּיעַ לְכָל חַי רָצוֹן.
בָּרוּךְ הַגֶּבֶר אֲשֶׁר יִבְטַח בַּיי, וְהָיָה יי מִבְטַחוֹ."

"I HAVE BEEN YOUNG and now I am old, but never have I seen the righteous forsaken, nor their children wanting bread." *(Psalm 37:25)* "Adonai will give strength to his people; Adonai will bless them with peace." *(Psalms 29:11)*

*Na-ar ha-yeetee gam zakantee,
v'lo-raeeti tzaddik ne-e-zav
v'zaro m'vakesh la-chem.
Adonai oz l'amo yee-tein,
Adonai y'varech et amo va-shalom.*

נַעַר הָיִיתִי גַם זָקַנְתִּי
וְלֹא רָאִיתִי צַדִּיק נֶעֱזָב,
וְזַרְעוֹ מְבַקֶּשׁ לָחֶם.
יי עֹז לְעַמּוֹ יִתֵּן,
יי יְבָרֵךְ אֶת עַמּוֹ בַשָּׁלוֹם.

The Third Cup

כּוֹס שְׁלִישִׁי

We conclude the Blessing over the Meal by drinking the Third Cup, the cup of Blessing, while reclining to the left.

HERE I AM, ready to perform the mitzvah of the third cup of wine, which concludes this Pesach meal.

הִנְנִי מוּכָן וּמְזֻמָּן לְקַיֵּם
מִצְוַת כּוֹס שְׁלִישִׁי
שֶׁל אַרְבַּע כּוֹסוֹת.

❖ BLESSED ARE YOU, Adonai, our God, Sovereign of the Universe, who creates the fruit of the vine.

*Ba-rukh ata Adonai
Elo-hei-nu me-lech ha-olam,
bo-rei pree ha-gafen.*

בָּרוּךְ אַתָּה יי,
אֱלֹהֵינוּ מֶלֶךְ הָעוֹלָם,
בּוֹרֵא פְּרִי הַגָּפֶן.

Cup of Elijah

כּוֹס אֵלִיָּהוּ

❖ 1. **Pour** *a large cup of wine in honor of Elijah.*

2. **Open** *the door for Elijah.*

   Now the seder *focuses on the hope for future redemption symbolized by Elijah the Prophet, bearer of good news.*
   In Egypt the doors of the house were shut tight on the night of the Tenth Plague. Blood marked the lintels and doorposts where we now place the mezuzah. However in the contemporary seder the doors are opened wide in expectation. This is no longer a night of terror but the dawn of hope. It is, as the Torah calls it, a **Night of Watching** *in expectation of great changes for the better.*

(See the tale of the African American Watch Night of December 31, 1862, in the supplement, Contemporary Seder Stories, S-27)

Marc Chagall,
Opening the Door for Elijah (1946)
© ADAGP, Paris (1996)

Kadesh

Urchatz

Karpas

Yachatz

Maggid

Rachtza

Motzi

Matza

Maror

Korech

Shulchan Orech

Tzafun

Barech

Elijah's Cup

138

An Open Door: A Menu of Meanings

THE OPENING of the door on Pesach is a universal custom in Jewish homes, but its explanations are as varied as can be. Here is a sample of its multiple meanings:

1. Trust in Divine Security. While night time is generally a time of fear and vulnerability to attack, on seder night the Jews show their confidence in Divine surveillance. Seder night is called **the Night of Watching** (*leil sheemureem*) in which God protected us from the plague of the first born and the persecution of the Egyptians. Therefore, there is no reason to lock one's doors or even to keep them closed tonight. Our electronic security systems can be switched off.

2. Expectation of Redemption. The door is opened in expectation of redemption. As Rabbi Joshua said, "Just as Israel was redeemed from Egypt in the month of Nisan (on Pesach), so are we destined to be redeemed again — once and for all — in Nisan in the future." Elijah is expected to visit, bringing good tidings of the coming of the Messiah.

3. Fear of the Blood Libel. Medieval folklore suggests a pragmatic reason for opening the door: the fear of spies and informers who might accuse the Jews of drinking the blood of a Christian child or using it for making matza. The Jews wanted to see who might be **eavesdropping** and spreading malicious — in fact, deadly — rumors about the seder.

Anne Frank: I Still Believe

That's the difficulty in these times: ideals, dreams, and cherished hopes rise within us, only to meet the horrible truth and be shattered.

It's really a wonder that I haven't dropped all my ideals, because they seem so absurd and impossible to carry out. Yet I keep them, because in spite of everything I still believe that people are really good at heart. I simply can't build up my hopes on a foundation consisting of confusion, misery, and death. I see the world gradually being turned into a wilderness. I hear the ever-approaching thunder, which will destroy us, too. I can feel the suffering of millions — and yet, if I look up into the heavens, I think it will come out all right, that this cruelty too will end, and that peace and tranquility will return again.

In the meantime, I must uphold my ideals, for perhaps the time will come when I shall be able to carry them out.

(Diary of Anne Frank, Amsterdam 1944)

Filling the Cup of Redemption Ourselves

The Hassidic rebbe Naftali Tzvi Horowitz (died 1817) used to invite all the participants of the seder — in order of their place at the table — to pour from their personal cup into Elijah's cup. This symbolizes the need for everyone to make their own personal contribution to awaken the divine forces of redemption by beginning with human efforts (*heet-o-ra-rut dee-l'ta-ta*).

In some families, each participant helps to fill Elijah's cup of future redemption while expressing a particular wish for a better year.

Welcoming Elijah

בָּרוּךְ הַבָּא

Welcome Elijah *with the traditional greeting "Baruch Ha-Ba" and a prayer or song.*

Kadesh
Urchatz
Karpas
Yachatz
Maggid
Rachtza
Motzi
Matza
Maror
Korech
Shulchan
Orech
Tzafun
Barech
Elijah's
Cup

THE PRAYER FOR ELIJAH

by The Maharal of Prague (16th C. — associated with the legend of the Golem, the Jewish precursor of Frankenstein)

HaRachaman! May the Merciful One send Elijah the prophet to announce good news about redemption and comfort — just as You promised: *"Here, I will send you Elijah the prophet before Adonai's great and awesome day.* **He will reconcile the hearts of parents to their children and children to their parents . . . ."** *(Malachi 3:24)*

הָרַחֲמָן, הוּא יִשְׁלַח לָנוּ אֶת אֵלִיָּהוּ
הַנָּבִיא זָכוּר לַטוֹב, וִיבַשֶּׂר לָנוּ בְּשׂוֹרוֹת
טוֹבוֹת יְשׁוּעוֹת וְנֶחָמוֹת. כָּאָמוּר: "הִנֵּה
אָנֹכִי שֹׁלֵחַ לָכֶם אֶת אֵלִיָּה הַנָּבִיא לִפְנֵי
בוֹא יוֹם יְהוָה הַגָּדוֹל וְהַנּוֹרָא, וְהֵשִׁיב לֵב
אָבוֹת עַל בָּנִים וְלֵב בָּנִים עַל אֲבוֹתָם."

(מלאכי ג, כג–כד)

MESSIANIC SONGS OF HOPE

ELIJAH the prophet,	*Eliyahu ha-navee*	אֵלִיָּהוּ הַנָּבִיא
Elijah the Tishbee,	*Eliyahu ha-Tish-bee*	אֵלִיָּהוּ הַתִּשְׁבִּי,
Elijah the Giladee!	*Eliyahu ha-Giladee*	אֵלִיָּהוּ הַגִּלְעָדִי
May he soon come to us	*beem-hei-ra v'ya-mei-nu yavo ei-leinu*	בִּמְהֵרָה בְיָמֵינוּ יָבוֹא אֵלֵינוּ
Along with the Messiah, son of David.	*eem ma-shee-ach ben David.*	עִם מָשִׁיחַ בֶּן דָּוִד.

I BELIEVE with a perfect faith	*Anee ma-a-meen b'eh-eh-mu-na shlei-ma*	אֲנִי מַאֲמִין בֶּאֱמוּנָה שְׁלֵמָה
in the coming of the Messiah	*b'vee-at ha-ma-shee-ach*	בְּבִיאַת הַמָּשִׁיחַ,
and even though he delays	*v'af-al-pee she-yeet-ma-mei-ah*	וְאַף עַל פִּי שֶׁיִּתְמַהֲמֵהַּ,
I will await	*eem kol zeh acha-keh lo*	עִם כָּל זֶה אֲחַכֶּה לוֹ
the day of his coming.	*b'chol yom she-yavo.*	בְּכָל יוֹם שֶׁיָּבוֹא.

AS THE SEDER winds down, the memory of the historic Exodus gives way to hopes for the messianic future. During thousands of years since the original liberation from Egypt, the Jews have often been forced to commemorate the origins of their national freedom in conditions of oppression and even extermination. The memory of past miracles reinforced their belief that rescue could come again in the most unexpected ways.

But what is the vision we desire for the future? How does the experience of being a victim shape our dream of being a victor? The **cup of Elijah** came to represent two possibilities. The primary motif embodied in the Biblical verses of *"Pour out Your Wrath"* is the pain-nourished demand for bringing the persecutors to justice. "Never again" merges with a desire for Divine wrath and for righteous vengeance to assuage the pain of humiliation and to silence the sadism of the oppressor. Yet the Zionist national poet H.N. Bialik wrote, *"The appropriate vengeance for the murder of a child has not been conceived even by Satan himself."* Such dark thoughts tend to polarize Jew and gentile and to perpetuate the memory of pain.

However, the messianic vision can also encompass reconciliation and a forward-looking justice for Israel and for all nations. Elijah also symbolizes the reconciliation of parent and child, of those alienated one from another.

Holocaust and Hope

At the darkest moment, the Warsaw Ghetto Uprising revived Jewish hope and honor. After 450,000 Jews had already been deported, the Jewish youth movements mounted armed resistance that reached its climax on seder night, 1943.

The Last Passover in the Warsaw Ghetto

Read the following dramatization, drawn from authentic memoirs by Vladislav Pavlak. It captures the conflicting views of Passover, 1943. You may assign a narrator and three voices (A,B,C) to read it in parts.

N: It was April 19, 1943, the first day in the renewed defense of the ghetto.

A: Do you know what day this is?

B: Monday. The 19th of April.

A: No, no, I don't mean that. But do you know that today is a holiday?

B: What, is he crazy? We're dying and he blabbers about holidays.

A: I am telling you, today is a great holiday. It is Passover, the seder night.

B: If it makes you happy, why don't you conduct seder for yourself? Passover without matza and maror! What kind of Passover is that?

A: We need no bitter herbs. Sufficient bitterness and humiliation have been our lot. Are we not slaves? Are we not orphans who have been forsaken? We need no wine, let us drink water. We need no matzot. Our bread is the bread of affliction.

N: They read the Haggadah aloud. When they came to the words:

"And Adonai has freed us from the bondage of Egypt," someone interrupted.

B: It's a lie, I'm telling you. God has never freed us from bondage, for it follows us wherever we go. We were slaves by the rivers of Babylon, in Spain and now, again we are slaves, and as slaves do we die.

C: The commander spoke: Quiet! Fools! He was right when he said that today we celebrate a holiday. Passover is a holiday of freedom. Don't you see that we are free? No longer do we listen to orders. They tell us: Come out of your hiding — and we refuse to come out. They lure us with promises, and we answer with gunfire. We have thrown off the armbands which they made us wear for our humiliation and we turned them into banners. Today is the day of freedom, and that freedom is within us. We will go down in defeat but we will die as free men and women.

Pour Out Your Wrath

שְׁפֹךְ חֲמָתְךָ

1. *As the seder* comes to an end, not only do we recall the moment of the liberation from Egypt, but we also pray for redemption from our contemporary persecutors.

2. *Stand and read* the demand that our oppressors be brought to the bench of Divine Justice.

"**POUR OUT** your fury on the nations
that do not know you,
upon the kingdoms
that do not invoke your name,
for they have devoured Jacob
and desolated his home." *(Psalms 79:6,7)*

Sh'foch cha-mat-cha
el ha-goyim asher lo y'da-ucha,
v'al ha-mam-la-chot asher
b'sheem-cha lo ka-ra-u.
Kee achal et Ya-acov
ve'et na-vei-hu hei-shamu.

"שְׁפֹךְ חֲמָתְךָ
אֶל הַגּוֹיִם, אֲשֶׁר לֹא יְדָעוּךָ,
וְעַל מַמְלָכוֹת אֲשֶׁר
בְּשִׁמְךָ לֹא קָרָאוּ.
כִּי אָכַל אֶת יַעֲקֹב.
וְאֶת נָוֵהוּ הֵשַׁמּוּ."

"**POUR OUT** your wrath on them;
may your blazing anger overtake them." *(Psalms 69:25)*

Sh'foch alei-hem za-a-me-cha
va-cha-ron ap-cha ya-see-geim.

"שְׁפֹךְ עֲלֵיהֶם זַעְמֶךָ,
וַחֲרוֹן אַפְּךָ יַשִּׂיגֵם."

"**PURSUE** them in wrath and destroy them from under the heavens of Adonai!" *(Lamentations 3:66)*

Teer-dof b'af v'tash-mee-deim
mee-tachat shmei Adonai.

"תִּרְדֹּף בְּאַף וְתַשְׁמִידֵם,
מִתַּחַת שְׁמֵי יְיָ."

Pour Out Your Love
On Our Allies: The Righteous Gentiles

POUR OUT your love on the nations who have known you and on the kingdoms who call upon your name. For they show loving-kindness to the seed of Jacob and they defend your people Israel from those who would devour them alive. May they live to see the sukkah of peace spread over your chosen ones and to participate in the joy of your nations.

שְׁפֹךְ אַהֲבָתְךָ עַל הַגּוֹיִם אֲשֶׁר
יְדָעוּךָ וְעַל מַמְלָכוֹת אֲשֶׁר
בְּשִׁמְךָ קוֹרְאִים בִּגְלַל חֲסָדִים
שֶׁהֵם עוֹשִׂים עִם יַעֲקֹב וּמְגִנִּים
עַל עַמְּךָ יִשְׂרָאֵל מִפְּנֵי
אוֹכְלֵיהֶם. יִזְכּוּ לִרְאוֹת בְּסֻכַּת
בְּחִירֶיךָ וְלִשְׂמוֹחַ בְּשִׂמְחַת גּוֹיֶיךָ.

Kadesh
Urchatz
Karpas
Yachatz
Maggid
Rachtza
Motzi
Matza
Maror
Korech
Shulchan Orech
Tzafun
Barech

Pour Out Your Wrath

'Your Wrath':
A Late Addition

IT WAS NOT until the bloody Crusades that Biblical verses of Divine anger were added to the Haggadah, for pogroms typically occurred on Easter/Passover.

'Your Love':
A Later Addition

THIS UNIQUE addition to a medieval Haggadah appears side by side with *"Pour out your wrath"* in a manuscript from Worms (1521) attributed to the descendants of Rashi. Scholars today debate its authenticity but its sentiment for righteous gentiles is genuine.

Righteous Gentiles

IN 1942 THE DANISH KING Christian X wrote in his diary that if Danish Jewry had to wear the yellow star, then "we would best meet it by all wearing the Star of David." On Rosh HaShanah 1943, the Germans planned a secret roundup of all the Jews. But the Danish underground spirited away almost all of the 8,000 Danish Jews the night before. They crossed the sea in little boats to neutral Sweden. An activist pastor explained:

"We are Christians; Abraham is our spiritual father and the Jews are our brothers. How could it be possible to be Christians without helping? People who called themselves Christians in other countries were really not Christians!"

Opening the Door for Elijah   *Moritz Oppenheim (19th C. Germany)*

The Fourth Cup and the Festival Hallel

כּוֹס רְבִיעִי וְהַלֵּל

1. **The Pesach seder** is divided into two parts by the meal itself. In fact, Hallel (*Psalms 113-118*) itself is split. While the first half of the seder and of the Hallel (*Psalms 113-114*) is dedicated to the past, to historical memory of the redemption from Egypt, the second half looks forward to the **future** and ends with the wish: "Next year in Jerusalem." Messianic hope inspires the singing from now through to the completion of the seder. Our mood is joyful anticipation of a better world.

2. **Fill the fourth cup** of wine and place it before you and conclude singing the Festival Hallel.

NOT TO US, Adonai, not to us,
but to your name bring glory
for the sake of your love and your faithfulness.
    Let the nations not say, "Where, now, is their God?"
    when our God is in heaven and
    all that God wills, God accomplishes.
Their idols are silver and gold, the work of human hands.
They have mouths, but cannot speak, eyes, but cannot see;
    they have ears, but cannot hear, noses, but cannot smell;
    they have hands, but cannot touch, feet, but cannot walk;
    they can make no sound in their throats.
Those who fashion them, all who trust in them, shall become like them.
Israel, trust in Adonai! God is your help and shield.

לֹא לָנוּ יי לֹא לָנוּ
כִּי לְשִׁמְךָ תֵּן כָּבוֹד,
עַל חַסְדְּךָ עַל אֲמִתֶּךָ.
לָמָּה יֹאמְרוּ הַגּוֹיִם, אַיֵּה נָא אֱלֹהֵיהֶם.
וֵאלֹהֵינוּ בַשָּׁמָיִם
כֹּל אֲשֶׁר חָפֵץ עָשָׂה.
עֲצַבֵּיהֶם כֶּסֶף וְזָהָב, מַעֲשֵׂה יְדֵי אָדָם.
פֶּה לָהֶם וְלֹא יְדַבֵּרוּ, עֵינַיִם לָהֶם וְלֹא יִרְאוּ.
אָזְנַיִם לָהֶם וְלֹא יִשְׁמָעוּ, אַף לָהֶם וְלֹא יְרִיחוּן.
יְדֵיהֶם וְלֹא יְמִישׁוּן, רַגְלֵיהֶם וְלֹא יְהַלֵּכוּ,
לֹא יֶהְגּוּ בִּגְרוֹנָם.
כְּמוֹהֶם יִהְיוּ עֹשֵׂיהֶם, כֹּל אֲשֶׁר בֹּטֵחַ בָּהֶם.
יִשְׂרָאֵל בְּטַח בַּיי, עֶזְרָם וּמָגִנָּם הוּא. בֵּית אַהֲרֹן בִּטְחוּ בַיי,
עֶזְרָם וּמָגִנָּם הוּא. יִרְאֵי יי בִּטְחוּ בַיי, עֶזְרָם וּמָגִנָּם הוּא.

ADONAI is mindful of us. God will bless us;
God will bless the house of Israel;
God will bless the house of Aaron;
God will bless those who fear Adonai, small and great alike.
    May Adonai increase your numbers, yours and your children's also.
    May you be blessed by Adonai, Maker of heaven and earth.
The heavens belong to Adonai,
but the earth God gave over to humankind.
    The dead cannot praise Adonai, nor any who go down into silence.
    But we will bless Adonai, now and forever, HALLELUJAH. (*Psalm 115*)

יי זְכָרָנוּ יְבָרֵךְ,
יְבָרֵךְ אֶת בֵּית יִשְׂרָאֵל,
יְבָרֵךְ אֶת בֵּית אַהֲרֹן.
יְבָרֵךְ יִרְאֵי יי, הַקְּטַנִּים עִם הַגְּדֹלִים.
יֹסֵף יי, עֲלֵיכֶם, עֲלֵיכֶם וְעַל בְּנֵיכֶם.
בְּרוּכִים אַתֶּם לַיי, עֹשֵׂה שָׁמַיִם וָאָרֶץ.
הַשָּׁמַיִם שָׁמַיִם לַיי,
וְהָאָרֶץ נָתַן לִבְנֵי אָדָם.
לֹא הַמֵּתִים יְהַלְלוּ יָהּ, וְלֹא כָּל יֹרְדֵי דוּמָה.
וַאֲנַחְנוּ נְבָרֵךְ יָהּ, מֵעַתָּה וְעַד עוֹלָם, הַלְלוּיָהּ.

Kadesh
Urchatz
Karpas
Yachatz
Maggid
Rachtza
Motzi
Matza
Maror
Korech
Shulchan Orech
Tzafun
Barech
Hallel
Festival Psalms

I LOVE Adonai

for God hears my voice, my pleas;

for God turns an ear to me, whenever I call.

    The bonds of death encompassed me;

    the torments of Sheol overtook me.

I came upon trouble and sorrow

and I invoked the name of Adonai,

"Adonai, save my life!"

    Adonai is gracious and beneficent;

    our God is compassionate.

Adonai protects the simple;

I was brought low and God saved me.

    Be at rest, once again, my soul,

    for Adonai has been good to you.

You have delivered me from death,

my eyes from tears, my feet from stumbling.

    I shall walk before Adonai in the lands of the living.

    I trust [in Adonai];

out of great suffering I spoke and said rashly,

"All human beings are false."

    How can I repay Adonai

    for all God's bounties to me?

I raise the cup of deliverance

and invoke the name of Adonai.

    I will pay my vows to Adonai

    in the presence of all God's people.

The death of God's faithful ones is grievous in Adonai's sight.

    O Adonai, I am your servant,

    your servant, the child of your maid-servant;

    You have undone the cords that bound me.

I will sacrifice a thanks offering

to You and invoke the name of Adonai.

    I will pay my vows to Adonai

    in the presence of all God's people,

    in the courts of the house of the Adonai,

    in the midst of Jerusalem. HALLELUJAH. (Psalm 116)

PRAISE ADONAI, all you nations; extol God, all you peoples,

for great is Divine love toward us;

the faithfulness of Adonai endures forever. HALLELUJAH. (Psalm 117)

אָהַבְתִּי כִּי יִשְׁמַע יי,

אֶת קוֹלִי תַּחֲנוּנָי.

כִּי הִטָּה אָזְנוֹ לִי וּבְיָמַי אֶקְרָא:

אֲפָפוּנִי חֶבְלֵי מָוֶת,

וּמְצָרֵי שְׁאוֹל מְצָאוּנִי

צָרָה וְיָגוֹן אֶמְצָא.

וּבְשֵׁם יי אֶקְרָא,

אָנָּה יי מַלְּטָה נַפְשִׁי.

חַנּוּן יי וְצַדִּיק,

וֵאלֹהֵינוּ מְרַחֵם.

שֹׁמֵר פְּתָאִים יי

דַּלּוֹתִי וְלִי יְהוֹשִׁיעַ.

שׁוּבִי נַפְשִׁי לִמְנוּחָיְכִי,

כִּי יי גָּמַל עָלָיְכִי.

כִּי חִלַּצְתָּ נַפְשִׁי מִמָּוֶת

אֶת עֵינִי מִן דִּמְעָה, אֶת רַגְלִי מִדֶּחִי.

אֶתְהַלֵּךְ לִפְנֵי יי, בְּאַרְצוֹת הַחַיִּים.

הֶאֱמַנְתִּי כִּי אֲדַבֵּר,

אֲנִי עָנִיתִי מְאֹד. אֲנִי אָמַרְתִּי בְחָפְזִי

כָּל הָאָדָם כֹּזֵב.

מָה אָשִׁיב לַיי,

כָּל תַּגְמוּלוֹהִי עָלָי.

כּוֹס יְשׁוּעוֹת אֶשָּׂא,

וּבְשֵׁם יי אֶקְרָא.

נְדָרַי לַיי אֲשַׁלֵּם,

נֶגְדָה נָּא לְכָל עַמּוֹ.

יָקָר בְּעֵינֵי יי הַמָּוְתָה לַחֲסִידָיו.

אָנָּה יי כִּי אֲנִי עַבְדֶּךָ

אֲנִי עַבְדְּךָ, בֶּן אֲמָתֶךָ

פִּתַּחְתָּ לְמוֹסֵרָי.

לְךָ אֶזְבַּח זֶבַח תּוֹדָה

וּבְשֵׁם יי אֶקְרָא.

נְדָרַי לַיי אֲשַׁלֵּם

נֶגְדָה נָּא לְכָל עַמּוֹ.

בְּחַצְרוֹת בֵּית יי

בְּתוֹכֵכִי יְרוּשָׁלַיִם הַלְלוּיָהּ.

הַלְלוּ אֶת יי, כָּל גּוֹיִם, שַׁבְּחוּהוּ כָּל הָאֻמִּים.

כִּי גָבַר עָלֵינוּ חַסְדּוֹ,

וֶאֱמֶת יי לְעוֹלָם הַלְלוּיָהּ.

GIVE THANKS TO ADONAI, for God is good, God's kindness is forever.
Let Israel declare, "God's kindness is eternal."
Let the house of Aaron declare, "God's kindness is forever."
Let those who fear Adonai declare, "God's kindness is forever."

הוֹדוּ לַיְיָ כִּי טוֹב, כִּי לְעוֹלָם חַסְדּוֹ.
יֹאמַר נָא יִשְׂרָאֵל, כִּי לְעוֹלָם חַסְדּוֹ.
יֹאמְרוּ נָא בֵית אַהֲרֹן, כִּי לְעוֹלָם חַסְדּוֹ.
יֹאמְרוּ נָא יִרְאֵי יְיָ, כִּי לְעוֹלָם חַסְדּוֹ.

I CALLED to Adonai from my narrow prison,
God answered me in the freedom of space.
Adonai is on my side, I have no fear; what can mortals do to me?
With Adonai on my side as my helper, 1 will see the downfall of my foes.
It is better to take refuge in Adonai than to trust in mortals;
it is better to take refuge in Adonai than to trust in the great.
All nations have surrounded me;
in the name of Adonai I will surely cut them off.
They surrounded me;
in the name of Adonai 1 will surely cut them off.
They have surrounded me like bees; they shall be extinguished like burning thorns;
in the name of Adonai I will surely cut them off.
You pressed me hard, I nearly fell; but Adonai helped me.
Adonai is my strength and might; God has become my deliverance.
The tents of the victorious resound with shouts of deliverance:

"The right hand of Adonai is triumphant!
The right hand of Adonai is exalted!
The right hand of Adonai is triumphant!"
I shall not die but live and proclaim the works of Adonai.
Adonai punished me severely, but did not hand me over to death.

מִן הַמֵּצַר קָרָאתִי יָּהּ,
עָנָנִי בַמֶּרְחָב יָהּ.
יְיָ לִי לֹא אִירָא, מַה יַּעֲשֶׂה לִי אָדָם.
יְיָ לִי בְּעֹזְרָי, וַאֲנִי אֶרְאֶה בְשֹׂנְאָי.
טוֹב לַחֲסוֹת בַּיְיָ, מִבְּטֹחַ בָּאָדָם.
טוֹב לַחֲסוֹת בַּיְיָ מִבְּטֹחַ בִּנְדִיבִים.
כָּל גּוֹיִם סְבָבוּנִי
בְּשֵׁם יְיָ כִּי אֲמִילַם.
סַבּוּנִי גַם סְבָבוּנִי
בְּשֵׁם יְיָ כִּי אֲמִילַם.
סַבּוּנִי כִדְבֹרִים דֹּעֲכוּ כְּאֵשׁ קוֹצִים,
בְּשֵׁם יְיָ כִּי אֲמִילַם.
דָּחֹה דְחִיתַנִי לִנְפֹּל, וַיְיָ עֲזָרָנִי.
עָזִּי וְזִמְרָת יָהּ, וַיְהִי לִי לִישׁוּעָה.
קוֹל רִנָּה וִישׁוּעָה בְּאָהֳלֵי צַדִּיקִים,
יְמִין יְיָ עֹשָׂה חָיִל.
יְמִין יְיָ רוֹמֵמָה,
יְמִין יְיָ עֹשָׂה חָיִל.
לֹא אָמוּת כִּי אֶחְיֶה, וַאֲסַפֵּר מַעֲשֵׂי יָהּ.
יַסֹּר יִסְּרַנִּי יָּהּ, וְלַמָּוֶת לֹא נְתָנָנִי.

OPEN THE GATES of victory for me that I may enter them and praise Adonai.
This is the gateway to Adonai — the victorious shall enter through it.
I praise You, for You have answered me, and have become my deliverance.
The stone that the builders rejected has become the chief cornerstone.
This is Adonai's doing; it is marvelous in our sight.
This is the day that Adonai has made — let us exult and rejoice on it.

פִּתְחוּ לִי שַׁעֲרֵי צֶדֶק, אָבֹא בָם אוֹדֶה יָהּ.
זֶה הַשַּׁעַר לַיְיָ, צַדִּיקִים יָבֹאוּ בוֹ.
אוֹדְךָ כִּי עֲנִיתָנִי, וַתְּהִי לִי לִישׁוּעָה. (2x)
אֶבֶן מָאֲסוּ הַבּוֹנִים, הָיְתָה לְרֹאשׁ פִּנָּה. (2x)
מֵאֵת יְיָ הָיְתָה זֹּאת, הִיא נִפְלָאת בְּעֵינֵינוּ. (2x)
זֶה הַיּוֹם עָשָׂה יְיָ, נָגִילָה וְנִשְׂמְחָה בוֹ. (2x)

ADONAI, deliver us!
ADONAI, let us prosper!

אָנָּא יְיָ הוֹשִׁיעָה נָּא. אָנָּא יְיָ הוֹשִׁיעָה נָּא.
אָנָּא יְיָ הַצְלִיחָה נָא. אָנָּא יְיָ הַצְלִיחָה נָא.

May one who enters be blessed in the name of Adonai;
we bless you from the House of Adonai.
Adonai is God; God has given us light;
bind the festival offering to the horns of the altar with cords.
You are my God and I will praise You;
You are my God and I will extol You.
Give thanks to Adonai for God is good,
God's kindness is forever. *(Psalm 118)*

בָּרוּךְ הַבָּא בְּשֵׁם יְיָ, בֵּרַכְנוּכֶם מִבֵּית יְיָ. (2x)
אֵל יְיָ וַיָּאֶר לָנוּ, אִסְרוּ חַג בַּעֲבֹתִים, עַד קַרְנוֹת הַמִּזְבֵּחַ. (2x)
אֵלִי אַתָּה וְאוֹדֶךָּ אֱלֹהַי אֲרוֹמְמֶךָּ. (2x)
הוֹדוּ לַיְיָ כִּי טוֹב, כִּי לְעוֹלָם חַסְדּוֹ. (2x)

יְהַלְלוּךָ יְיָ אֱלֹהֵינוּ כָּל מַעֲשֶׂיךָ, וַחֲסִידֶיךָ צַדִּיקִים עוֹשֵׂי רְצוֹנֶךָ,
וְכָל עַמְּךָ בֵּית יִשְׂרָאֵל בְּרִנָּה יוֹדוּ וִיבָרְכוּ וִישַׁבְּחוּ וִיפָאֲרוּ
וִירוֹמְמוּ וְיַעֲרִיצוּ וְיַקְדִּישׁוּ וְיַמְלִיכוּ אֶת שִׁמְךָ מַלְכֵּנוּ, כִּי לְךָ טוֹב
לְהוֹדוֹת וּלְשִׁמְךָ נָאֶה לְזַמֵּר, כִּי מֵעוֹלָם וְעַד עוֹלָם אַתָּה אֵל.

Kadesh
Urchatz
Karpas
Yachatz
Maggid
Rachtza
Motzi
Matza
Maror
Korech
Shulchan Orech
Tzafun
Barech
Hallel

Great Hallel

The Great Hallel

1. *In addition to* the usual Festival Hallel, on seder night we add the Great Hallel (*Psalm 136*). Both of them feature the famous refrain: *"Give thanks to Adonai, for God is good! God's kindness is forever!"* — *"Kee l'olam chas-do!"*

2. *Some rabbis* require or at least permit that an extra cup be drunk with the Great Hallel. Some people dedicate this fifth cup to the reestablishment of the State of Israel and the ingathering of the exiles. They see Pesach not only as a celebration of liberation from servitude but also as the first step to independence.

Psalm 136: Selected Verses

GIVE THANKS to Adonai for God is good,
For God's kindness is forever.
God struck Egypt's first born,
And brought Israel out of their midst,
With a strong hand and outstretched arm,
God split apart the Sea of Reeds,
And made Israel pass through it,
God hurled Pharaoh and his army
into the Sea of Reeds,
God led the people through the wilderness,
God took note of us in our degradation,
And rescued us from our enemies.
God provides food for all living things,
For God's kindness is forever.

כִּי לְעוֹלָם חַסְדּוֹ!	הוֹדוּ לַיָי כִּי טוֹב,
כִּי לְעוֹלָם חַסְדּוֹ!	הוֹדוּ לֵאלֹהֵי הָאֱלֹהִים,
כִּי לְעוֹלָם חַסְדּוֹ!	הוֹדוּ לַאֲדֹנֵי הָאֲדֹנִים,
כִּי לְעוֹלָם חַסְדּוֹ!	לְעֹשֵׂה נִפְלָאוֹת גְּדֹלוֹת לְבַדּוֹ,
כִּי לְעוֹלָם חַסְדּוֹ!	לְעֹשֵׂה הַשָּׁמַיִם בִּתְבוּנָה,
כִּי לְעוֹלָם חַסְדּוֹ!	לְרוֹקַע הָאָרֶץ עַל הַמָּיִם,
כִּי לְעוֹלָם חַסְדּוֹ!	לְעֹשֵׂה אוֹרִים גְּדֹלִים,
כִּי לְעוֹלָם חַסְדּוֹ!	אֶת הַשֶּׁמֶשׁ לְמֶמְשֶׁלֶת בַּיּוֹם,
כִּי לְעוֹלָם חַסְדּוֹ!	אֶת הַיָּרֵחַ וְכוֹכָבִים לְמֶמְשְׁלוֹת בַּלָּיְלָה,
כִּי לְעוֹלָם חַסְדּוֹ!	לְמַכֵּה מִצְרַיִם בִּבְכוֹרֵיהֶם,
כִּי לְעוֹלָם חַסְדּוֹ!	וַיּוֹצֵא יִשְׂרָאֵל מִתּוֹכָם,
כִּי לְעוֹלָם חַסְדּוֹ!	בְּיָד חֲזָקָה וּבִזְרוֹעַ נְטוּיָה,
כִּי לְעוֹלָם חַסְדּוֹ!	לְגֹזֵר יַם סוּף לִגְזָרִים,
כִּי לְעוֹלָם חַסְדּוֹ!	וְהֶעֱבִיר יִשְׂרָאֵל בְּתוֹכוֹ,
כִּי לְעוֹלָם חַסְדּוֹ!	וְנִעֵר פַּרְעֹה וְחֵילוֹ בְיַם סוּף,
כִּי לְעוֹלָם חַסְדּוֹ!	לְמוֹלִיךְ עַמּוֹ בַּמִּדְבָּר,
כִּי לְעוֹלָם חַסְדּוֹ!	לְמַכֵּה מְלָכִים גְּדֹלִים,
כִּי לְעוֹלָם חַסְדּוֹ!	וַיַּהֲרֹג מְלָכִים אַדִּירִים,
כִּי לְעוֹלָם חַסְדּוֹ!	לְסִיחוֹן מֶלֶךְ הָאֱמֹרִי,
כִּי לְעוֹלָם חַסְדּוֹ!	וּלְעוֹג מֶלֶךְ הַבָּשָׁן,
כִּי לְעוֹלָם חַסְדּוֹ!	וְנָתַן אַרְצָם לְנַחֲלָה,
כִּי לְעוֹלָם חַסְדּוֹ!	נַחֲלָה לְיִשְׂרָאֵל עַבְדּוֹ,
כִּי לְעוֹלָם חַסְדּוֹ!	שֶׁבְּשִׁפְלֵנוּ זָכַר לָנוּ,
כִּי לְעוֹלָם חַסְדּוֹ!	וַיִּפְרְקֵנוּ מִצָּרֵינוּ,
כִּי לְעוֹלָם חַסְדּוֹ!	נוֹתֵן לֶחֶם לְכָל בָּשָׂר,
כִּי לְעוֹלָם חַסְדּוֹ!	הוֹדוּ לְאֵל הַשָּׁמַיִם,

The Blessing After the Hallel

"The Breath of Life Praises You"
Selected Translation

THE LIFE BREATH of every living thing will bless your name, God. Without you we have no king and redeemer, no one to rescue us and to take pity on us in times of trouble and strife.

God, you will not sleep or slumber, you wake the sleeping, give speech to the mute, release prisoners, support the fallen and raise up straight those bent over.

Even if our mouths were as full of song as the sea, our tongues like the waves, our lips like the wide expanses, our eyes like the sun and the moon, our hands spread like the eagles and our feet as light as gazelles, still we could never suffice to praise you for even one of the thousands and tens of thousands of favors you have granted our people.

FROM EGYPT You redeemed us, from the house of bondage . . . You rescue the poor from the strong, the poverty-stricken from those who rob them.

TENS OF THOUSANDS of Jewish communities praise your name in every generation.

BLESSED ARE YOU, Adonai, God and Sovereign, great in praises, Master of wonders, who chooses the songs of praise, Life of the universe.

נִשְׁמַת כָּל-חַי

נִשְׁמַת כָּל חַי, תְּבָרֵךְ אֶת שִׁמְךָ יי אֱלֹהֵינוּ. וְרוּחַ כָּל בָּשָׂר, תְּפָאֵר וּתְרוֹמֵם זִכְרְךָ מַלְכֵּנוּ תָּמִיד, מִן הָעוֹלָם וְעַד הָעוֹלָם אַתָּה אֵל. וּמִבַּלְעָדֶיךָ אֵין לָנוּ מֶלֶךְ גּוֹאֵל וּמוֹשִׁיעַ, פּוֹדֶה וּמַצִּיל וּמְפַרְנֵס וּמְרַחֵם, בְּכָל עֵת צָרָה וְצוּקָה. אֵין לָנוּ מֶלֶךְ אֶלָּא אָתָּה. אֱלֹהֵי הָרִאשׁוֹנִים וְהָאַחֲרוֹנִים, אֱלוֹהַּ כָּל בְּרִיּוֹת, אֲדוֹן כָּל תּוֹלָדוֹת, הַמְהֻלָּל בְּרֹב הַתִּשְׁבָּחוֹת, הַמְנַהֵג עוֹלָמוֹ בְּחֶסֶד, וּבְרִיּוֹתָיו בְּרַחֲמִים. וַיי לֹא יָנוּם וְלֹא יִישָׁן, הַמְעוֹרֵר יְשֵׁנִים וְהַמֵּקִיץ נִרְדָּמִים, וְהַמֵּשִׂיחַ אִלְּמִים, וְהַמַּתִּיר אֲסוּרִים, וְהַסּוֹמֵךְ נוֹפְלִים, וְהַזּוֹקֵף כְּפוּפִים, לְךָ לְבַדְּךָ אֲנַחְנוּ מוֹדִים. אִלּוּ פִינוּ מָלֵא שִׁירָה כַּיָּם, וּלְשׁוֹנֵנוּ רִנָּה כַּהֲמוֹן גַּלָּיו, וְשִׂפְתוֹתֵינוּ שֶׁבַח כְּמֶרְחֲבֵי רָקִיעַ, וְעֵינֵינוּ מְאִירוֹת כַּשֶּׁמֶשׁ וְכַיָּרֵחַ, וְיָדֵינוּ פְרוּשׂוֹת כְּנִשְׁרֵי שָׁמָיִם, וְרַגְלֵינוּ קַלּוֹת כָּאַיָּלוֹת, אֵין אֲנַחְנוּ מַסְפִּיקִים, לְהוֹדוֹת לְךָ יי אֱלֹהֵינוּ וֵאלֹהֵי אֲבוֹתֵינוּ, וּלְבָרֵךְ אֶת שְׁמֶךָ עַל אַחַת מֵאָלֶף אֶלֶף אַלְפֵי אֲלָפִים וְרִבֵּי רְבָבוֹת פְּעָמִים, הַטּוֹבוֹת שֶׁעָשִׂיתָ עִם אֲבוֹתֵינוּ וְעִמָּנוּ.

מִמִּצְרַיִם גְּאַלְתָּנוּ יי אֱלֹהֵינוּ, וּמִבֵּית עֲבָדִים פְּדִיתָנוּ, בְּרָעָב זַנְתָּנוּ, וּבְשָׂבָע כִּלְכַּלְתָּנוּ, מֵחֶרֶב הִצַּלְתָּנוּ, וּמִדֶּבֶר מִלַּטְתָּנוּ, וּמֵחֳלָיִם רָעִים וְנֶאֱמָנִים דִּלִּיתָנוּ.

עַד הֵנָּה עֲזָרוּנוּ רַחֲמֶיךָ, וְלֹא עֲזָבוּנוּ חֲסָדֶיךָ וְאַל תִּטְּשֵׁנוּ יי אֱלֹהֵינוּ לָנֶצַח. עַל כֵּן אֵבָרִים שֶׁפִּלַּגְתָּ בָּנוּ, וְרוּחַ וּנְשָׁמָה שֶׁנָּפַחְתָּ בְּאַפֵּינוּ, וְלָשׁוֹן אֲשֶׁר שַׂמְתָּ בְּפִינוּ, הֵן הֵם יוֹדוּ וִיבָרְכוּ וִישַׁבְּחוּ וִיפָאֲרוּ וִירוֹמְמוּ וְיַעֲרִיצוּ וְיַקְדִּישׁוּ וְיַמְלִיכוּ אֶת שִׁמְךָ מַלְכֵּנוּ, כִּי כָל פֶּה לְךָ יוֹדֶה, וְכָל לָשׁוֹן לְךָ תִשָּׁבַע, וְכָל בֶּרֶךְ לְךָ תִכְרַע, וְכָל קוֹמָה לְפָנֶיךָ תִשְׁתַּחֲוֶה, וְכָל לְבָבוֹת יִירָאוּךָ, וְכָל קֶרֶב וּכְלָיוֹת יְזַמְּרוּ לִשְׁמֶךָ. כַּדָּבָר שֶׁכָּתוּב, כָּל עַצְמוֹתַי תֹּאמַרְנָה יי מִי כָמוֹךָ. מַצִּיל עָנִי מֵחָזָק מִמֶּנּוּ, וְעָנִי וְאֶבְיוֹן מִגֹּזְלוֹ. מִי יִדְמֶה לָךְ, וּמִי יִשְׁוֶה לָּךְ וּמִי יַעֲרָךְ לָךְ. הָאֵל הַגָּדוֹל הַגִּבּוֹר וְהַנּוֹרָא, אֵל עֶלְיוֹן קֹנֵה שָׁמַיִם וָאָרֶץ. נְהַלֶּלְךָ וּנְשַׁבֵּחֲךָ וּנְפָאֶרְךָ וּנְבָרֵךְ אֶת שֵׁם קָדְשֶׁךָ. כָּאָמוּר, לְדָוִד, בָּרְכִי נַפְשִׁי אֶת יי, וְכָל קְרָבַי אֶת שֵׁם קָדְשׁוֹ.

הָאֵל בְּתַעֲצֻמוֹת עֻזֶּךָ, הַגָּדוֹל בִּכְבוֹד שְׁמֶךָ. הַגִּבּוֹר לָנֶצַח וְהַנּוֹרָא בְּנוֹרְאוֹתֶיךָ. הַמֶּלֶךְ הַיּוֹשֵׁב עַל כִּסֵּא רָם וְנִשָּׂא.

שׁוֹכֵן עַד, מָרוֹם וְקָדוֹשׁ שְׁמוֹ. וְכָתוּב, רַנְּנוּ צַדִּיקִים בַּיי, לַיְשָׁרִים נָאוָה תְהִלָּה. בְּפִי יְשָׁרִים תִּתְהַלָּל. וּבְדִבְרֵי צַדִּיקִים תִּתְבָּרַךְ. וּבִלְשׁוֹן חֲסִידִים תִּתְרוֹמָם. וּבְקֶרֶב קְדוֹשִׁים תִּתְקַדָּשׁ.

וּבְמַקְהֲלוֹת רִבְבוֹת עַמְּךָ בֵּית יִשְׂרָאֵל, בְּרִנָּה יִתְפָּאֵר שִׁמְךָ מַלְכֵּנוּ, בְּכָל דּוֹר וָדוֹר, שֶׁכֵּן חוֹבַת כָּל הַיְצוּרִים, לְפָנֶיךָ יי אֱלֹהֵינוּ, וֵאלֹהֵי אֲבוֹתֵינוּ, לְהוֹדוֹת לְהַלֵּל לְשַׁבֵּחַ לְפָאֵר לְרוֹמֵם לְהַדֵּר לְבָרֵךְ לְעַלֵּה וּלְקַלֵּס, עַל כָּל דִּבְרֵי שִׁירוֹת וְתִשְׁבָּחוֹת דָּוִד בֶּן יִשַׁי עַבְדְּךָ מְשִׁיחֶךָ.

יִשְׁתַּבַּח שִׁמְךָ לָעַד מַלְכֵּנוּ, הָאֵל הַמֶּלֶךְ הַגָּדוֹל וְהַקָּדוֹשׁ בַּשָּׁמַיִם וּבָאָרֶץ. כִּי לְךָ נָאֶה, יי אֱלֹהֵינוּ וֵאלֹהֵי אֲבוֹתֵינוּ, שִׁיר וּשְׁבָחָה, הַלֵּל וְזִמְרָה, עֹז וּמֶמְשָׁלָה, נֶצַח, גְּדֻלָּה וּגְבוּרָה, תְּהִלָּה וְתִפְאֶרֶת, קְדֻשָּׁה וּמַלְכוּת. בְּרָכוֹת וְהוֹדָאוֹת מֵעַתָּה וְעַד עוֹלָם.

בָּרוּךְ אַתָּה יי, אֵל מֶלֶךְ גָּדוֹל בַּתִּשְׁבָּחוֹת, אֵל הַהוֹדָאוֹת, אֲדוֹן הַנִּפְלָאוֹת, הַבּוֹחֵר בְּשִׁירֵי זִמְרָה, מֶלֶךְ, אֵל, חַי הָעוֹלָמִים.

Kadesh
Urchatz
Karpas
Yachatz
Maggid
Rachtza
Motzi
Matza
Maror
Korech
Shulchan Orech
Tzafun
Barech
Hallel

Blessing After Hallel and Fourth Cup

The Fourth Cup

כּוֹס רְבִיעִי

***Raise the fourth** cup of wine, recite the blessing over it and recline to the left while drinking.*

HERE I AM, ready to perform the mitzvah of the fourth cup of wine, which concludes the Hallel songs of thanks.

הִנְנִי מוּכָן וּמְזֻמָּן לְקַיֵּם מִצְוַת כּוֹס רְבִיעִי שֶׁל אַרְבַּע כּוֹסוֹת.

❖ BLESSED ARE YOU, Adonai, our God, Sovereign of the Universe, who created the Fruit of the Vine.

Ba-rukh ata Adonai, Elo-hei-nu me-lech ha-olam, bo-rei pree ha-gafen.

בָּרוּךְ אַתָּה יי, אֱלֹהֵינוּ מֶלֶךְ הָעוֹלָם, בּוֹרֵא פְּרִי הַגָּפֶן.

Blessing after Drinking Wine:

BLESSED ARE YOU, Adonai, for the vine and the fruit, for the beautiful and spacious land You gave us. Have mercy on us and bring us there to eat its fruits. Grant us happiness on this Feast of Matzot. Blessed are You, Adonai, for the land and for the fruit of the vine.

Ba-ruch ata Adonai, al ha-aretz v'al pree ha-gafen.

בָּרוּךְ אַתָּה יי אֱלֹהֵינוּ מֶלֶךְ הָעוֹלָם עַל הַגֶּפֶן וְעַל פְּרִי הַגֶּפֶן. וְעַל תְּנוּבַת הַשָּׂדֶה, וְעַל אֶרֶץ חֶמְדָּה טוֹבָה וּרְחָבָה, שֶׁרָצִיתָ וְהִנְחַלְתָּ לַאֲבוֹתֵינוּ, לֶאֱכוֹל מִפִּרְיָהּ וְלִשְׂבּוֹעַ מִטּוּבָהּ. רַחֶם נָא יי אֱלֹהֵינוּ עַל יִשְׂרָאֵל עַמֶּךָ, וְעַל יְרוּשָׁלַיִם עִירֶךָ, וְעַל צִיּוֹן מִשְׁכַּן כְּבוֹדֶךָ, וְעַל מִזְבְּחֶךָ וְעַל הֵיכָלֶךָ. וּבְנֵה יְרוּשָׁלַיִם עִיר הַקֹּדֶשׁ בִּמְהֵרָה בְיָמֵינוּ, וְהַעֲלֵנוּ לְתוֹכָהּ, וְשַׂמְּחֵנוּ בְּבִנְיָנָהּ וְנֹאכַל מִפִּרְיָהּ וְנִשְׂבַּע מִטּוּבָהּ, וּנְבָרֶכְךָ עָלֶיהָ בִּקְדֻשָּׁה וּבְטָהֳרָה

(בשבת – וּרְצֵה וְהַחֲלִיצֵנוּ בְּיוֹם הַשַּׁבָּת הַזֶּה)

The Four Cups and the Four Verbs

The Rabbis identified each cup of wine with the fourfold promise of redemption: "God spoke to Moshe: Tell the children of Israel: I will bring you out . . . I will rescue you . . . I will redeem you . . . I will take you for me as a people and I will be for you as a God . . . ." *(Exodus 6:2-7)*

וְשַׂמְּחֵנוּ בְּיוֹם חַג הַמַּצּוֹת הַזֶּה. כִּי אַתָּה יי טוֹב וּמֵטִיב לַכֹּל, וְנוֹדֶה לְּךָ עַל הָאָרֶץ וְעַל פְּרִי הַגָּפֶן. בָּרוּךְ אַתָּה יי, עַל הָאָרֶץ וְעַל פְּרִי הַגָּפֶן.

On the second night of Pesach only:

Counting the Omer

סְפִירַת הָעֹמֶר

1. **On the second night** of Pesach we begin counting the 50 days from the Exodus to Sinai, from Pesach, the harvest of barley, until Shavuot, the harvest of wheat. Traditionally, the Rabbis interpret the counting as reflecting Israel's eager anticipation of the giving of the Torah at Sinai on Shavuot.

The physical liberation is not an end in itself, but must be wedded to a life of values and responsibility.

2. **Please rise** and count off the first day of the Omer.

Kadesh
Urchatz
Karpas
Yachatz
Maggid
Rachtza
Motzi
Matza
Maror
Korech
Shulchan Orech
Tzafun
Barech
Hallel
Hallel

Counting the Omer

HERE I AM, ready to perform the mitzvah of counting the Omer.

הִנְנִי מוּכָן וּמְזֻמָּן לְקַיֵּם מִצְוַת עֲשֵׂה שֶׁל סְפִירַת הָעֹמֶר.

BLESSED ARE YOU, Adonai,
Sovereign of the Universe,
who has sanctified us with Divine laws
and commanded us to count the Omer.

Ba-ruch ata Adonai,
Elo-heinu me-lech ha-olam,
asher keed'shanu b'meetz-vo-tav
v'tzee-vanu al s'feerat ha-omer.

בָּרוּךְ אַתָּה יי,
אֱלֹהֵינוּ מֶלֶךְ הָעוֹלָם,
אֲשֶׁר קִדְּשָׁנוּ בְּמִצְוֹתָיו
וְצִוָּנוּ עַל סְפִירַת הָעֹמֶר.

TODAY is the first day of the Omer.

Ha-yom yom echad la-omer.

הַיּוֹם יוֹם אֶחָד לָעֹמֶר.

The Double Jubilee

IN THE BIBLICAL ERA Israel counted off seven times seven sabbatical years and concluded with the fiftieth year, the Jubilee, which was marked with the blowing of the shofar. The word Jubilee means shofar and "it proclaimed liberty throughout the land to all the inhabitants thereof." *(Lev. 25)*

Annually the minor Jubilee was the counting off of seven times seven weeks *(shavuot)* concluded on the fiftieth day with the holiday of Shavuot (Festival of the Weeks) or Pentecost. Every day one measure *(omer)* of the new barley was offered in the Temple, until Shavuot when the first "fruits" of the wheat harvest were offered.

The rabbis later reinterpreted the fifty day count-down as a reliving of the most important spiritual journey in Jewish history. The original 50 day itinerary brought Israel geographically from Egypt to Mount Sinai, politically from slavery to the ratification of its Divine constitution, and spiritually from idolatry to the status of "a kingdom of priests and a holy nation."

In a sense, the whole purpose of the Exodus is to prepare Israel to accept the Torah. The true meaning of liberation is fulfilled in choosing freely to enter into a commitment to God as a community. Rabbi Y.M. Epstein interprets the barley offering, the *"omer,"* as animal fodder and the wheat offering of the Holiday of the Giving of the Torah as the food of civilized human beings. He took that to symbolize that through Torah we cultivate our new freedom into the spiritual liberty befitting a dignified human being. *(Aruch HaShulchan O. H. 489:3)*

IN CONTEMPORARY Israel the journey from Pesach to Shavuot has become a reiteration of our national autobiography in the 20th century. While Pesach recalls our ancient enslavement in Egypt, it also serves as a prelude for the Holocaust in which Jewish suffering in exile reaches its heights.

Yom HaShoah (whose date commemorates the Warsaw Ghetto Uprising that climaxed on seder night, 1943) is used to honor the activism of the ghetto fighters and to memorialize the slaughtered millions and their courage. Out of the vulnerability of Diaspora Jews emerged the Zionist attempt to return to the land, to political autonomy and to military independence.

Yom HaZikaron honors the soldiers who gave their lives so Jews could achieve independence and celebrate *Yom HaAtzmaut* (1948).

Yom Yerushalayim (1967) marks the reunification of David's city Jerusalem (1000 B.C.E.) completing a 3,000 year cycle of building, destruction, exile and finally return.

Shavuot in Israel adds the dimension of the return to the land and the first fruits of a nation that has returned to its agricultural roots.

A Preview of Upcoming Jewish Holidays

Pesach is the beginning of a 50-day period filled with Jewish commemorations — ancient and contemporary.

12th Day of Omer	*Yom HaShoah* (Holocaust and Heroism Day).
19th Day of Omer	*Yom HaZikaron* (Memorial Day for Fallen Israeli Soldiers)
20th Day of Omer	*Yom HaAtzmaut* (Israel Independence Day; May 15, 1948)
33rd Day of Omer	*Lag BaOmer* (All-Night Campfire Celebration commemorating the Bar Kochba Revolt against Rome, 132 C.E. and the death of the mystical hero, Rabbi Shimon Bar Yochai)
43rd Day of Omer	*Yom Yerushalayim* (Jerusalem's Day of Reunification since the Six Day War, June, 1967)
50th Day	*Shavuot* (Pentecost, the Anniversary of the Giving of the Torah at Sinai, and the bringing of First Fruits of Wheat to the Temple)

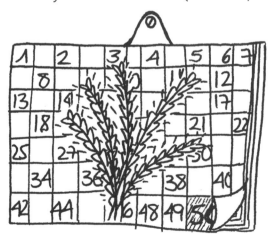

Concluding Songs

פִּיּוּט

At the end of the seder, the Ashkenazi Haggadah includes two poems sung alternatively on the first and second seder night. The **first** recalls all the **night rescues**, "in the middle of the night." At night God saved Israel with the tenth plague, helped Jacob when he was pursued by Lavan, and Mordechai when pursued by Haman.

The **second poem** reviews the many redemptions that occurred according to tradition on Pesach: the angels announced the birth of Isaac, the conquest of Jericho, the hanging of Haman, and so on.

Kadesh
Urchatz
Karpas
Yachatz
Maggid
Rachtza
Motzi
Matza
Maror
Korech
Shulchan Orech
Tzafun
Barech
Hallel
Nirtza
Medieval Poems

For the first night only:

"It Happened in the Middle of the Night"
(Ex. 12:29) (Yannai, 5th C. Israel)

"וּבְכֵן וַיְהִי בַּחֲצִי הַלַּיְלָה."

אָז רוֹב נִסִּים הִפְלֵאתָ בַּלַּיְלָה,
בְּרֹאשׁ אַשְׁמוּרוֹת זֶה הַלַּיְלָה,
גֵּר צֶדֶק נִצַּחְתּוֹ כְּנֶחֱלַק לוֹ לַיְלָה,
וַיְהִי בַּחֲצִי הַלַּיְלָה.

דַּנְתָּ מֶלֶךְ גְּרָר בַּחֲלוֹם הַלַּיְלָה,
הִפְחַדְתָּ אֲרַמִּי בְּאֶמֶשׁ לַיְלָה,
וַיָּשַׂר יִשְׂרָאֵל לְמַלְאָךְ וַיּוּכַל לוֹ לַיְלָה,
וַיְהִי בַּחֲצִי הַלַּיְלָה.

זֶרַע בְּכוֹרֵי פַתְרוֹס מָחַצְתָּ בַּחֲצִי הַלַּיְלָה,
חֵילָם לֹא מָצְאוּ בְּקוּמָם בַּלַּיְלָה,
טִיסַת נְגִיד חֲרֹשֶׁת סִלִּיתָ בְּכוֹכְבֵי לַיְלָה,
וַיְהִי בַּחֲצִי הַלַּיְלָה.

יָעַץ מְחָרֵף לְנוֹפֵף אִוּוּי, הוֹבַשְׁתָּ פְגָרָיו בַּלַּיְלָה,
כָּרַע בֵּל וּמַצָּבוֹ בְּאִישׁוֹן לַיְלָה,
לְאִישׁ חֲמוּדוֹת נִגְלָה רָז חֲזוֹת לַיְלָה,
וַיְהִי בַּחֲצִי הַלַּיְלָה.

מִשְׁתַּכֵּר בִּכְלֵי קֹדֶשׁ נֶהֱרַג בּוֹ בַּלַּיְלָה,
נוֹשַׁע מִבּוֹר אֲרָיוֹת פּוֹתֵר בְּעִתוּתֵי לַיְלָה,
שִׂנְאָה נָטַר אֲגָגִי וְכָתַב סְפָרִים לַיְלָה,
וַיְהִי בַּחֲצִי הַלַּיְלָה.

For the second night only:

"And You Shall Say: It is the Passover Sacrifice"
(Ex. 12:27) (Elazar haKalir, 8th C. Israel)

"וַאֲמַרְתֶּם זֶבַח פֶּסַח."

אֹמֶץ גְּבוּרוֹתֶיךָ הִפְלֵאתָ בַּפֶּסַח,
בְּרֹאשׁ כָּל מוֹעֲדוֹת נִשֵּׂאתָ פֶּסַח,
גִּלִּיתָ לְאֶזְרָחִי חֲצוֹת לֵיל פֶּסַח,
וַאֲמַרְתֶּם זֶבַח פֶּסַח.

דְּלָתָיו דָּפַקְתָּ כְּחֹם הַיּוֹם בַּפֶּסַח,
הִסְעִיד נוֹצְצִים עֻגוֹת מַצּוֹת בַּפֶּסַח,
וְאֶל הַבָּקָר רָץ זֵכֶר לְשׁוֹר עֵרֶךְ פֶּסַח,
וַאֲמַרְתֶּם זֶבַח פֶּסַח.

עוֹרַרְתָּ נִצְחֲךָ עָלָיו בְּנֶדֶד שְׁנַת לַיְלָה,
פּוּרָה תִדְרוֹךְ לְשׁוֹמֵר מַה מִּלַּיְלָה,
צָרַח כַּשֹּׁמֵר וְשָׂח אָתָא בֹקֶר וְגַם לַיְלָה,
וַיְהִי בַּחֲצִי הַלַּיְלָה.

קָרֵב יוֹם אֲשֶׁר הוּא לֹא יוֹם וְלֹא לַיְלָה,
רָם הוֹדַע כִּי לְךָ הַיּוֹם אַף לְךָ הַלַּיְלָה,
שׁוֹמְרִים הַפְקֵד לְעִירְךָ כָּל הַיּוֹם וְכָל הַלַּיְלָה,
תָּאִיר כְּאוֹר יוֹם חֶשְׁכַּת לַיְלָה,
וַיְהִי בַּחֲצִי הַלַּיְלָה.

זֹעֲמוּ סְדוֹמִים וְלֹהֲטוּ בָּאֵשׁ בַּפֶּסַח,
חֻלַּץ לוֹט מֵהֶם, וּמַצּוֹת אָפָה בְּקֵץ פֶּסַח,
טִאטֵאתָ אַדְמַת מֹף וְנֹף בְּעָבְרְךָ בַּפֶּסַח,
וַאֲמַרְתֶּם זֶבַח פֶּסַח.

יָהּ, רֹאשׁ כָּל אוֹן מָחַצְתָּ בְּלֵיל שִׁמּוּר פֶּסַח,
כַּבִּיר, עַל בֵּן בְּכוֹר פָּסַחְתָּ בְּדַם פֶּסַח,
לְבִלְתִּי תֵת מַשְׁחִית לָבֹא בִּפְתָחַי בַּפֶּסַח,
וַאֲמַרְתֶּם זֶבַח פֶּסַח.

מְסֻגֶּרֶת סֻגָּרָה בְּעִתּוֹתֵי פֶּסַח,
נִשְׁמְדָה מִדְיָן בִּצְלִיל שְׂעוֹרֵי עֹמֶר פֶּסַח,
שֹׂרְפוּ מִשְׁמַנֵּי פּוּל וְלוּד בִּיקַד יְקוֹד פֶּסַח,
וַאֲמַרְתֶּם זֶבַח פֶּסַח.

עוֹד הַיּוֹם בְּנֹב לַעֲמֹד, עַד גָּעָה עוֹנַת פֶּסַח,
פַּס יַד כָּתְבָה לְקַעֲקֵעַ צוּל בַּפֶּסַח,
צָפֹה הַצָּפִית עָרוֹךְ הַשֻּׁלְחָן, בַּפֶּסַח,
וַאֲמַרְתֶּם זֶבַח פֶּסַח.

קָהָל כִּנְּסָה הֲדַסָּה צוֹם לְשַׁלֵּשׁ בַּפֶּסַח,
רֹאשׁ מִבֵּית רָשָׁע מָחַצְתָּ בְּעֵץ חֲמִשִּׁים בַּפֶּסַח,
שְׁתֵּי אֵלֶּה רֶגַע, תָּבִיא לְעוּצִית בַּפֶּסַח,
תָּעֹז יָדְךָ וְתָרוּם יְמִינְךָ, כְּלֵיל הִתְקַדֶּשׁ חַג פֶּסַח,
וַאֲמַרְתֶּם זֶבַח פֶּסַח.

Kee Lo Naeh

It is Proper to Praise Him

כִּי לוֹ נָאֶה

This table song, by Jacob, a German poet, is an alphabetical acrostic praising God's many attributes. Though it has no connection to Pesach at all, it entered the Ashkenazi Haggadah after the 12th C. as a popular religious song.

The first verse typifies the style: "Mighty in royalty, Beautiful in stature, God's angels exclaim: To God alone belongs the Kingdom, for all this is becoming and fitting to God."

Refrain:

L'cha u-l'cha, l'cha kee l'cha, l'cha af l'cha.

L'cha Adonai ha-mam-lacha.

Kee lo na-eh, kee lo ya-eh.

אַדִּיר בִּמְלוּכָה, **בָּחוּר** כַּהֲלָכָה, **גְּדוּדָיו** יֹאמְרוּ לוֹ:
לְךָ וּלְךָ, לְךָ כִּי לְךָ, לְךָ אַף לְךָ,
לְךָ יי הַמַּמְלָכָה.
כִּי לוֹ נָאֶה, כִּי לוֹ יָאֶה.

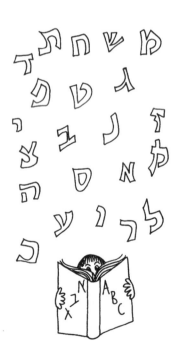

מוֹשֵׁל בִּמְלוּכָה, **נוֹרָא** כַּהֲלָכָה, **סְבִיבָיו** יֹאמְרוּ לוֹ:
לְךָ וּלְךָ, לְךָ כִּי לְךָ, לְךָ אַף לְךָ, לְךָ יי הַמַּמְלָכָה.
כִּי לוֹ נָאֶה, כִּי לוֹ יָאֶה.

עָנָו בִּמְלוּכָה, **פּוֹדֶה** כַּהֲלָכָה, **צַדִּיקָיו** יֹאמְרוּ לוֹ:
לְךָ וּלְךָ, לְךָ כִּי לְךָ, לְךָ אַף לְךָ, לְךָ יי הַמַּמְלָכָה.
כִּי לוֹ נָאֶה, כִּי לוֹ יָאֶה.

קָדוֹשׁ בִּמְלוּכָה, **רַחוּם** כַּהֲלָכָה, **שִׁנְאַנָּיו** יֹאמְרוּ לוֹ:
לְךָ וּלְךָ, לְךָ כִּי לְךָ, לְךָ אַף לְךָ, לְךָ יי הַמַּמְלָכָה.
כִּי לוֹ נָאֶה, כִּי לוֹ יָאֶה.

תַּקִּיף בִּמְלוּכָה, **תּוֹמֵךְ** כַּהֲלָכָה, **תְּמִימָיו** יֹאמְרוּ לוֹ:
לְךָ וּלְךָ, לְךָ כִּי לְךָ, לְךָ אַף לְךָ, לְךָ יי הַמַּמְלָכָה.
כִּי לוֹ נָאֶה, כִּי לוֹ יָאֶה.

דָּגוּל בִּמְלוּכָה, **הָדוּר** כַּהֲלָכָה, **וָתִיקָיו** יֹאמְרוּ לוֹ:
לְךָ וּלְךָ, לְךָ כִּי לְךָ, לְךָ אַף לְךָ, לְךָ יי הַמַּמְלָכָה.
כִּי לוֹ נָאֶה, כִּי לוֹ יָאֶה.

זַכַּאי בִּמְלוּכָה, **חָסִין** כַּהֲלָכָה, **טַפְסְרָיו** יֹאמְרוּ לוֹ:
לְךָ וּלְךָ, לְךָ כִּי לְךָ, לְךָ אַף לְךָ, לְךָ יי הַמַּמְלָכָה.
כִּי לוֹ נָאֶה, כִּי לוֹ יָאֶה.

יָחִיד בִּמְלוּכָה, **כַּבִּיר** כַּהֲלָכָה, **לִמּוּדָיו** יֹאמְרוּ לוֹ:
לְךָ וּלְךָ, לְךָ כִּי לְךָ, לְךָ אַף לְךָ, לְךָ יי הַמַּמְלָכָה.
כִּי לוֹ נָאֶה, כִּי לוֹ יָאֶה.

Adeer Hu
Mighty is God

The poet (15th C. Germany) recounts the Divine attributes in alphabetical order, and prays for the building of the third Temple.

*A*deer hu, adeer hu

Refrain: Yeev-neh veito b'ka-rov,
beem-hei-ra, beem-hei-ra, b'ya-mei-nu b'ka-rov,
Eil b'nei, Eil b'nei, B'nei veit-cha b'ka-rov.

*B*a-chur hu, *G*a-dol hu, *D*a-gul hu,
Yeev-neh vei-to b'ka-rov . . . .

*H*a-dur hu, *V*a-teek hu, *Z*a-kai hu,
Yeev-neh vei-to b'ka-rov . . . .

*CH*a-sid hu, *T*a-hor hu, *Y*a-cheed hu,
Yeev-neh vei-to b'ka-rov . . . .

*K*a-beer hu, *L*a-mud hu, *M*e-lech hu,
Yeev-neh vei-to b'ka-rov . . . .

*N*o-ra hu, *S*a-geev hu, *EE*-zuz hu,
Yeev-neh vei-to b'ka-rov . . . .

*P*o-deh hu, *TZ*a-deek hu, *K*a-dosh hu,
Yeev-neh vei-to b'ka-rov . . . .

*R*a-chum hu, *SH*a-dai hu, *T*a-keef hu,
Yeev-neh vei-to b'ka-rov...

אַדִּיר הוּא, אַדִּיר הוּא,
יִבְנֶה בֵיתוֹ בְּקָרוֹב,
בִּמְהֵרָה בִּמְהֵרָה, בְּיָמֵינוּ בְּקָרוֹב.
אֵל בְּנֵה, בְּנֵה בֵיתְךָ בְּקָרוֹב.

בָּחוּר הוּא, גָּדוֹל הוּא, דָּגוּל הוּא,
יִבְנֶה בֵיתוֹ בְּקָרוֹב . . . .

הָדוּר הוּא, וָתִיק הוּא, זַכַּאי הוּא,
יִבְנֶה בֵיתוֹ בְּקָרוֹב . . . .

חָסִיד הוּא, טָהוֹר הוּא, יָחִיד הוּא,
יִבְנֶה בֵיתוֹ בְּקָרוֹב . . . .

כַּבִּיר הוּא, לָמוּד הוּא, מֶלֶךְ הוּא,
יִבְנֶה בֵיתוֹ בְּקָרוֹב . . . .

נוֹרָא הוּא, סַגִּיב הוּא, עִזּוּז הוּא,
יִבְנֶה בֵיתוֹ בְּקָרוֹב . . . .

פּוֹדֶה הוּא, צַדִּיק הוּא, קָדוֹשׁ הוּא,
יִבְנֶה בֵיתוֹ בְּקָרוֹב . . . .

רַחוּם הוּא, שַׁדַּי הוּא, תַּקִּיף הוּא,
יִבְנֶה בֵיתוֹ בְּקָרוֹב . . . .

אַדִּיר הוּא

154

Echad Mee Yodei-a
Who Knows One?

אֶחָד מִי יוֹדֵעַ

*"**Who Knows One?**" is modeled on a German non-Jewish folksong (15th or 16th C.). It consists of a numerical quiz* *written like a basic Jewish trivia game. You may test your knowledge on the advanced quiz below.*

❖ The Jewish Trivia Song

1 Who knows **one**?
  I know **one**.
  One is our God, who is in heaven and on earth.
2 Who knows **two**?
  I know **two**.
  Two are the tablets of the Covenant.
  One is our God, who is in heaven and on earth.
3 **Three** are the Fathers.

4 **Four** are the Mothers.
5 **Five** are the books of the Torah.
6 **Six** are the Mishnah sections.
7 **Seven** are the days of the week.
8 **Eight** are the days before circumcision.
9 **Nine** are the months of pregnancy.
10 **Ten** are the Ten Commandments.
11 **Eleven** are the stars in Joseph's dream.
12 **Twelve** are the tribes of Israel.
13 **Thirteen** are God's attributes of mercy.

Singing Activity

Since the song is written in question and answer form, you may assign the answers to different participants. The whole "chorus" sings the question: **"Who knows one (two, etc.)?"** and the preassigned respondent sings the answer **"I know one, One is our God . . ."** every time that number comes up. No one dare fall asleep and miss a turn in the rotation.

The Advanced 'Who Knows One?'

Who knows three?
Name the three fathers of Israel.
(Hint: A..., I..., J...)

Who knows the four mothers of the Torah?
(Hint: S..., R..., R ..., L...)

Who knows the "fours" of the seder?

Who knows the five books of the Torah in English and in Hebrew?
(Hint: G..., E..., L..., N..., D...)

Who knows the ten commandments? (See Exodus 20)

Who knows the ten plagues?

*Who knows Jacob's twelve sons?**
Hint: Leah's sons: R..., Sh..., L...,
        J..., Y..., Z...
    Rachel's: J..., B...,
    Zilpah's: G..., A...
    Bilhah's: D..., N...

Who knows 613?

ECHAD MEE YO-DEI-A?

Echad anee yo-dei-a.
Echad Elo-hei-nu
she-ba-sha-ma-yeem uva-aretz.

Shna-yeem mee yo-dei-a?

Shna-yeem anee yo-dei-a.
Shnei lu-chot ha-breet,
Echad Elo-hei-nu
she-ba-sha-ma-yeem uva-aretz.

Shlo-sha mee yo-dei-a?

Shlo-sha anee yo-dei-a.
Shlo-sha avot,
Shnei lu-chot ha-breet,
Echad Elo-hei-nu
she-ba-sha-ma-yeem uva-aretz.

Arba mee yo-dei-a?

Arba anee yo-dei-a.
Arba eema-hot,
Shlo-sha avot,
Shnei lu-chot ha-breet,
Echad Elo-hei-nu
she-ba-sha-ma-yeem uva-aretz.

Cha-mee-sha mee yo-dei-a?

Cha-mee-sha anee yo-dei-a.
Cha-mee-sha chum-shei Torah,
Arba eema-hot,
Shlo-sha avot,
Shnei lu-chot ha-breet,
Echad Elo-hei-nu
she-ba-sha-ma-yeem uva-aretz.

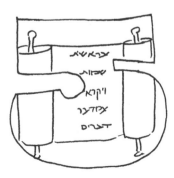

אֶחָד מִי יוֹדֵעַ?
אֶחָד אֲנִי יוֹדֵעַ!
אֶחָד אֱלֹהֵינוּ
שֶׁבַּשָּׁמַיִם וּבָאָרֶץ.

שְׁנַיִם מִי יוֹדֵעַ?
שְׁנַיִם אֲנִי יוֹדֵעַ!
שְׁנֵי לֻחוֹת הַבְּרִית,
אֶחָד אֱלֹהֵינוּ
שֶׁבַּשָּׁמַיִם וּבָאָרֶץ.

שְׁלֹשָׁה מִי יוֹדֵעַ?
שְׁלֹשָׁה אֲנִי יוֹדֵעַ!
שְׁלֹשָׁה אָבוֹת,
שְׁנֵי לֻחוֹת הַבְּרִית,
אֶחָד אֱלֹהֵינוּ
שֶׁבַּשָּׁמַיִם וּבָאָרֶץ.

אַרְבַּע מִי יוֹדֵעַ?
אַרְבַּע אֲנִי יוֹדֵעַ!
אַרְבַּע אִמָּהוֹת,
שְׁלֹשָׁה אָבוֹת,
שְׁנֵי לֻחוֹת הַבְּרִית,
אֶחָד אֱלֹהֵינוּ
שֶׁבַּשָּׁמַיִם וּבָאָרֶץ.

חֲמִשָּׁה מִי יוֹדֵעַ?
חֲמִשָּׁה אֲנִי יוֹדֵעַ!
חֲמִשָּׁה חוּמְשֵׁי תּוֹרָה,
אַרְבַּע אִמָּהוֹת,
שְׁלֹשָׁה אָבוֹת,
שְׁנֵי לֻחוֹת הַבְּרִית,
אֶחָד אֱלֹהֵינוּ
שֶׁבַּשָּׁמַיִם וּבָאָרֶץ.

Kadesh
Urchatz
Karpas
Yachatz
Maggid
Rachtza
Motzi
Matza
Maror
Korech
Shulchan
Orech
Tzafun
Barech
Hallel
Nirtza

Who
Knows
One

156

Shee-sha mee yo-dei-a?

Shee-sha anee yo-dei-a.
Shee-sha seedrei Mishna,
Cha-meesha chum-shei Torah,
Arba eema-hot,
Shlo-sha avot,
Shnei lu-chot ha-breet,
Echad Elo-hei-nu
she-ba-sha-ma-yeem uva-aretz.

שִׁשָּׁה מִי יוֹדֵעַ?
שִׁשָּׁה אֲנִי יוֹדֵעַ!
שִׁשָּׁה סִדְרֵי מִשְׁנָה,
חֲמִשָּׁה חוּמְשֵׁי תוֹרָה,
אַרְבַּע אִמָּהוֹת,
שְׁלֹשָׁה אָבוֹת,
שְׁנֵי לֻחוֹת הַבְּרִית,
אֶחָד אֱלֹהֵינוּ
שֶׁבַּשָּׁמַיִם וּבָאָרֶץ.

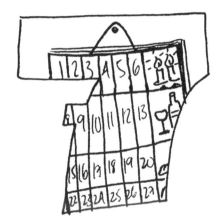

Shee-va mee yo-dei-a?

Shee-va anee yo-dei-a.
Shee-va y'mei Shab-ta,
Shee-sha seedrei Mishna,
Cha-meesha chum-shei Torah,
Arba eema-hot,
Shlo-sha avot,
Shnei lu-chot ha-breet,
Echad Elo-hei-nu
she-ba-sha-ma-yeem uva-aretz.

שִׁבְעָה מִי יוֹדֵעַ?
שִׁבְעָה אֲנִי יוֹדֵעַ!
שִׁבְעָה יְמֵי שַׁבַּתָּא,
שִׁשָּׁה סִדְרֵי מִשְׁנָה,
חֲמִשָּׁה חוּמְשֵׁי תוֹרָה,
אַרְבַּע אִמָּהוֹת,
שְׁלֹשָׁה אָבוֹת,
שְׁנֵי לֻחוֹת הַבְּרִית,
אֶחָד אֱלֹהֵינוּ
שֶׁבַּשָּׁמַיִם וּבָאָרֶץ.

Shmona mee yo-dei-a?

Shmona anee yo-dei-a.
Shmona y'mei mee-la,
Shee-va y'mei Shab-ta,
Shee-sha seedrei Mishna,
Cha-meesha chum-shei Torah,
Arba eema-hot,
Shlo-sha avot,
Shnei lu-chot ha-breet,
Echad Elo-hei-nu
she-ba-sha-ma-yeem uva-aretz.

שְׁמוֹנָה מִי יוֹדֵעַ?
שְׁמוֹנָה אֲנִי יוֹדֵעַ!
שְׁמוֹנָה יְמֵי מִילָה,
שִׁבְעָה יְמֵי שַׁבַּתָּא,
שִׁשָּׁה סִדְרֵי מִשְׁנָה,
חֲמִשָּׁה חוּמְשֵׁי תוֹרָה,
אַרְבַּע אִמָּהוֹת,
שְׁלֹשָׁה אָבוֹת,
שְׁנֵי לֻחוֹת הַבְּרִית,
אֶחָד אֱלֹהֵינוּ
שֶׁבַּשָּׁמַיִם וּבָאָרֶץ.

Tee-sha mee yo-dei-a?

Tee-sha anee yo-dei-a.
Tee-sha yar-chei lei-da,
Shmona y'mei mee-la,
Shee-va y'mei Shab-ta,
Shee-sha see-drei Mishna,
Cha-mee-sha chum-shei Torah,
Arba eema-hot,
Shlo-sha avot,
Shnei lu-chot ha-breet,
Echad Elo-hei-nu
she-ba-sha-ma-yeem uva-aretz.

תִּשְׁעָה מִי יוֹדֵעַ?
תִּשְׁעָה אֲנִי יוֹדֵעַ!
תִּשְׁעָה יַרְחֵי לֵדָה,
שְׁמוֹנָה יְמֵי מִילָה,
שִׁבְעָה יְמֵי שַׁבַּתָּא,
שִׁשָּׁה סִדְרֵי מִשְׁנָה,
חֲמִשָּׁה חוּמְשֵׁי תוֹרָה,
אַרְבַּע אִמָּהוֹת,
שְׁלֹשָׁה אָבוֹת,
שְׁנֵי לֻחוֹת הַבְּרִית,
אֶחָד אֱלֹהֵינוּ
שֶׁבַּשָּׁמַיִם וּבָאָרֶץ.

A-sa-ra mee yo-dei-a?

A-sa-ra anee yo-dei-a.
A-sa-ra dee-bra-ya,
Tee-sha yar-chei lei-da,
Shmona y'mei mee-la,
Shee-va y'mei Shab-ta,
Shee-sha see-drei Mishna,
Cha-mee-sha chum-shei Torah,
Arba eema-hot,
Shlo-sha avot,
Shnei lu-chot ha-breet,
Echad Elo-hei-nu
she-ba-sha-ma-yeem uva-aretz.

עֲשָׂרָה מִי יוֹדֵעַ?
עֲשָׂרָה אֲנִי יוֹדֵעַ!
עֲשָׂרָה דִּבְּרַיָּא,
תִּשְׁעָה יַרְחֵי לֵדָה,
שְׁמוֹנָה יְמֵי מִילָה,
שִׁבְעָה יְמֵי שַׁבַּתָּא,
שִׁשָּׁה סִדְרֵי מִשְׁנָה,
חֲמִשָּׁה חוּמְשֵׁי תוֹרָה,
אַרְבַּע אִמָּהוֹת,
שְׁלֹשָׁה אָבוֹת,
שְׁנֵי לֻחוֹת הַבְּרִית,
אֶחָד אֱלֹהֵינוּ
שֶׁבַּשָּׁמַיִם וּבָאָרֶץ.

Echad-asar mee yo-dei-a?

Echad-asar anee yo-dei-a.
Echad-asar koch-va-ya,
A-sa-ra dee-bra-ya,
Tee-sha yar-chei lei-da,
Shmona y'mei mee-la,
Shee-va y'mei Shab-ta,
Shee-sha see-drei Mishna,
Cha-mee-sha chum-shei Torah,
Arba eema-hot,
Shlo-sha avot,
Shnei lu-chot ha-breet,
Echad Elo-hei-nu
she-ba-sha-ma-yeem uva-aretz.

אַחַד עָשָׂר מִי יוֹדֵעַ?
אַחַד עָשָׂר אֲנִי יוֹדֵעַ!
אַחַד עָשָׂר כּוֹכְבַיָּא,
עֲשָׂרָה דִּבְּרַיָּא,
תִּשְׁעָה יַרְחֵי לֵדָה,
שְׁמוֹנָה יְמֵי מִילָה,
שִׁבְעָה יְמֵי שַׁבַּתָּא,
שִׁשָּׁה סִדְרֵי מִשְׁנָה,
חֲמִשָּׁה חוּמְשֵׁי תוֹרָה,
אַרְבַּע אִמָּהוֹת,
שְׁלֹשָׁה אָבוֹת,
שְׁנֵי לֻחוֹת הַבְּרִית,
אֶחָד אֱלֹהֵינוּ
שֶׁבַּשָּׁמַיִם וּבָאָרֶץ.

Kadesh
Urchatz
Karpas
Yachatz
Maggid
Rachtza
Motzi
Matza
Maror
Korech
Shulchan Orech
Tzafun
Barech
Hallel
Nirtza

Who
Knows
One

Shneim-asar mee yo-dei-a?

Shneim-asar anee yo-dei-a.
Shneim-asar sheev-ta-ya,
Echad-asar koch-va-ya,
A-sa-ra dee-bra-ya,
Tee-sha yar-chei lei-da,
Shmona y'mei mee-la,
Shee-va y'mei Shab-ta,
Shee-sha see-drei Mishna,
Cha-mee-sha chum-shei Torah,
Arba eema-hot,
Shlo-sha avot,
Shnei lu-chot ha-breet,
Echad Elo-hei-nu
she-ba-sha-ma-yeem uva-aretz.

שְׁנֵים עָשָׂר מִי יוֹדֵעַ?
שְׁנֵים עָשָׂר אֲנִי יוֹדֵעַ!
שְׁנֵים עָשָׂר שִׁבְטַיָּא,
אַחַד עָשָׂר כּוֹכְבַיָּא,
עֲשָׂרָה דִּבְּרַיָּא,
תִּשְׁעָה יַרְחֵי לֵדָה,
שְׁמוֹנָה יְמֵי מִילָה,
שִׁבְעָה יְמֵי שַׁבַּתָּא,
שִׁשָּׁה סִדְרֵי מִשְׁנָה,
חֲמִשָּׁה חוּמְשֵׁי תוֹרָה,
אַרְבַּע אִמָּהוֹת,
שְׁלֹשָׁה אָבוֹת,
שְׁנֵי לֻחוֹת הַבְּרִית,
אֶחָד אֱלֹהֵינוּ
שֶׁבַּשָּׁמַיִם וּבָאָרֶץ.

Shlo-sha-asar mee yo-dei-a?

Shlo-sha-asar anee yo-dei-a.
Shlo-sha-asar mee-da-ya,
Shneim-asar sheev-ta-ya,
Echad-asar koch-va-ya,
A-sa-ra dee-bra-ya,
Tee-sha yar-chei lei-da,
Shmona y'mei mee-la,
Shee-va y'mei Shab-ta,
Shee-sha see-drei Mishna,
Cha-mee-sha chum-shei Torah,
Arba eema-hot,
Shlo-sha avot,
Shnei lu-chot ha-breet,
Echad Elo-hei-nu
she-ba-sha-ma-yeem uva-aretz.

שְׁלֹשָׁה עָשָׂר מִי יוֹדֵעַ?
שְׁלֹשָׁה עָשָׂר אֲנִי יוֹדֵעַ!
שְׁלֹשָׁה עָשָׂר מִדַּיָּא,
שְׁנֵים עָשָׂר שִׁבְטַיָּא,
אַחַד עָשָׂר כּוֹכְבַיָּא,
עֲשָׂרָה דִּבְּרַיָּא,
תִּשְׁעָה יַרְחֵי לֵדָה,
שְׁמוֹנָה יְמֵי מִילָה,
שִׁבְעָה יְמֵי שַׁבַּתָּא,
שִׁשָּׁה סִדְרֵי מִשְׁנָה,
חֲמִשָּׁה חוּמְשֵׁי תוֹרָה,
אַרְבַּע אִמָּהוֹת,
שְׁלֹשָׁה אָבוֹת,
שְׁנֵי לֻחוֹת הַבְּרִית,
אֶחָד אֱלֹהֵינוּ
שֶׁבַּשָּׁמַיִם וּבָאָרֶץ.

Chad Gad-ya
Just One Kid

חַד גַּדְיָא

This is the Jewish *"Old MacDonald Had a Farm."*
Preassign a stanza to volunteers who must produce an
appropriate sound or gesture for each subsequent aggressor.
For example, the goat might say "maa," the cat "meow,"
and the dog "woof." The stick could make a banging sound,
the fire might "sizzle," and the water, "glug-glug." Think up
appropriate sounds for the ox and the slaughterer. The angel
of death and God require the greatest creativity and delicacy.
Everyone sings the verses, while the preassigned participant
adds a sound and/or visual effect each time. For example,
"ata shunra (meow) v'achla l'gad-ya (maa-maa) . . . ."
[The cat came (meow) and ate up the goat (maa-maa) that
my Abba bought for two zuzeem].
The song, translated below, appears in Hebrew on p. 162.

Chorus:

❖ Just one kid, just one kid
That my Abba bought for two zuzeem (two coins) . . .
CHAD GADYA, CHAD GADYA.

1 Along came the **cat** ("meow")
and ate the **kid** ("maa")
that my **Abba** bought for two zuzeem
CHAD GADYA, CHAD GADYA.

2 Along came the **dog** ("woof")
and bit the **cat** ("meow")
that ate the **kid** ("maa")
that my **Abba** bought for two zuzeem
CHAD GADYA, CHAD GADYA....

3 Along came the **stick** ("bang")
and hit the **dog** ("woof")

4 Along came the **fire** ("sizzle")
and burned the **stick** ("bang")

5 Along came the **water** ("gurgle")
and quenched the **fire** ("sizzle")

6 Along came the **ox** ("slurp")
and drank the **water** ("gurgle")

Final Verse:

9 Then came the **Holy One**
and destroyed the **angel of death**
that slew the **slaughterer**
that killed the **ox** ("slurp")
that drank the **water** ("gurgle")
that quenched the **fire** ("sizzle, crackle")
that burned the **stick** ("bang")
that beat the **dog** ("woof")
that bit the **cat** ("meow")
that ate the **kid** ("maa")
that my **Abba** bought for two zuzeem . . .
CHAD GADYA, CHAD GADYA.

Measure for Measure

WRITTEN IN ARAMAIC and modeled on German folksongs, this ballad — which has no overt connection to Pesach — entered the Ashkenazi Haggadah in the 15th-16th century. Hardpressed Jewish commentators have discovered a moral lesson between the lines: measure for measure, an oppressor will always be swallowed by a greater oppressor until God redeems the world from death.

Slipping in a Popular Tune

ALTHOUGH THERE ARE ancient Jewish melodies, many "Jewish" melodies are originally borrowed from the general musical world. The Hassidic movement made it a great virtue to borrow secular tunes and redirect their musical energies to the service of God. For example, French Habad (Lubavitch) Hassidim enjoy singing Shabbat songs to the music of the *Marseillaise* — the secularist anthem of the French Revolution. They believe that thereby they are redeeming the divine sparks of creativity that have been imprisoned in the encasing of a misguided militantly anti-religious movement.

You too may wish to set the words of the Pesach songs to well-known show-tunes or folksongs (for example, "*There was an old lady who swallowed a fly*").

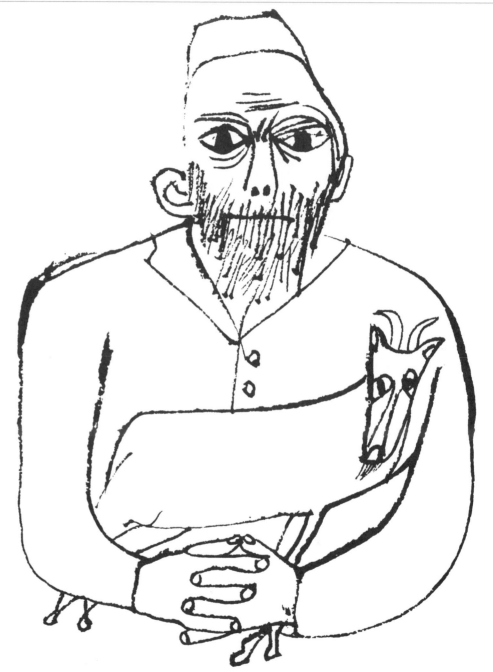

Ben Shahn, "Chad Gadya"   © *Ben Shahn Estate / Licensed by Vaga, NY, NY 1996*

CHAD GAD-YA, CHAD GAD-YA
D'zabeen abba bee-trei zu-zei
Chad gad-ya (2)

חַד גַּדְיָא, חַד גַּדְיָא
דְּזַבִּין אַבָּא בִּתְרֵי זוּזֵי,
חַד גַּדְיָא, חַד גַּדְיָא.

V'ata shun-ra v'ach-la l'gad-ya
D'zabeen abba bee-trei zu-zei
Chad gad-ya (2)

וְאָתָא שׁוּנְרָא, וְאָכְלָה לְגַדְיָא,
דְּזַבִּין אַבָּא בִּתְרֵי זוּזֵי,
חַד גַּדְיָא, חַד גַּדְיָא.

V'ata chal-ba v'na-scha-ch l'shun-ra
D'ach-la l'gad-ya
D'zabeen abba bee-trei zu-zei
Chad gad-ya (2)

וְאָתָא כַלְבָּא, וְנָשַׁךְ לְשׁוּנְרָא,
דְּאָכְלָה לְגַדְיָא,
דְּזַבִּין אַבָּא בִּתְרֵי זוּזֵי,
חַד גַּדְיָא, חַד גַּדְיָא.

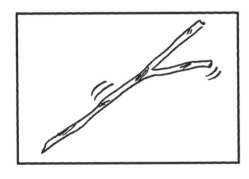

V'ata chu-tra v'hee-ka l'chal-ba
D'na-shach l'shun-ra
D'ach-la l'gad-ya
D'zabeen abba bee-trei zu-zei
Chad gad-ya (2)

וְאָתָא חוּטְרָא, וְהִכָּה לְכַלְבָּא,
דְּנָשַׁךְ לְשׁוּנְרָא,
דְּאָכְלָה לְגַדְיָא,
דְּזַבִּין אַבָּא בִּתְרֵי זוּזֵי,
חַד גַּדְיָא, חַד גַּדְיָא.

V'ata nura v'saraf l'chu-tra
D'hee-ka l'chal-ba
D'na-shach l'shun-ra
D'ach-la l'gad-ya
D'zabeen abba bee-trei zu-zei
Chad gad-ya (2)

וְאָתָא נוּרָא, וְשָׂרַף לְחוּטְרָא,
דְּהִכָּה לְכַלְבָּא,
דְּנָשַׁךְ לְשׁוּנְרָא,
דְּאָכְלָה לְגַדְיָא,
דְּזַבִּין אַבָּא בִּתְרֵי זוּזֵי,
חַד גַּדְיָא, חַד גַּדְיָא.

V'ata maya v'cha-va l'nura
D'saraf l'chu-tra
D'hee-ka l'chal-ba
D'na-shach l'shun-ra
D'ach-la l'gad-ya
D'zabeen abba bee-trei zu-zei
Chad gad-ya (2)

וְאָתָא מַיָּא, וְכָבָה לְנוּרָא,
דְּשָׂרַף לְחוּטְרָא,
דְּהִכָּה לְכַלְבָּא,
דְּנָשַׁךְ לְשׁוּנְרָא,
דְּאָכְלָה לְגַדְיָא,
דְזַבִּין אַבָּא בִּתְרֵי זוּזֵי,
חַד גַּדְיָא, חַד גַּדְיָא.

V'ata tora v'shata l'maya
D'chava l'nura
D'saraf l'chu-tra
D'hee-ka l'chal-ba
D'na-shach l'shun-ra
D'ach-la l'gad-ya
D'zabeen abba bee-trei zu-zei
Chad gad-ya(2)

וְאָתָא תוֹרָא, וְשָׁתָא לְמַיָּא,
דְּכָבָה לְנוּרָא,
דְּשָׂרַף לְחוּטְרָא,
דְּהִכָּה לְכַלְבָּא,
דְּנָשַׁךְ לְשׁוּנְרָא,
דְּאָכְלָה לְגַדְיָא,
דְזַבִּין אַבָּא בִּתְרֵי זוּזֵי,
חַד גַּדְיָא, חַד גַּדְיָא.

V'ata ha-sho-cheit V'sha-chat l'tora
D'shata l'maya
D'chava l'nura
D'saraf l'chu-tra
D'hee-ka l'chal-ba
D'na-shach l'shunra
D'ach-la l'gad-ya
D'zabeen abba bee-trei zu-zei
Chad gad-ya(2)

וְאָתָא הַשּׁוֹחֵט, וְשָׁחַט לְתוֹרָא,
דְּשָׁתָא לְמַיָּא,
דְּכָבָה לְנוּרָא,
דְּשָׂרַף לְחוּטְרָא,
דְּהִכָּה לְכַלְבָּא,
דְּנָשַׁךְ לְשׁוּנְרָא,
דְּאָכְלָה לְגַדְיָא,
דְזַבִּין אַבָּא בִּתְרֵי זוּזֵי,
חַד גַּדְיָא, חַד גַּדְיָא.

V'ata ma-lach ha-mavet
V'sha-chat l'sho-cheit
D'sha-chat l'tora
D'shata l'maya
D'chava l'nura
D'saraf l'chu-tra
D'hee-ka l'chal-ba
D'na-shach l'shunra
D'ach-la l'gad-ya
D'zabeen abba bee-trei zu-zei
Chad gad-ya (2)

וְאָתָא מַלְאַךְ הַמָּוֶת,
וְשָׁחַט לְשׁוֹחֵט,
דְּשָׁחַט לְתוֹרָא,
דְּשָׁתָא לְמַיָּא,
דְּכָבָה לְנוּרָא,
דְּשָׂרַף לְחוּטְרָא,
דְּהִכָּה לְכַלְבָּא,
דְּנָשַׁךְ לְשׁוּנְרָא,
דְּאָכְלָה לְגַדְיָא,
דְּזַבִּין אַבָּא בִּתְרֵי זוּזֵי,
חַד גַּדְיָא, חַד גַּדְיָא.

V'ata Ha-Ka-dosh Baruch Hu
V'sha-chat l'ma-lach ha-mavet
D'sha-chat l'sho-cheit
D'sha-chat l'tora
D'shata l'maya
D'chava l'nura
D'saraf l'chu-tra
D'hee-ka l'chal-ba
D'na-shach l'shunra
D'ach-la l'gad-ya
D'zabeen abba bee-trei zu-zei
Chad gad-ya (2)

וְאָתָא הַקָּדוֹשׁ בָּרוּךְ הוּא,
וְשָׁחַט לְמַלְאַךְ הַמָּוֶת,
דְּשָׁחַט לְשׁוֹחֵט,
דְּשָׁחַט לְתוֹרָא,
דְּשָׁתָא לְמַיָּא,
דְּכָבָה לְנוּרָא,
דְּשָׂרַף לְחוּטְרָא,
דְּהִכָּה לְכַלְבָּא,
דְּנָשַׁךְ לְשׁוּנְרָא,
דְּאָכְלָה לְגַדְיָא,
דְּזַבִּין אַבָּא בִּתְרֵי זוּזֵי,
חַד גַּדְיָא, חַד גַּדְיָא.

Arye Allweil
from the first Israeli army Haggadah, 1949

Kadesh
Urchatz
Karpas
Yachatz
Maggid
Rachtza
Motzi
Matza
Maror
Korech
Shulchan
Orech
Tzafun
Barech
Hallel
Nirtza
Concluding
Poem

Conclusion — Nirtza

נִרְצָה

1. **The Pesach seder** ends with a prayer that all our efforts to perform the seder properly may be pleasing and acceptable to God. (The prayer was composed by Rabbi Yosef Tov-Elem, 11th C. France).

2. **We also** look forward to next year's seder. Hopefully we will celebrate it in a more peaceful world and in a fully restored Jerusalem. We conclude with **Next Year in Jerusalem**.

The Concluding Poem:
Looking Forward to Next Year's Seder

CONCLUDED is the Pesach seder,
Finished down to the last detail
with all its laws and customs.
As we have been able to conduct this seder,
So may we someday perform it in Jerusalem.
Pure One who dwells in the palace,
Support your congregation countless in number.
May you soon lead the offshoots of your stock,
Bringing the redeemed to Zion in joy.

חֲסַל סִדּוּר פֶּסַח כְּהִלְכָתוֹ,
כְּכָל מִשְׁפָּטוֹ וְחֻקָתוֹ.
כַּאֲשֶׁר זָכִינוּ לְסַדֵּר אוֹתוֹ,
כֵּן נִזְכֶּה לַעֲשׂוֹתוֹ.

זָךְ שׁוֹכֵן מְעוֹנָה,
קוֹמֵם קְהַל עֲדַת מִי מָנָה.
בְּקָרוֹב נַהֵל נִטְעֵי כַנָּה,
פְּדוּיִם לְצִיּוֹן בְּרִנָּה.

❖ *All sing:*

לְשָׁנָה הַבָּאָה בִּירוּשָׁלָיִם

L'Shana Ha-ba-a Bee-Yeru-sha-layeem!
NEXT YEAR IN JERUSALEM

Next Year in Jerusalem

לְשָׁנָה הַבָּאָה בִּירוּשָׁלָיִם

1. **Aliyah,** the family pilgrimage to Jerusalem, was once central to every Pesach. At these festive gatherings, people from the world over met and sang the Songs of Ascent. Jerusalem, they said, was "a city that transforms all Jews into friends."

2. **Later,** "aliyah" came to mean ascending to Eretz Yisrael and settling there. "Hatikvah," the Jewish anthem expressing **hope** for return to Zion, is often sung at the end of the seder.

HATIKVAH: THE HOPE

The Jewish national anthem (written by N.H. Imber in 1878) became the Israeli anthem in 1948.

AS LONG as the Jewish soul	Kol od ba-lei-vav p'nee-ma,	כָּל עוֹד בַּלֵּבָב פְּנִימָה,
stirs within our heart,	Nefesh yehudee ho-mee'ya	נֶפֶשׁ יְהוּדִי הוֹמִיָּה.
And our eyes look with anticipation,	U'lefa'atei miz-rach ka-dee-ma,	וּלְפַאֲתֵי מִזְרָח קָדִימָה,
Towards the East, to Zion,	Ayeen l'Tzion tzo-fee'ya	עַיִן לְצִיּוֹן צוֹפִיָּה.
Then our hope is not yet lost —	Od lo av-da teek-vatei-nu,	עוֹד לֹא אָבְדָה תִּקְוָתֵנוּ,
the hope of two thousand years —	Hatikva bat sh'not al-pa-yeem	הַתִּקְוָה בַּת שְׁנוֹת אַלְפַּיִם,
To be a free people in our land,	Leeh'yot am chof-shee be'art-zei-nu,	לִהְיוֹת עַם חָפְשִׁי בְּאַרְצֵנוּ,
the land of Zion and Jerusalem.	Eretz Tzion v'Yeru-sha-la-yeem.	אֶרֶץ צִיּוֹן וִירוּשָׁלָיִם.

JERUSALEM OF GOLD

composed by Naomi Shemer in 1967 before the Six Day War and popularized when the wall dividing Jerusalem fell.

MOUNTAIN air as pure as wine;	Aveer ha-reem tza-lul ka-ya-yeen	אֲוִיר הָרִים צָלוּל כַּיַּיִן
The scent of pines	v'rei-ach o-ra-neem	וְרֵיחַ אֳרָנִים
Carried by the wind at dusk	Nee-sa b'ru-ach ha-ar-ba-yeem	נִשָּׂא בְּרוּחַ הָעַרְבַּיִם
Along with the sound of bells.	Eem kol pa-a-mo-neem	עִם קוֹל פַּעֲמוֹנִים
In the slumber of tree and stone,	Uv'tar-dei-mat ee-lan va'eh-ven	וּבְתַרְדֵּמַת אִילָן וָאֶבֶן
A captive in her dream,	Shvu-yah ba-cha-lo-mah	שְׁבוּיָה בַּחֲלוֹמָהּ
The city sat in solitude,	Ha'eer a-sher ba-dad yo-she-vet	הָעִיר אֲשֶׁר בָּדָד יוֹשֶׁבֶת
A wall through her heart.	Uv'lee-bah cho-mah	וּבְלִבָּהּ חוֹמָה.
JERUSALEM OF GOLD,	Ye-ru-sha-la-yeem shel za-hav	יְרוּשָׁלַיִם שֶׁל זָהָב
of bronze and of light.	Ve'shel ne-cho-shet v'shel or	וְשֶׁל נְחשֶׁת וְשֶׁל אוֹר
I am the harp for all your songs.	Ha-lo l'chol shee-ra-yeech a-nee kee-nor.	הֲלֹא לְכָל שִׁירַיִךְ אֲנִי כִּנּוֹר.

Kadesh
Urchatz
Karpas
Yachatz
Maggid
Rachtza
Motzi
Matza
Maror
Korech
Shulchan Orech
Tzafun
Barech
Hallel
Nirtza

Next
Year in
Jerusalem

Song of Ascents (Aliyah): The City of Shalom

I rejoiced when they said to me: "We are going to the House of Adonai." Our feet stood inside your gates, Jerusalem — Jerusalem built up, a city bonded together. Pray for the SHALOM of JERUSALEM: "May those who love you be at peace." *(Psalm 122)*

David Sharir, Solomon's Temple (CL. S-234 © 1985 Safrai Gallery). For the artist, the pilgrimage to Solomon's First Temple also symbolizes the yearning for a return to the exotic Garden of Eden. (Isaiah 57:3)

In the Days to Come . . .

"I will give peace in the land,
and you will lie down,
and no one will make
you afraid." *(Leviticus 26:6)*

"And they shall beat their swords
into plowshares
And their spears into pruning
shears.
Nation shall not take up
Sword against nation;
They shall never again learn war."

(Isaiah 2)

David Sharir, Isaiah II:
"Spears into Pruning Shears"
(SS, Cat. S-71 © 1971 Safrai Gallery)

Messianic Visions

Peace Songs

1. NATION shall not take up
Sword against nation;
They shall never again learn war. *(Isaiah 2)*

לֹא יִשָּׂא גוֹי אֶל גּוֹי חֶרֶב
וְלֹא יִלְמְדוּ עוֹד מִלְחָמָה.

Lo-yee-sa goy el goy che-rev
V'lo yeel-m'du od meel-chama.

2. GOD who makes peace in heaven,
May God make peace over us
and all Israel. Amen.

עוֹשֶׂה שָׁלוֹם בִּמְרוֹמָיו,
הוּא יַעֲשֶׂה שָׁלוֹם עָלֵינוּ
וְעַל כָּל יִשְׂרָאֵל, וְאִמְרוּ אָמֵן.

Oseh shalom beem-romav
hu ya-aseh shalom aleinu
v'al kol Yisrael v'eemru amen.

3. DOWN BY THE RIVERSIDE
Gonna lay down my sword and shield
Down by the riverside (3x)
Gonna lay down my sword and shield
Down by the riverside (2x)
Refrain:
I ain't gonna study war no more (6x)

I'm gonna lay down that atom bomb
Down by the riverside (3x)
I'm gonna lay down that atom bomb
Down by the riverside (2x)

Maimonides: The Messianic World Vision

The rabbis and prophets did not long for the days of the Messiah that Israel might exercise dominion over the world, or rule over other peoples, or be exalted by the nations. Nor that the Jewish people might eat and drink and rejoice. Their aspiration was that the people of Israel be free to devote themselves to the Torah and its wisdom, with no one to oppress or disturb them, and thus earn the life in the world to come. In that era there will be neither famine nor war, neither jealousy nor strife. Blessings will be abundant, comforts within the reach of all. The one preoccupation of the whole world will be to know Adonai. Hence Jews will be very wise, they will know the things that are now concealed and will attain an understanding of their Creator to the utmost capacity of the human mind, "For the earth shall be full of the knowledge of Adonai, as the waters cover the sea." *(Isaiah 11:9) (Maimonides, Laws of Kings 12:4-5)*

Swords Into Plowshares

In the days to come,
The mount of Adonai's house
Shall stand firm above the mountains
And tower above the hills;
And all the nations shall gaze on it with joy.
Many peoples shall go and say: "Come,
Let us go up to the mount of Adonai,
To the house of the God of Jacob;
That God may instruct us in Divine ways.
And that we may walk in God's paths.

For Torah shall come forth from Zion,
The word of Adonai from Jerusalem.
Thus God will judge among the nations
And arbitrate for many peoples.
And they shall beat their swords into plowshares
And their spears into pruning shears.
Nation shall not take up
Sword against nation;
They shall never again learn war. *(Isaiah 2)*

Permissions *"Don't violate the borders of your neighbor's property" (Deuteronomy 19:14)*

We wish to thank all those who allowed us to use their creative work in this family Haggadah. We apologize to those whom we were unable to locate to request their permission and to offer them copyright fees.

1. **Yariv Ben Aharon**, *HaKibbutz*.
2. **Marc Chagall**, © ADAGP, Paris, 1996.
3. Professor **Stanley Chyet**, "Waitings," *Texts and Responses*, edited by M. Fishbane in honor of the 70th Birthday of Nahum Glatzer.
4. **Dick Codor**, "The Marx Brothers," *The Big Book of Jewish Humor*.
5. **Diana Craig** and **Leon Baxter**, *The Young Moses and The Flight from Egypt*, MacDonald Co., London.
6. **The Reubeni Foundation**, POB 7113, Jerusalem 91070, Mordechai Dwek, Chronicles Vol., I Editors, Israel Eldad and Moshe Aumann by permission.
7. **Judy Israel Elkin** for the "Even Harsher" exercise.
8. **Leonard Fein**, writer and teacher, founder of MOMENT Magazine (1975) and founder of MAZON: A Jewish Response to Hunger (1985) shared selections from his family Haggadah.
9. **Tully Filmus**, from the JPS book of his drawings.
10. **Asher Finkel**, *Responsa Anthology* by permission of the publisher Jason Aronson Inc. Northvale, NJ © 1990.
11. **Paul Freeman, Nota Koslowsky** and **Siegmund Forst**, illustrations published by the Shulsinger Brothers.
12. **Otto Geismar**, B. Cohen, Berlin Jalkut. By permission of his daughters.
13. **Everett Gendler**, translation of Shmuel Tamares from *The Freedom Haggadah*.
14. **Rabbis Irving Greenberg, Steven Greenberg** and **David Nelson**, CLAL, *Freedom Haggadah for Soviet Jewry*.
15. **Robert Grudin**, "Time and the Art of Living," *The Family Networker*, Jan. 1995.
16. **Rabbi Menahem HaCohen**, *Haggadah La'Am*, by generous permission of Amos Modan, Modan Publishers.
17. **Rabbi David Hartman**, reflections on Pesach from the transcripts of his Hebrew University lectures and from *Joy and Responsibility*.
18. **Heinrich Heine**, "Rabbi of Bacharach," © 1947; Pantheon Books.
19. **Robert Hieronimus**, *The History of America's Great Seal*.
20. **Tzvi Livni**, Yavneh Publishers.
21. **William and Mary Morris**, *Dictionary of Word and Phrase Origins*.
22. **David Moss**, *The Moss Haggadah*, courtesy of Bet Alpha Editions and the artist.
23. **National Conference of Synagogue Youth**, © Union of Orthodox Jewish Congregations of America, "Brocha of Moror" in "Our Way."
24. **Henry Noerdlinger**, *Moses and Egypt*.
25. **Dov Noy**, *The Beautiful Girl and the Three Princes* (Hebrew, 1965) contains the Iraqi folktale, "Rags to Riches."
26. **Rony Oren**, figures from *The Animated Haggadah* by the generous permission of Scopus Films © Jonathan Lubell.
27. **W. Pawlak**, "The Last Passover in Warsaw," *Passover Anthology* by Philip Goodman.
28. **Rabbi Joachim Prinz**, from his oral archives by the generous permission of his daughter Lucie Prinz.
29. **Dan Reisinger**, *Feast of Freedom*, ed. Rachel Anne Rabinowicz, © Rabbinical Assembly of America 1982, reprinted by permission.
30. **David Sharir** and **Shraga Weil** by the generous permission of the Safrai Gallery, 19 King David St., Jerusalem.
31. **Ben Shahn** ©1996 Estate of Ben Shahn/Licensed by Vaga, NY, NY.
32. **I.B. Singer**, *Zlateh the Goat and Other Stories* © 1966 and **Ira Steingroot** © 1995, *Keeping Passover*, by permission of Harper Collins Publishers.
33. **Jakob Steinhardt, Moses Lilien, Joseph Horna** and **Arye Allweil** illustrations of the Haggadah.
34. **Arthur Szyk** by permission of Mrs. Alexandra Bracie.
35. The **Tanakh** as published by The Jewish Publication Society served as a model for our own revised translations of Hallel.
36. **David Wander**, *The Haggadah in Memory of the Holocaust*, designed and illustrated by David Wander ©1988; calligraphy by Yonah Weinrib, commissioned by Zygfred Wolloch; by the generous permission of the artist.
37. **Shraga Weil**, "Song of Songs" © 1968 Sifriat HaPoalim, by permission of the artist.
38. **Istavan Zador**, Budapest "Omike."

Notes and References

p.13 The ingenious idea of **hiding pictures of the afikoman** in illustrations within the Haggadah derives from the *Moss Haggadah* by David Moss.

p.16 **Candle-lighting** (covering the eyes). Rabbi Falk, the Drisha, Arba Turim; Shulchan Aruch O.H. 263:5.

p.22 **Here I am**: Maimonides, Laws of Chametz uMatza 7:1.

p.23 **Who Pours the Wine?** Maimonides, Commentary on Mishna Pesachim 10:1; T.B. Pesachim 108; Tosefta Pesachim; T.B. Shabbat 128a; Sefer Dinim and Minhagim 222:505; Aruch HaShulchan O.H. 473.

p.23 **Reclining:** Tosafot Berachot 42a "They reclined"; Menachem Kasher, *Haggadah Shlema*, 68-69; Aruch HaShulchan O.H. 472:3.

p.27 **Happy Birthday** was reported by Rabbi Moshe Tutenauer as a true story. January 27, 1945 is reported as the day of liberation from Auschwitz in Primo Levi's autobiography.

p.30 **Karpas:** Daniel Goldschmidt notes that in the oldest manuscript of the Haggadah discovered in the Cairo Geniza, "karpas" consists of at least three dips including eggs and meat appetizers (Goldschmidt, *Haggadah*, 76-79). Medieval rabbis debated over whether to say a special blessing after hors d'oeuvres served before the meal or to include them under the full Birkat HaMazon. The custom of eating less than an olive's worth is a compromise between two positions.

p.31 **Why Karpas?** Eliezer Shmueli, *Mahzor Hatzomeah V'hachai B'Yisrael*. Philo, Special Laws, Book II. T.B. Rosh Hashana 11a. John Ayto, *Dictionary of Word Origins*, 496. *Sefer Dinim and Minhagim*, 230:524.

p.84 **"Spiritually naked"** is based on the midrash in Exodus Rabbah 19:15.

p.96 **Drops for the 10 Plagues:** *Darchei Moshe Isserles*, O.H. 473:18 describes this wine spilling custom; Maharil (See Kasher, 126-127) Rabbi Shalom (See Drisha and Prisha on Tur O.H. 490). The complete Hallel is not said on the last six days of Pesach. See Pesikta de Rav Kahana, 458, and Beit Yosef O.H. 490.

p.107 **Dayeinu:** The Afghani custom is reported in Reuven Kashani, *Duchan* Vol. 8, p. 48 and its Biblical explanation in Ira Steingroot, *Keeping Passover*, p. 139.

p.119 **Bernarda Shahn**. Introduction of *The Hallelujah Suite*.

p.121 **Great Seal.** See *Permissions*: Robert Hieronimus.

p.123 **"God will surely help"**: Joel Ziff. *Mirrors in Time*, p.76.

p.124 **1/2 - 1/3 of a Matza**: See Gershom Harpenes, *Geresh Yerachim Haggadah*, p. 23. **With or Without Haroset**. See Rabbi Zeev Whitman *"On Eating Matza B'Chipazon,"* HaMaayan 5741 Vol. 21, pp. 59-70 and Kasher, 157-158. **Bergen Belsen Blessing**: Yona Emanuel, Ha-Maayan #14, 5734, Volume 3, p. 3.

p.128 **Korech. Hillel's Sandwich**. Most rabbis in the days of the Temple disagreed with Hillel's custom believing that even in the days of the Temple, the ingredients of the sandwich should be eaten separately.
Reclining. Some important rabbis object to reclining while eating the sandwich, because this contradicts the spirit of slavery which maror and matza are intended to evoke. Others object to dipping the sandwich in charoset (Kasher, pp.170-171).

p.130 **Afikoman Directions.** Rashi, Rashbam TB Pesachim 119b; Maimonides, Laws of Chametz and Matza 8:9; The minority view of Rashi-Rashbam holds that matza eaten at the end of the seder is the obligatory matza of mitzvah. Therefore, Rabbi Asher requires two portions of matza be eaten at the end of the meal — one as a substitute for the Pesach lamb and one for matza; Ovadia Yosef, *Haggadah Chazon Ovadia*, p. 180.

p.131 **Afikoman: It's Greek to Me!**: See Sefer HaChinuch and Tosafot, TB Pesachim 120a; Rashbam TB Pesachim 119b and Saul Lieberman, *Tosefta Kifshuta*, Pesachim 10:4.

p.141 **Filling the Cup of Redemption Ourselves**: Zecharia Goren, *Mehkarei HeChag* 5754, p. 100; **An Open Door: Trust in Divine Security**: R. Moshe Isserles see Kasher, p. 180; **Expectation of Redemption**: R. Yehoshua identifies the date of the creation with the month of Nisan (B.T. Rosh Hashana 11a).

p.142 **Pour Out Your Love**: See *Machanaim* Vol. #80; Zecharia Goren, *Mechkarei Hag* (5744), pp. 94-105.

p.166 **"A City that Makes All Israel Friends"** based on J.T. Hagigah 3:6.

p.170 **The Song of Songs** is sung on various dates in the Jewish calendar depending on the local custom. See *Mahzor Vitry* (Part I, p.304) and *Tractate Soferim* (p. 251).